MEMORANDUM

DATE: January 14, 2007
TO: Dr. Radislav Portek
FROM: Bill Lee
RE: Project Monolith Recruitment Case Files 2001-2002

TOP SECRET
SENSITIVE COMPARTMENTED INFORMATION

DR. PORTEK—

As requested, I have assembled summaries of the recruitment efforts for the majority of the *Clarke* crew. The attached dossier includes details of my attempts during 2001 and 2002 to source appropriate parties for a mission with Project Monolith's unique requirements. The information included here should give you an appropriate overview of the reasons we selected each candidate.

I understand that you wish to review this information in light of the upcoming change in administration from President Francis Carroll to President Stephen Blades, as much of the work described herein was undertaken before you became head of Project Monolith, under the auspices of your predecessor Edward Stinton. I think this goal is admirable, and I am confident that this information will enable you to adequately brief our new President and assist him with any inquiries he may have.

In addition to the *Clarke* recruitment files, I have appended one additional document—a summary of our top people's speculation as to the history and motivations of the alien presence in our solar system. I hope you will find it equally informative and useful.

Please do not hesitate to reach out if I can be of any additional help here. While my duties with respect to Project Monolith essentially ended once the recruitment phase was complete, I remain available to serve in any capacity as needed.

BILL LEE

LETTER 44 VOLUME V: BLUESHIFT

WRITTEN BY
CHARLES SOULE

CHAPTER 1 ILLUSTRATED BY
JOËLLE JONES

CHAPTER 2 ILLUSTRATED BY
DREW MOSS

CHAPTER 3 ILLUSTRATED BY
RYAN KELLY

CHAPTER 4 ILLUSTRATED BY
ALISE GLUŠKOVA

CHAPTER 5 ILLUSTRATED BY
LANGDON FOSS

COLORED BY
DAN JACKSON

CHAPTER 1 LETTERED BY
SHAWN DEPASQUALE

CHAPTERS 2-5 LETTERED BY
CRANK!

BOOK DESIGNED BY
JASON STOREY WITH **KATE Z. STONE**

COVER ILLUSTRATED BY
ALBERTO JIMÉNEZ ALBURQUERQUE

EDITED BY
ROBIN HERRERA

LETTER 44

SOULE ★ ALBURQUERQUE ★ JACKSON

VOLUME V: BLUESHIFT

05

LETTER 44

THIS VOLUME COLLECTS ISSUES 7, 14, 21, 28, AND 32
OF THE ONI PRESS SERIES *LETTER 44*

Oni Press, Inc.

Publisher /// **Joe Nozemack**
Editor In Chief /// **James Lucas Jones**
Director of Operations /// **Brad Rooks**
Director of Sales /// **David Dissanayake**
Publicity Manager /// **Rachel Reed**
Marketing Assistant /// **Melissa Meszaros MacFadyen**
Director of Design and Production /// **Troy Look**
Graphic Designer /// **Hilary Thompson**
Junior Graphic Designer /// **Kate Z. Stone**
Digital Prepress Technician /// **Angie Knowles**
Managing Editor /// **Ari Yarwood**
Senior Editor /// **Charlie Chu**
Editor /// **Robin Herrera**
Administrative Assistant /// **Alissa Sallah**
Logistics Associate /// **Jung Lee**

1319 SE Martin Luther King Jr. Blvd. Suite 240
Portland, OR 97214

onipress.com
facebook.com/onipress | twitter.com/onipress | onipress.tumblr.com

charlessoule.com | @charlessoule
ajaalbertojimenezalburquerque.blogspot.com
joellejones.com
facebook.com/DrewerdMoss
funrama.blogspot.com
alisegluskova.tumblr.com
lllama.com

FIRST EDITION: NOVEMBER 2017

Letter 44 Volume 5. November 2017. Published by Oni Press, Inc. 1319 SE
Martin Luther King Jr. Blvd., Suite 240, Portland, OR 97214. Letter 44 is ™
& © 2017 Charles Soule. All rights reserved. Oni Press logo and icon ™ & ©
2017 Oni Press, Inc. Oni Press logo and icon artwork created by Keith A. Wood.
The events, institutions, and characters presented in this book are fictional.
Any resemblance to actual persons, living or dead, is purely coincidental.
No portion of this publication may be reproduced, by any means, without the
express written permission of the copyright holders.

ISBN: 978-1-62010-446-0 | eISBN: 978-1-62010-447-7

Library of Congress Control Number: 2014931101

10 8 6 4 2 1 3 5 7 9

Printed in China

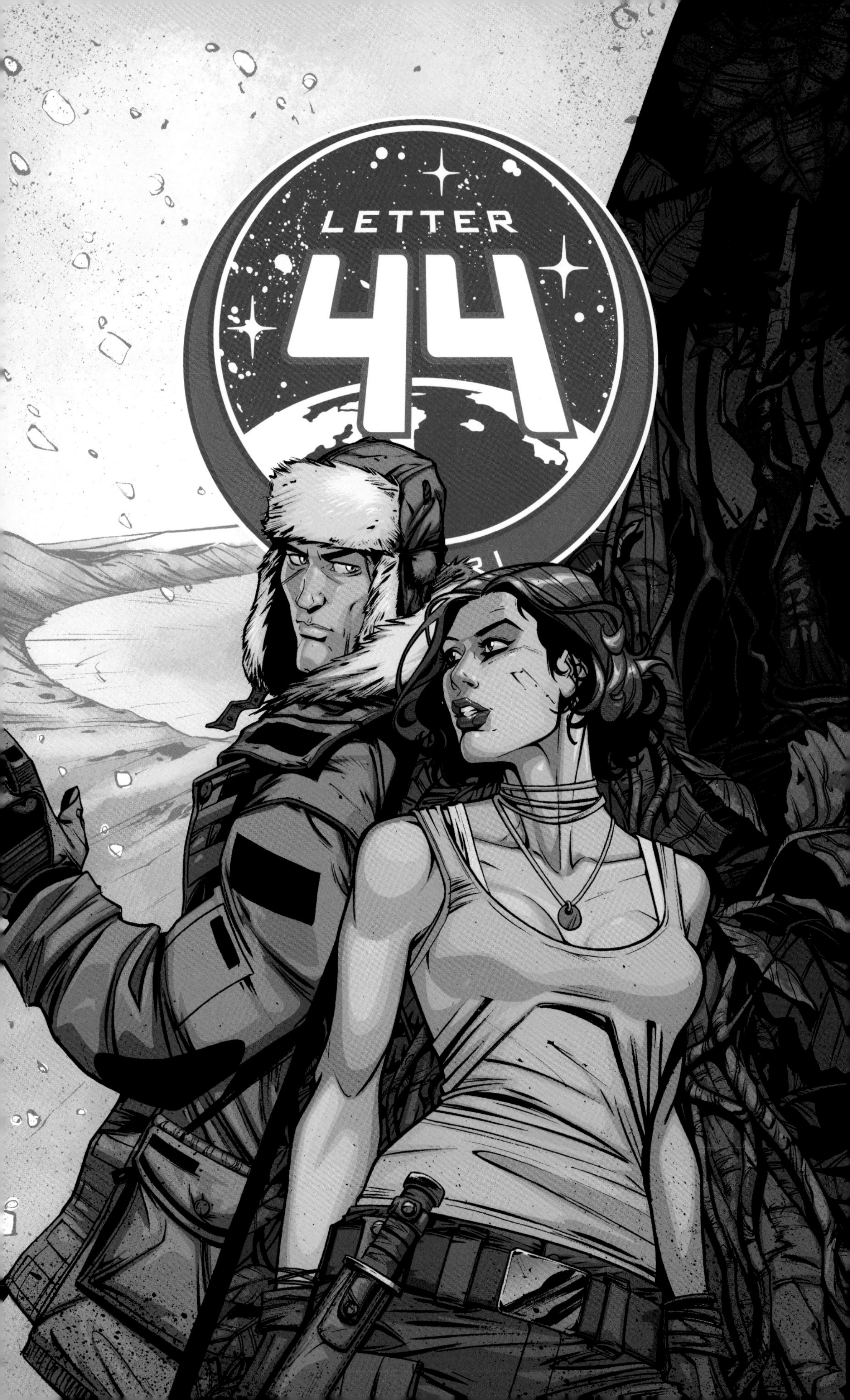
LETTER
44

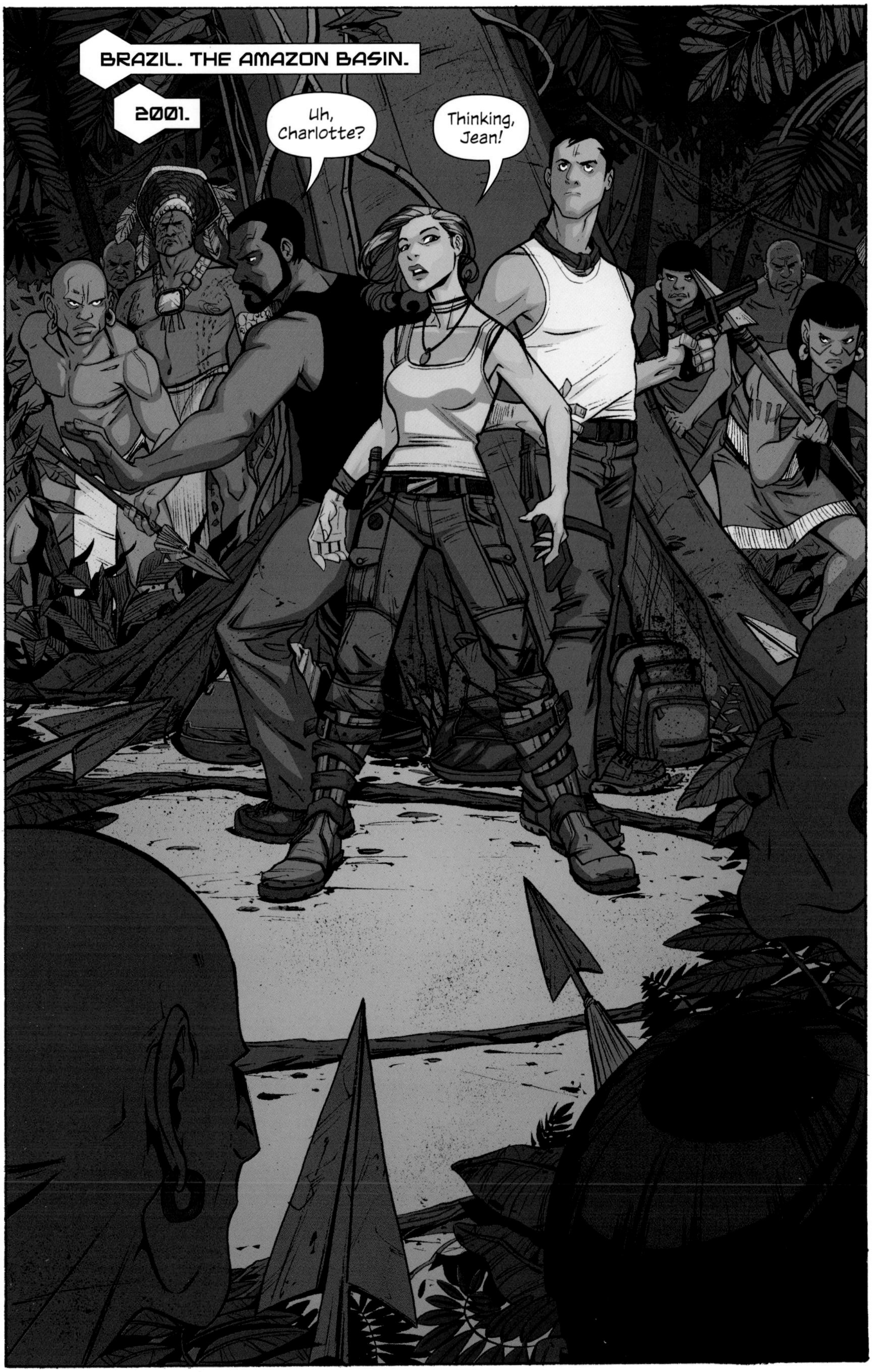
BRAZIL. THE AMAZON BASIN.
2001.
Uh, Charlotte?
Thinking, Jean!

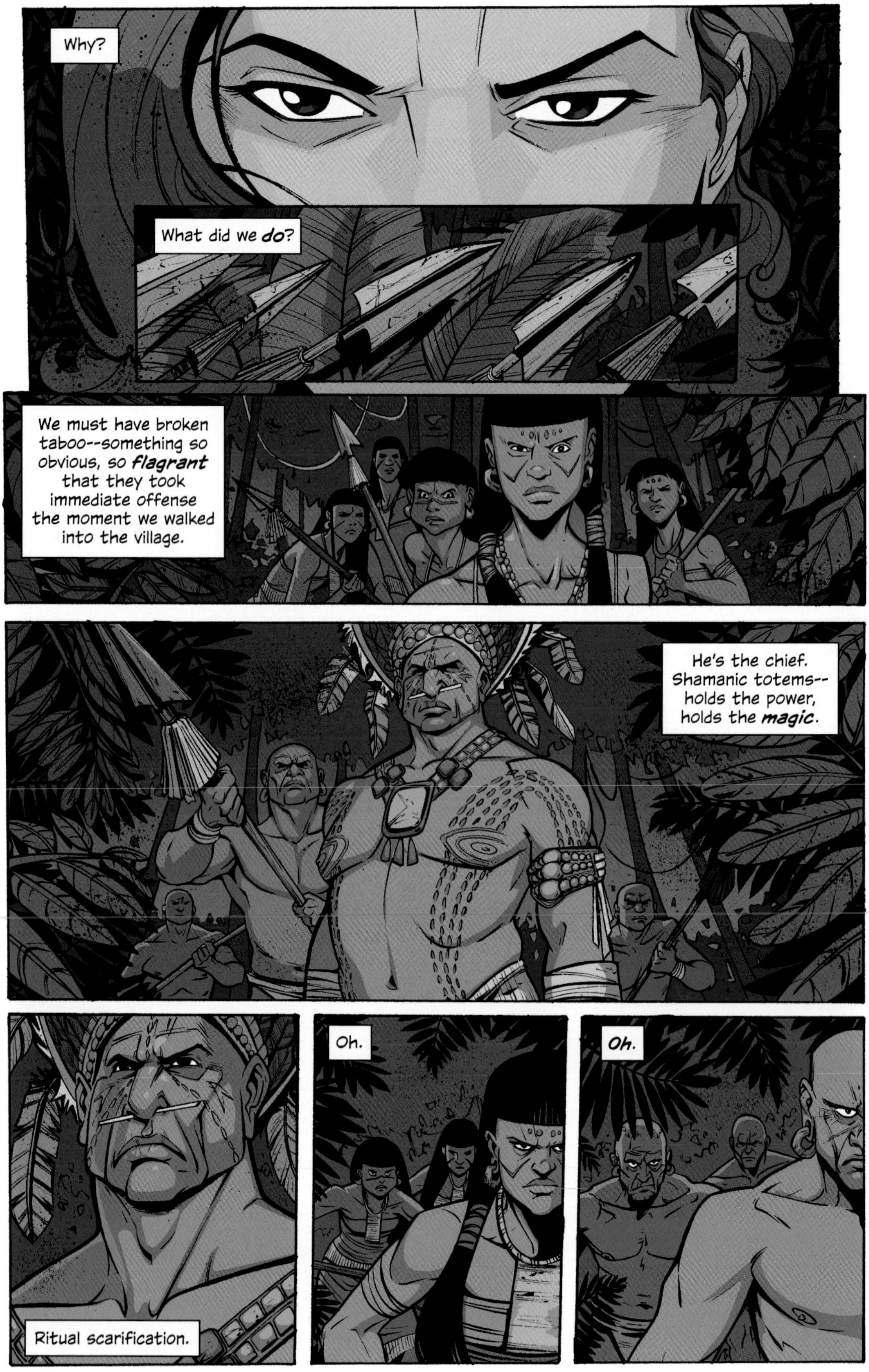
Why?
What did we *do*?
We must have broken taboo--something so obvious, so *flagrant* that they took immediate offense the moment we walked into the village.
He's the chief. Shamanic totems--holds the power, holds the *magic*.
Ritual scarification.
Oh.
Oh.

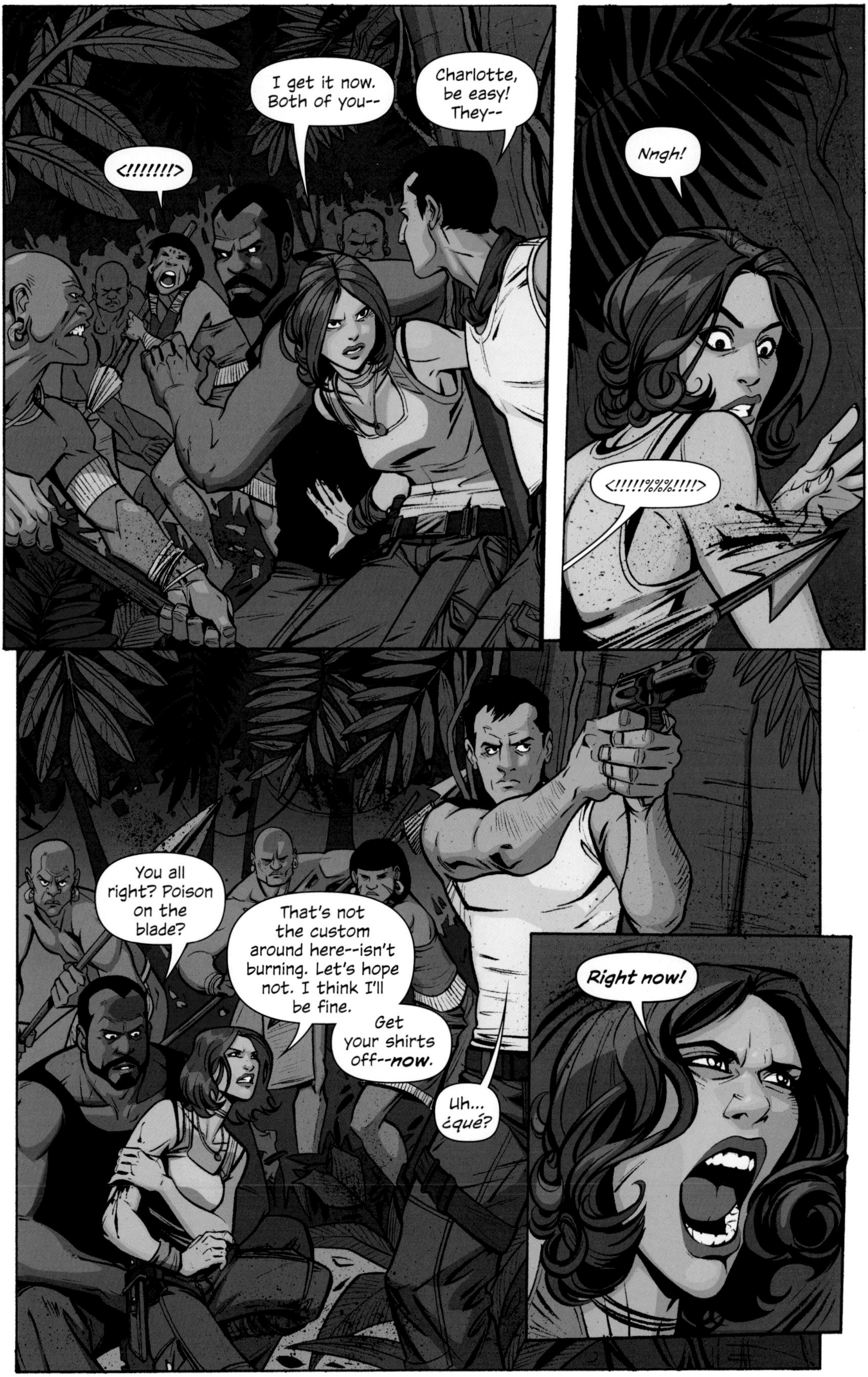
I get it now. Both of you--
Charlotte, be easy! They--
<!!!!!!!>
Nngh!
<!!!!!%%%!!!!>
You all right? Poison on the blade?
That's not the custom around here--isn't burning. Let's hope not. I think I'll be fine.
Get your shirts off--*now*.
Uh... ¿qué?
Right now!

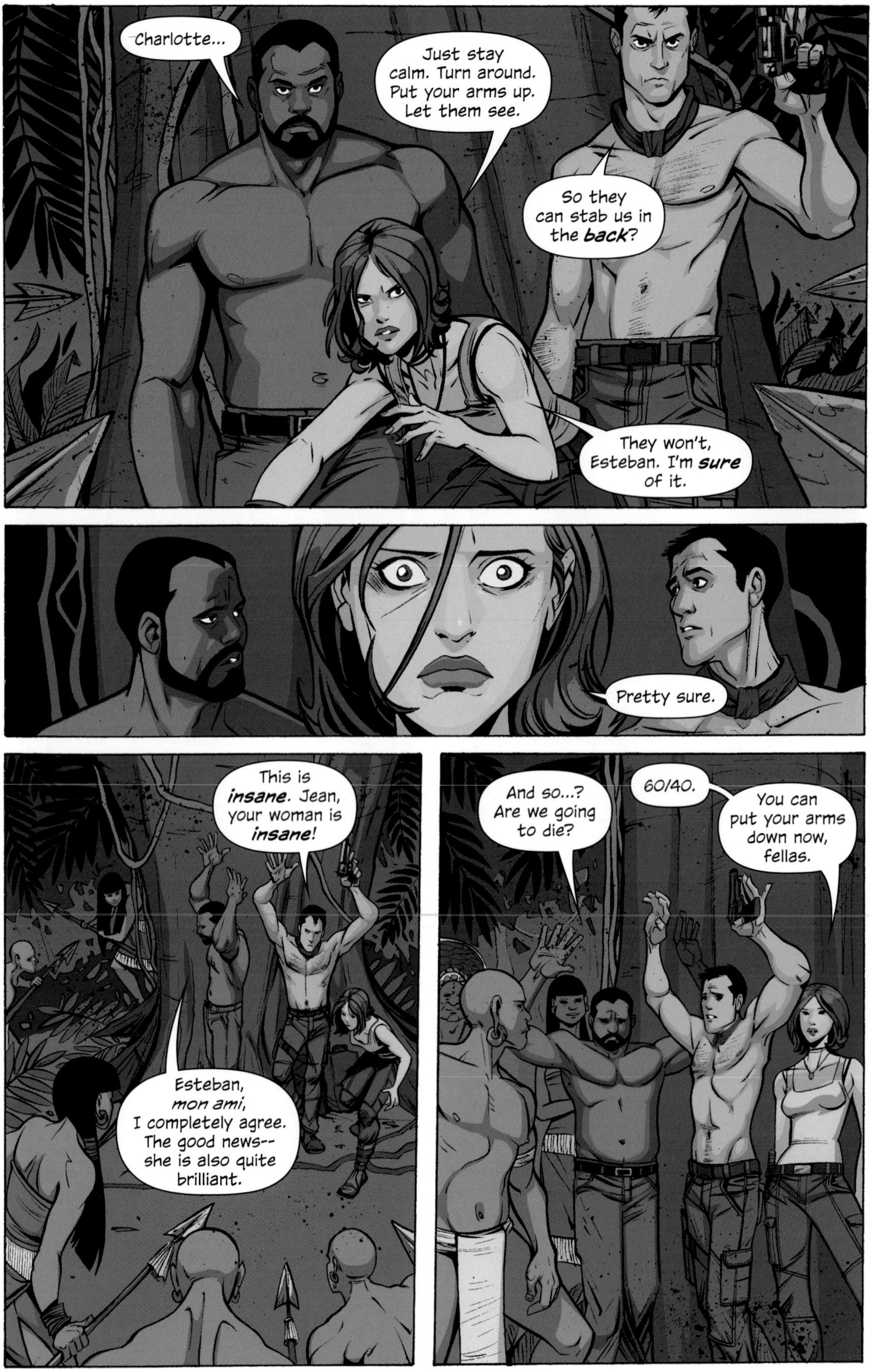
Charlotte...
Just stay calm. Turn around. Put your arms up. Let them see.
So they can stab us in the *back*?
They won't, Esteban. I'm *sure* of it.
Pretty sure.
This is *insane*. Jean, your woman is *insane*!
Esteban, *mon ami*, I completely agree. The good news--she is also quite brilliant.
And so...? Are we going to die?
60/40.
You can put your arms down now, fellas.

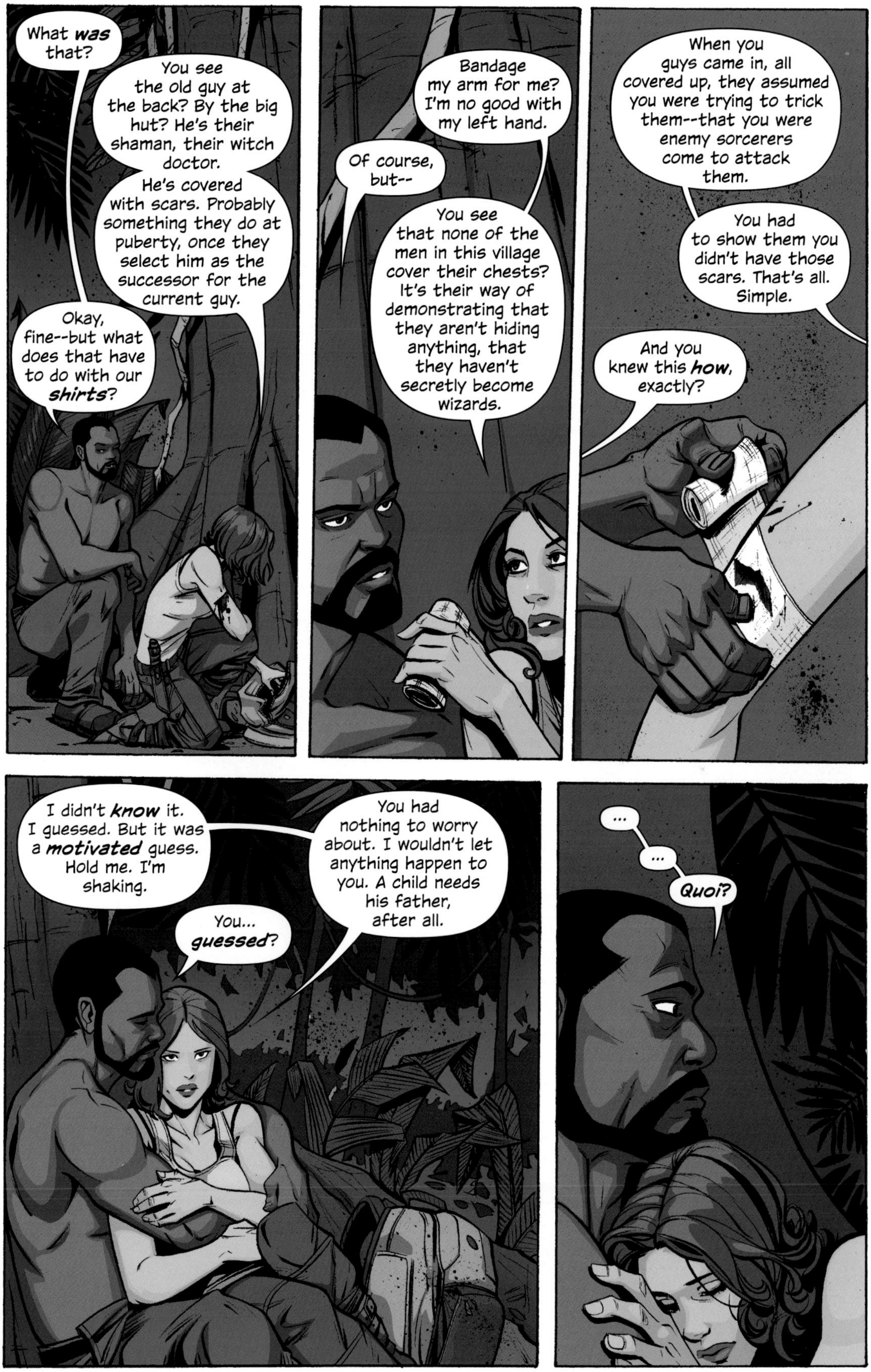
What *was* that?
You see the old guy at the back? By the big hut? He's their shaman, their witch doctor.
He's covered with scars. Probably something they do at puberty, once they select him as the successor for the current guy.
Okay, fine--but what does that have to do with our *shirts*?
Bandage my arm for me? I'm no good with my left hand.
Of course, but--
You see that none of the men in this village cover their chests? It's their way of demonstrating that they aren't hiding anything, that they haven't secretly become wizards.
When you guys came in, all covered up, they assumed you were trying to trick them--that you were enemy sorcerers come to attack them.
You had to show them you didn't have those scars. That's all. Simple.
And you knew this *how*, exactly?
I didn't *know* it. I guessed. But it was a *motivated* guess. Hold me. I'm shaking.
You... *guessed*?
You had nothing to worry about. I wouldn't let anything happen to you. A child needs his father, after all.
...
...
Quoi?

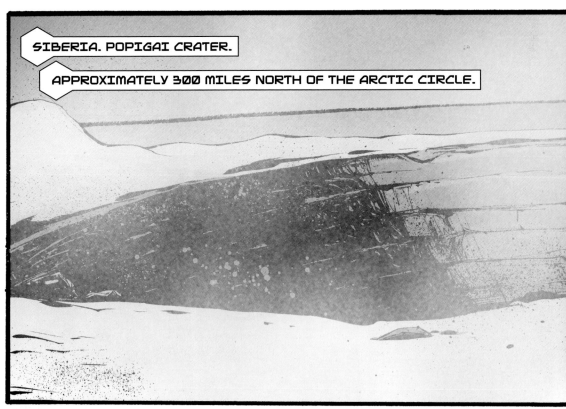

SIBERIA. POPIGAI CRATER.

APPROXIMATELY 300 MILES NORTH OF THE ARCTIC CIRCLE.

How bad is it out there, Pavel?

32 below. Celsius. Very bad.

Could be worse. It gets down into the negative 50s here, sometimes.

Zip up. We're going out.

All right, you know what you'll be doing out there? Jokes aside, this is an extremely dangerous environment.

Four samples, then right back inside. You won't have to ask me twice.

Good. Let's go.

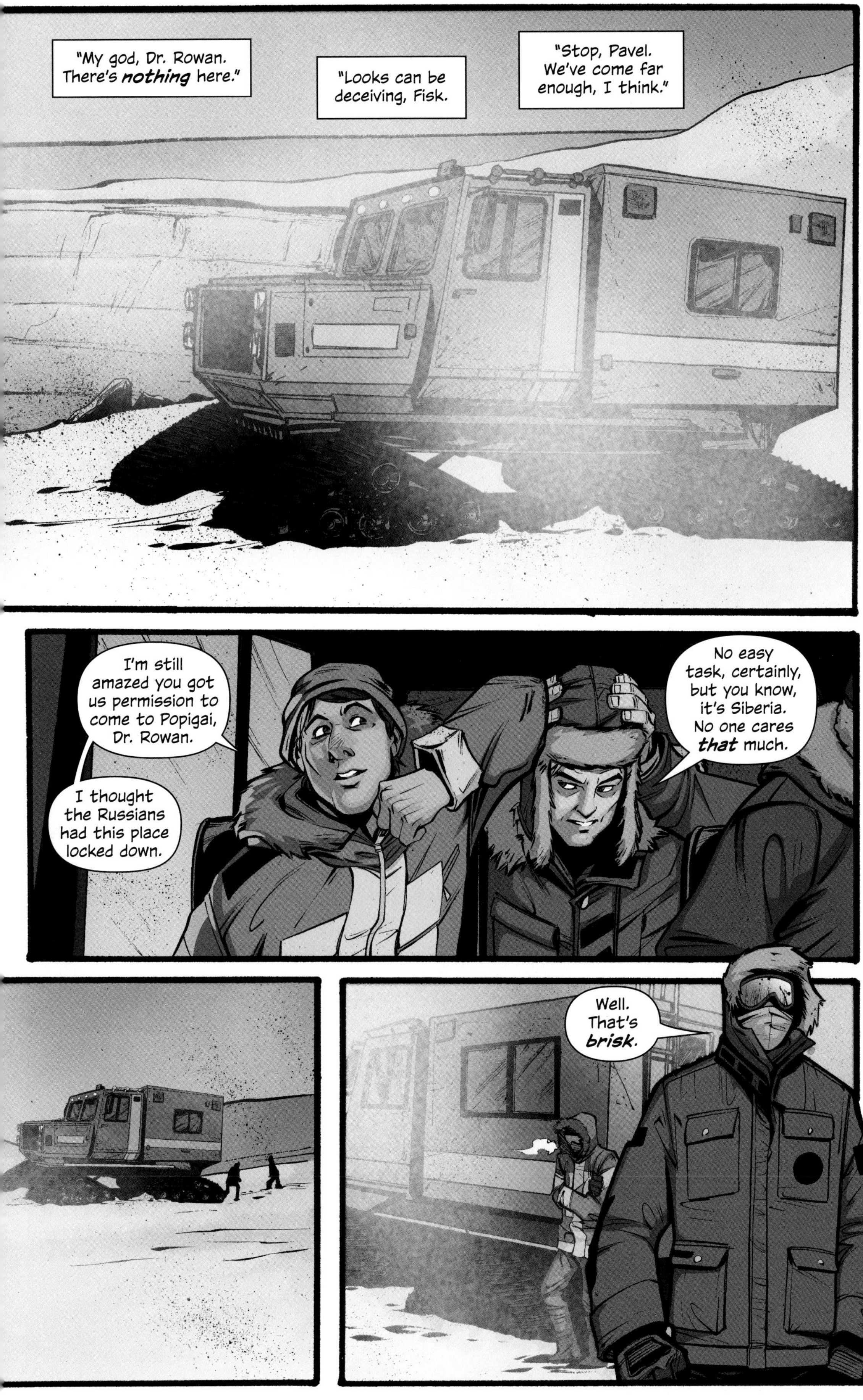
"My god, Dr. Rowan. There's **nothing** here."
"Looks can be deceiving, Fisk.
"Stop, Pavel. We've come far enough, I think."
I'm still amazed you got us permission to come to Popigai, Dr. Rowan.
I thought the Russians had this place locked down.
No easy task, certainly, but you know, it's Siberia. No one cares **that** much.
Well. That's **brisk**.

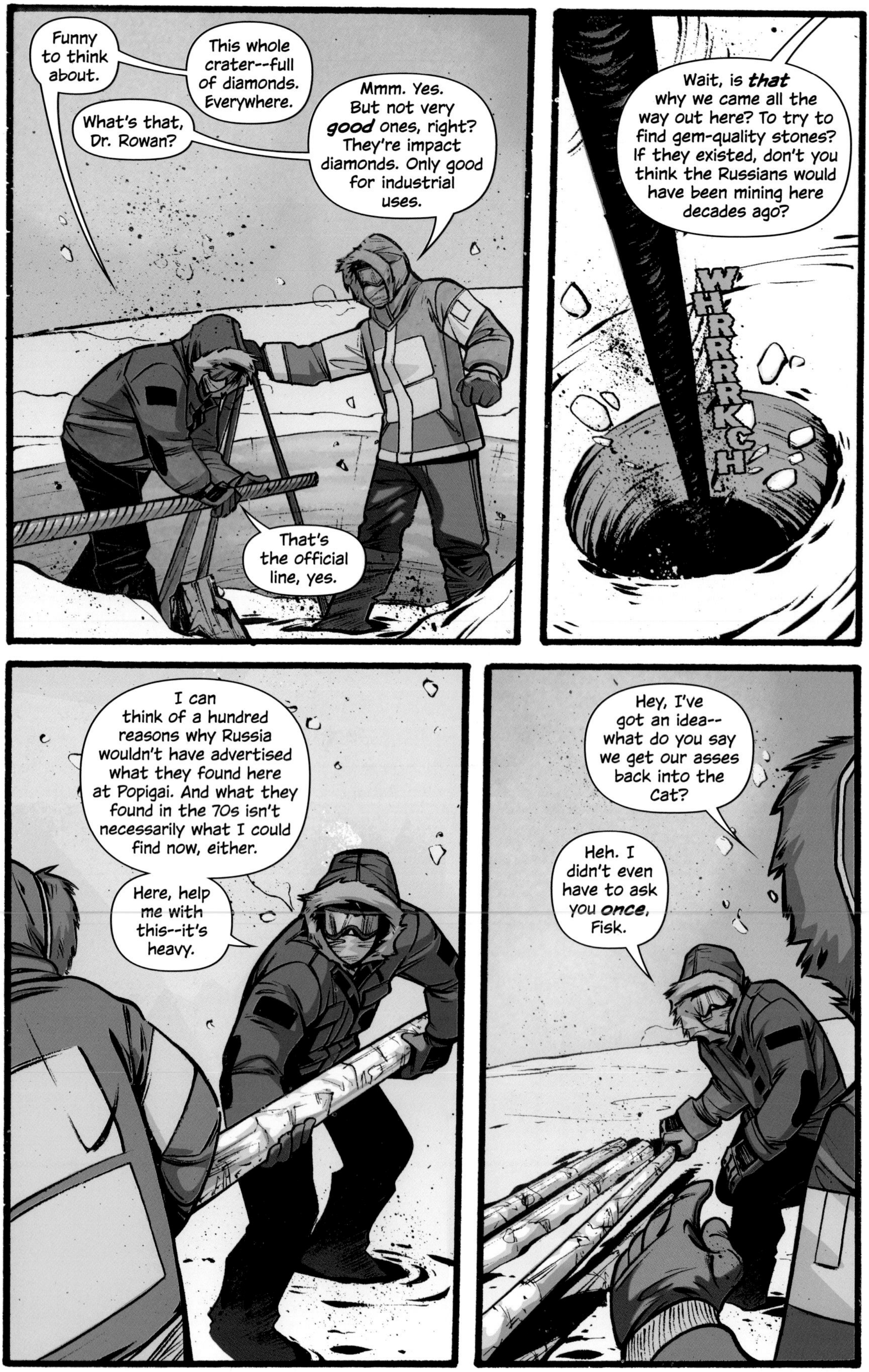
Funny to think about.
This whole crater--full of diamonds. Everywhere.
What's that, Dr. Rowan?
Mmm. Yes. But not very *good* ones, right? They're impact diamonds. Only good for industrial uses.
That's the official line, yes.
Wait, is *that* why we came all the way out here? To try to find gem-quality stones? If they existed, don't you think the Russians would have been mining here decades ago?
WHRRRRKCH
I can think of a hundred reasons why Russia wouldn't have advertised what they found here at Popigai. And what they found in the 70s isn't necessarily what I could find now, either.
Here, help me with this--it's heavy.
Hey, I've got an idea--what do you say we get our asses back into the Cat?
Heh. I didn't even have to ask you *once*, Fisk.

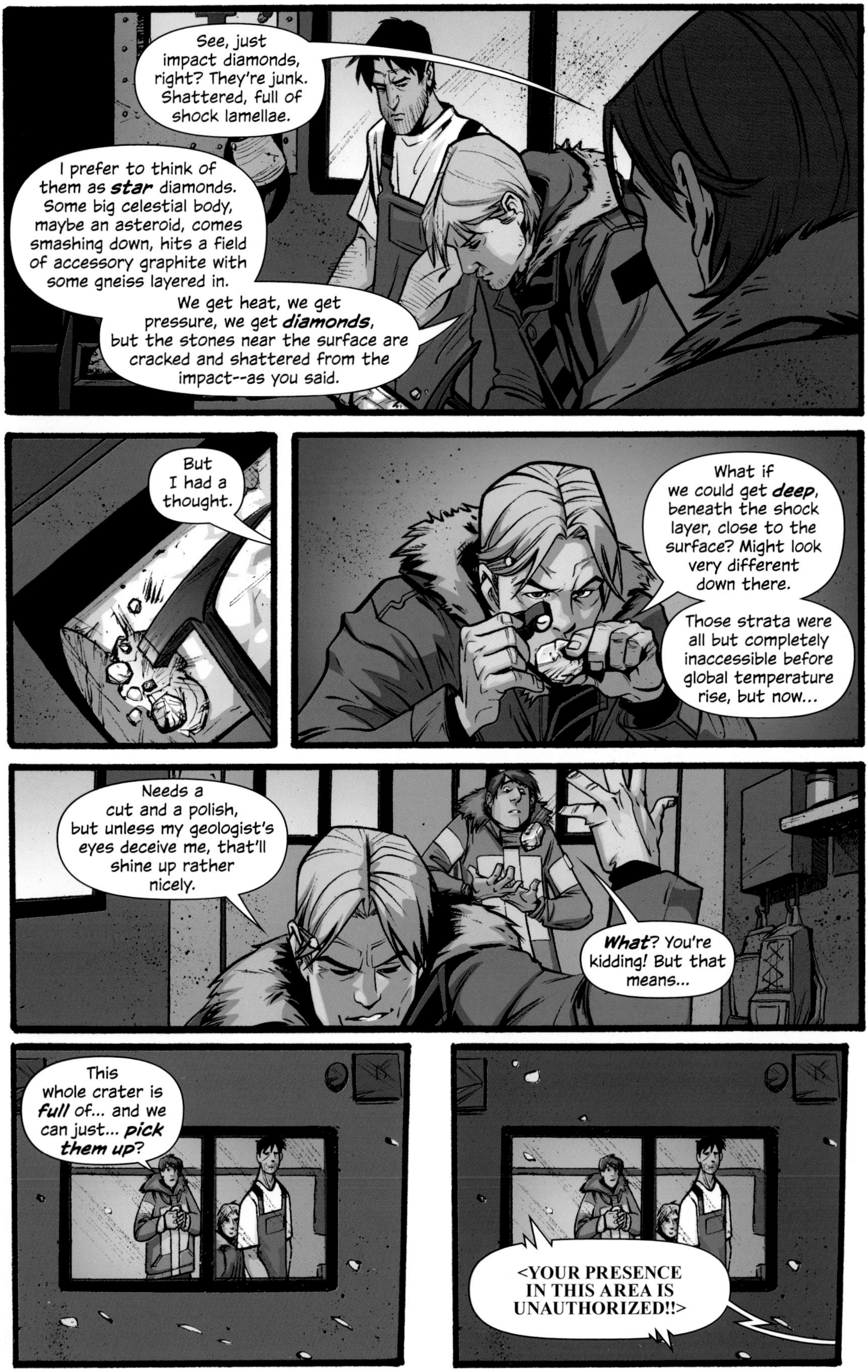
See, just impact diamonds, right? They're junk. Shattered, full of shock lamellae.
I prefer to think of them as **star** diamonds. Some big celestial body, maybe an asteroid, comes smashing down, hits a field of accessory graphite with some gneiss layered in.
We get heat, we get pressure, we get **diamonds**, but the stones near the surface are cracked and shattered from the impact--as you said.
But I had a thought.
What if we could get **deep**, beneath the shock layer, close to the surface? Might look very different down there.
Those strata were all but completely inaccessible before global temperature rise, but now...
Needs a cut and a polish, but unless my geologist's eyes deceive me, that'll shine up rather nicely.
What? You're kidding! But that means...
This whole crater is **full** of... and we can just... **pick them up**?
<YOUR PRESENCE IN THIS AREA IS UNAUTHORIZED!!>

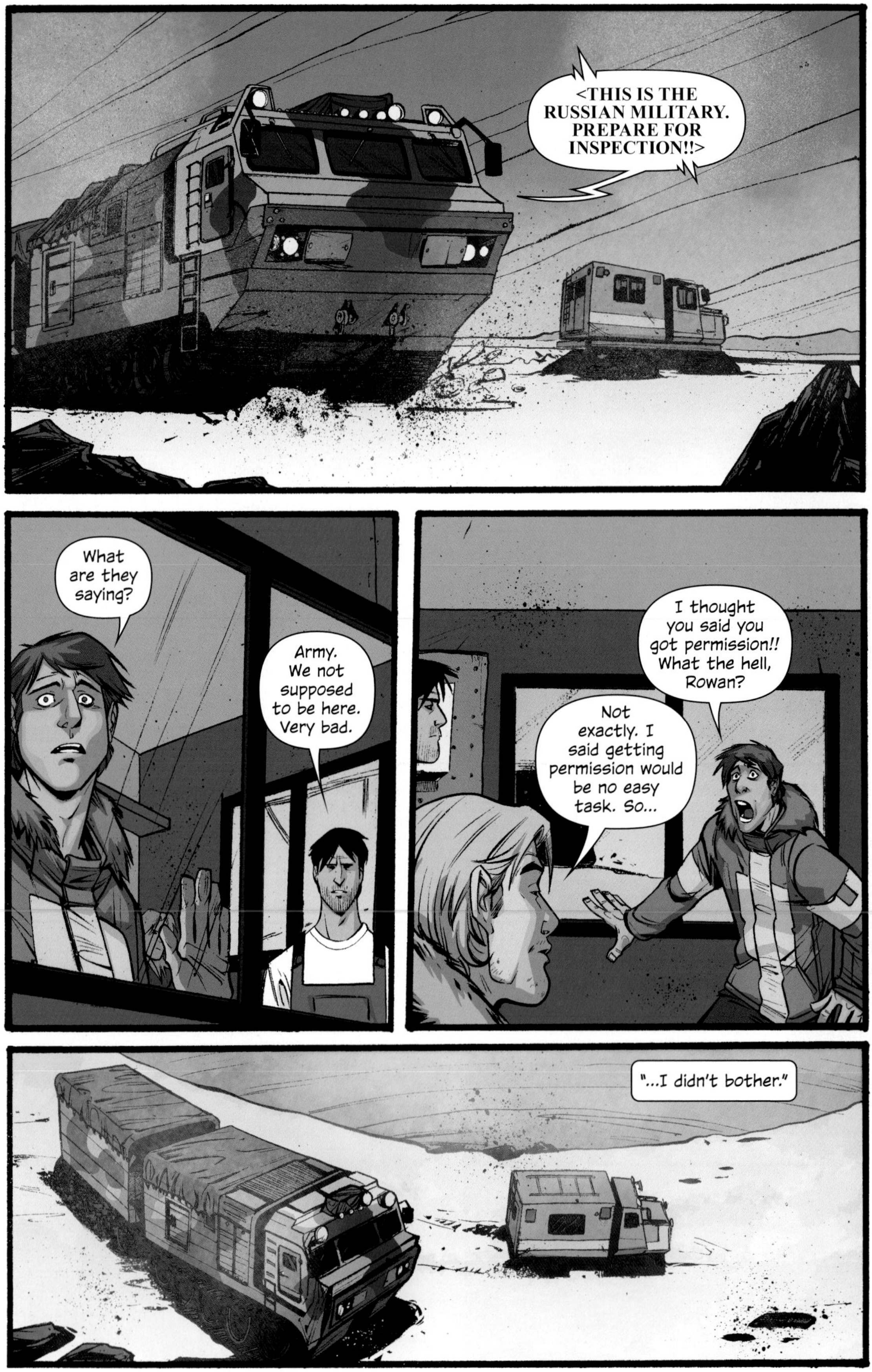
<THIS IS THE RUSSIAN MILITARY. PREPARE FOR INSPECTION!!>
What are they saying?
Army. We not supposed to be here. Very bad.
I thought you said you got permission!! What the hell, Rowan?
Not exactly. I said getting permission would be no easy task. So...
"...I didn't bother."

STOCKHOLM, SWEDEN.

"Receiving the 2002 Nobel Prize in Physics, for her contributions to astrophysical analysis of near-Earth asteroids and related advanced detection techniques, Dr. Charlotte Hayden, United States of America."

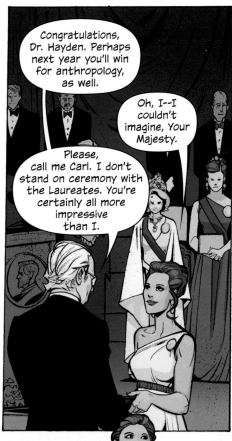

Congratulations, Dr. Hayden. Perhaps next year you'll win for anthropology, as well.

Oh, I--I couldn't imagine, Your Majesty.

Please, call me Carl. I don't stand on ceremony with the Laureates. You're certainly all more impressive than I.

Best wishes on the upcoming addition to your family, as well. Please, bring the child back to Sweden some time. My grandchildren need playmates.

I... honestly, I can't believe any of this is happening!

It wouldn't be if you didn't deserve it, my dear. Now, address your admirers--they're all waiting.

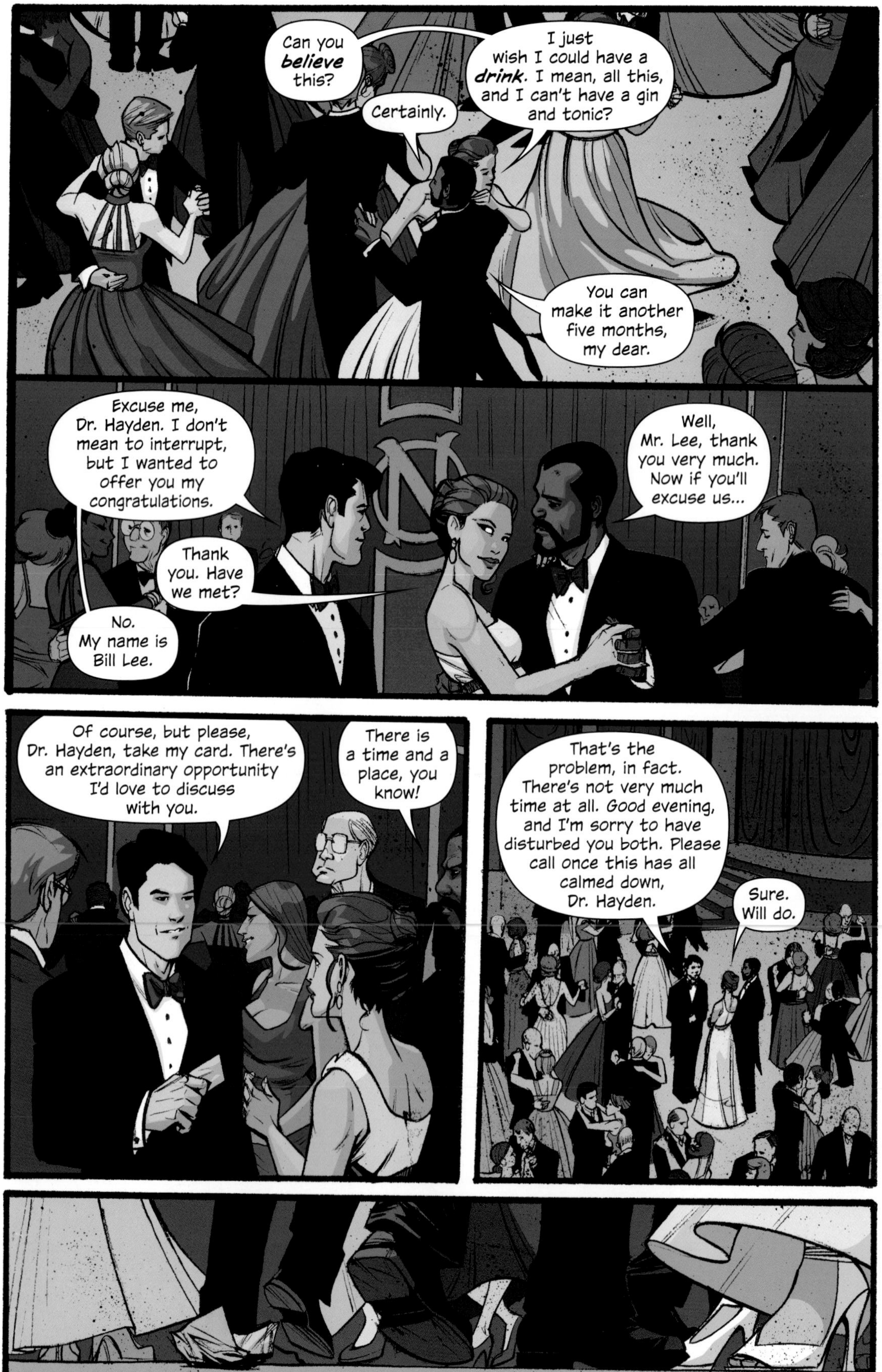
Can you *believe* this?
Certainly.
I just wish I could have a *drink*. I mean, all this, and I can't have a gin and tonic?
You can make it another five months, my dear.
Excuse me, Dr. Hayden. I don't mean to interrupt, but I wanted to offer you my congratulations.
Thank you. Have we met?
No. My name is Bill Lee.
Well, Mr. Lee, thank you very much. Now if you'll excuse us...
Of course, but please, Dr. Hayden, take my card. There's an extraordinary opportunity I'd love to discuss with you.
There is a time and a place, you know!
That's the problem, in fact. There's not very much time at all. Good evening, and I'm sorry to have disturbed you both. Please call once this has all calmed down, Dr. Hayden.
Sure. Will do.

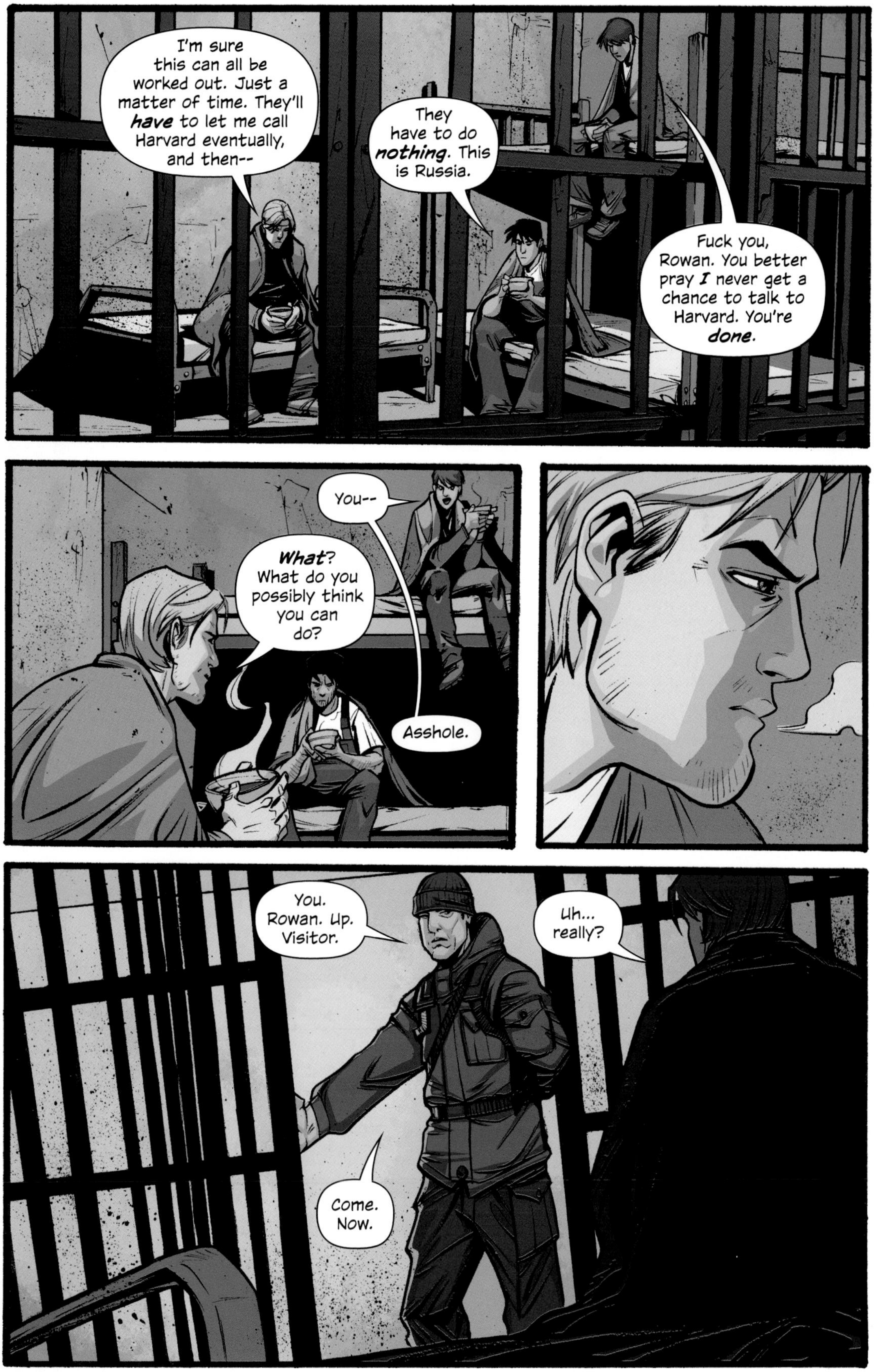
I'm sure this can all be worked out. Just a matter of time. They'll *have* to let me call Harvard eventually, and then--
They have to do *nothing*. This is Russia.
Fuck you, Rowan. You better pray *I* never get a chance to talk to Harvard. You're *done*.
You--
What? What do you possibly think you can do?
Asshole.
You. Rowan. Up. Visitor.
Uh... really?
Come. Now.

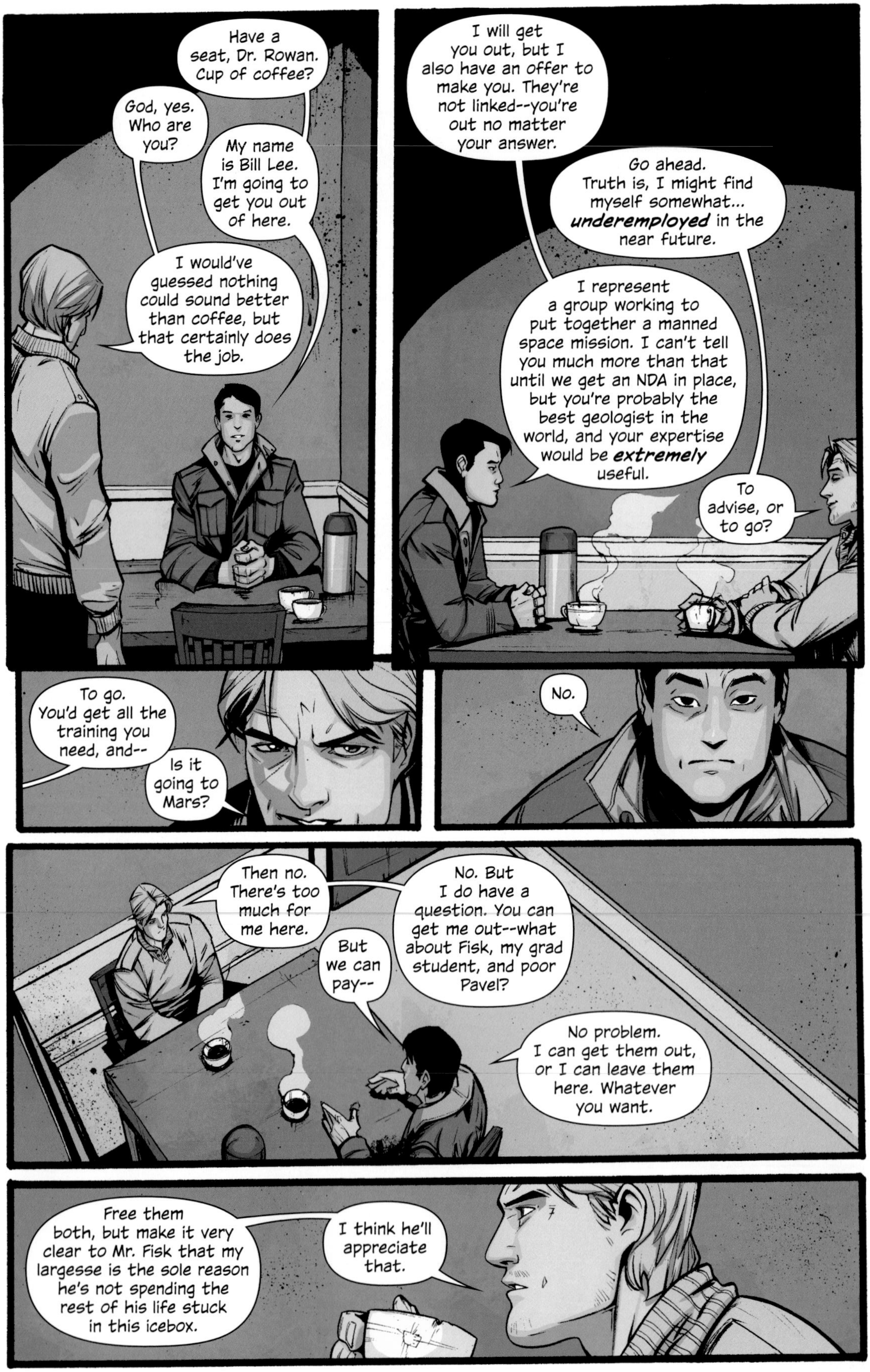
Have a seat, Dr. Rowan. Cup of coffee?
God, yes. Who are you?
My name is Bill Lee. I'm going to get you out of here.
I would've guessed nothing could sound better than coffee, but that certainly does the job.
I will get you out, but I also have an offer to make you. They're not linked--you're out no matter your answer.
Go ahead. Truth is, I might find myself somewhat... *underemployed* in the near future.
I represent a group working to put together a manned space mission. I can't tell you much more than that until we get an NDA in place, but you're probably the best geologist in the world, and your expertise would be *extremely* useful.
To advise, or to go?
To go. You'd get all the training you need, and--
Is it going to Mars?
No.
Then no. There's too much for me here.
But we can pay--
No. But I do have a question. You can get me out--what about Fisk, my grad student, and poor Pavel?
No problem. I can get them out, or I can leave them here. Whatever you want.
Free them both, but make it very clear to Mr. Fisk that my largesse is the sole reason he's not spending the rest of his life stuck in this icebox.
I think he'll appreciate that.

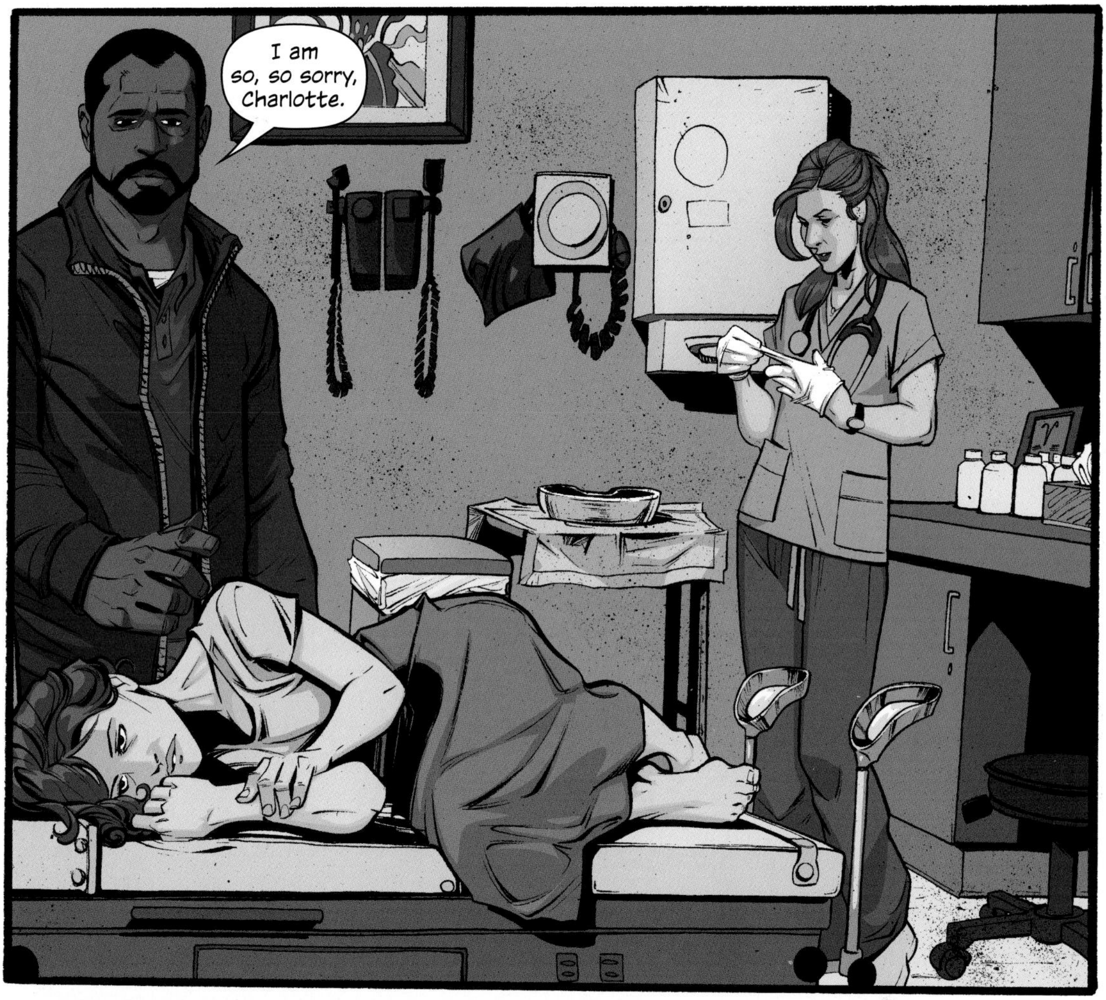
I am so, so sorry, Charlotte.

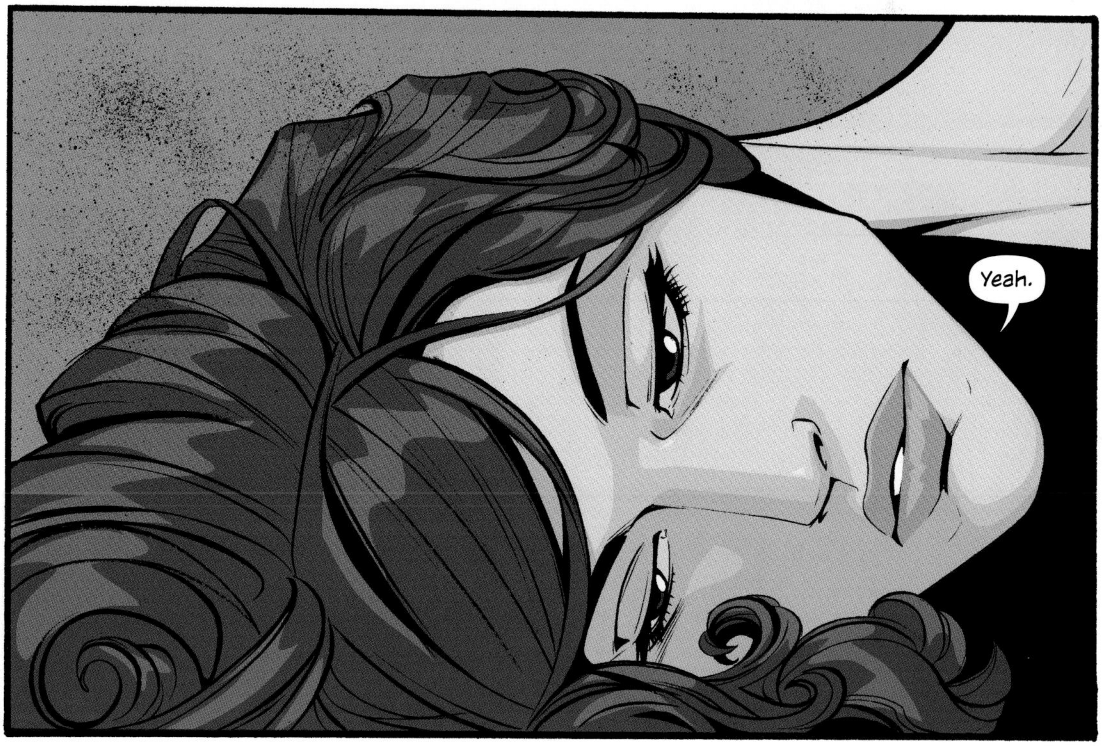
Yeah.

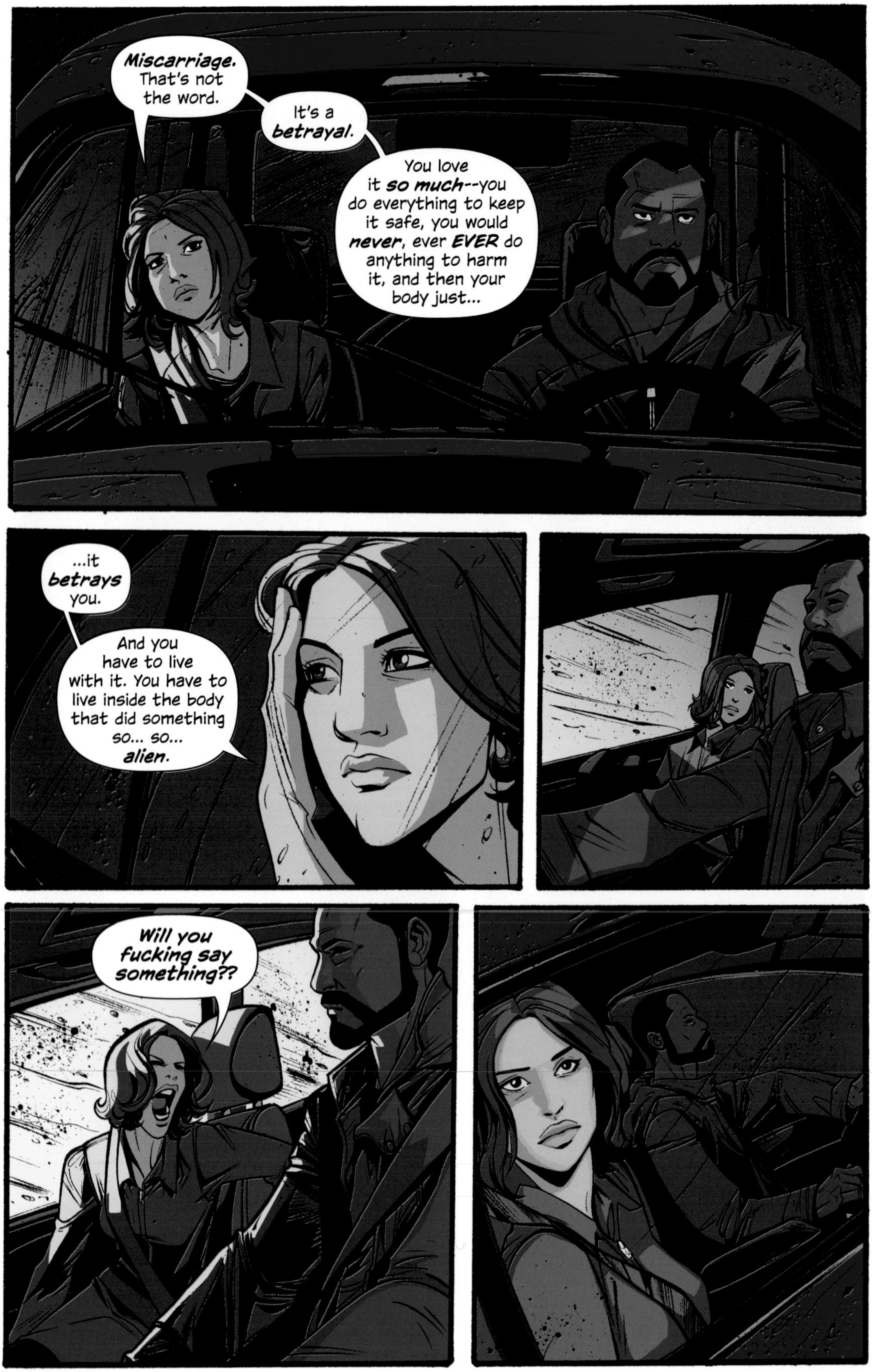

Miscarriage. That's not the word.
It's a betrayal.
You love it so much--you do everything to keep it safe, you would never, ever EVER do anything to harm it, and then your body just...
...it betrays you.
And you have to live with it. You have to live inside the body that did something so... so... alien.
Will you fucking say something??

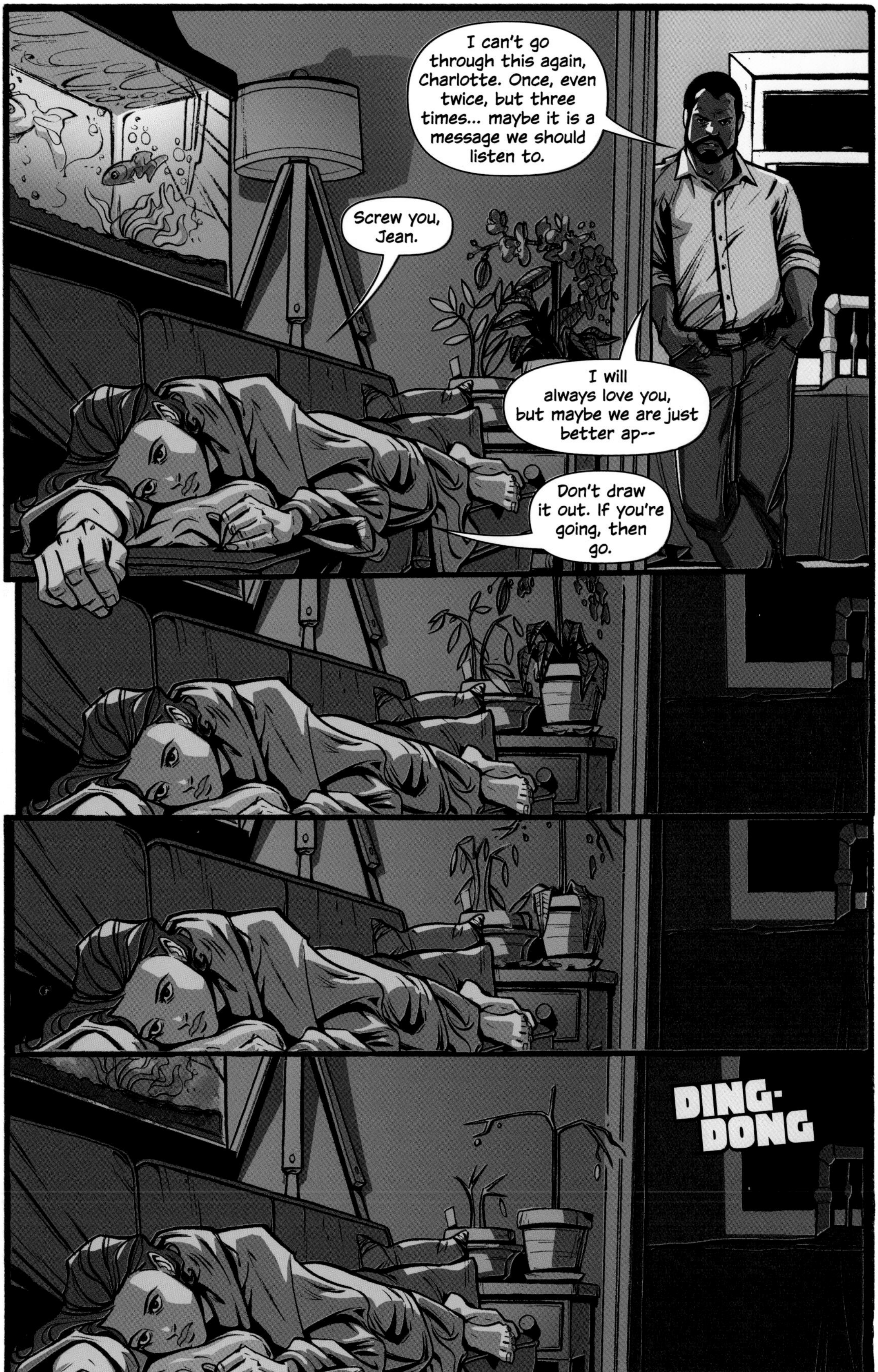
I can't go through this again, Charlotte. Once, even twice, but three times... maybe it is a message we should listen to.
Screw you, Jean.
I will always love you, but maybe we are just better ap--
Don't draw it out. If you're going, then go.
DING-DONG

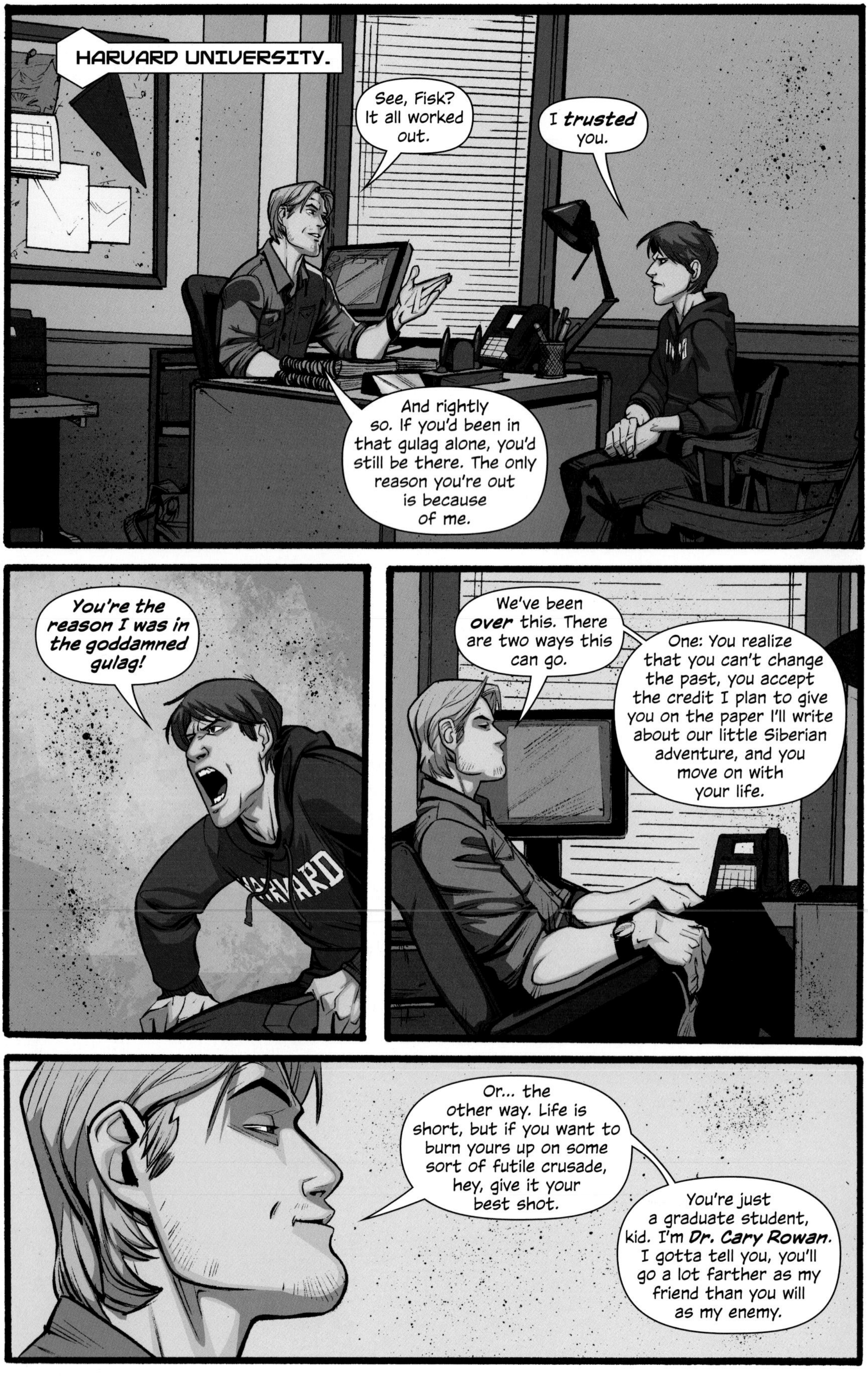
HARVARD UNIVERSITY.
See, Fisk? It all worked out.
I *trusted* you.
And rightly so. If you'd been in that gulag alone, you'd still be there. The only reason you're out is because of me.
You're the reason I was in the goddamned gulag!
We've been *over* this. There are two ways this can go.
One: You realize that you can't change the past, you accept the credit I plan to give you on the paper I'll write about our little Siberian adventure, and you move on with your life.
Or... the other way. Life is short, but if you want to burn yours up on some sort of futile crusade, hey, give it your best shot.
You're just a graduate student, kid. I'm *Dr. Cary Rowan.* I gotta tell you, you'll go a lot farther as my friend than you will as my enemy.
HARVARD

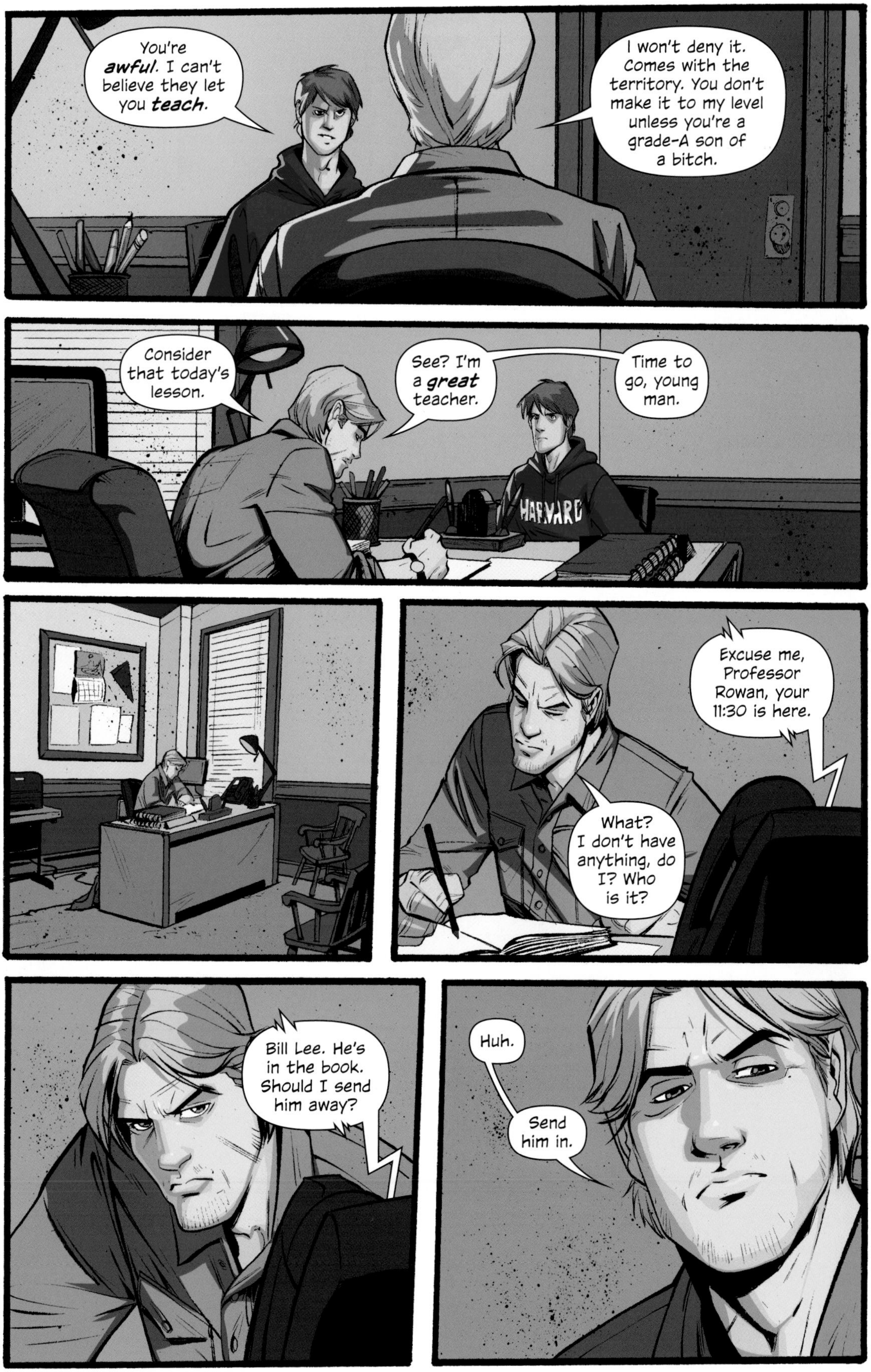
You're *awful*. I can't believe they let you *teach*.
I won't deny it. Comes with the territory. You don't make it to my level unless you're a grade-A son of a bitch.
Consider that today's lesson.
See? I'm a *great* teacher.
Time to go, young man.
HARVARD
Excuse me, Professor Rowan, your 11:30 is here.
What? I don't have anything, do I? Who is it?
Bill Lee. He's in the book. Should I send him away?
Huh.
Send him in.

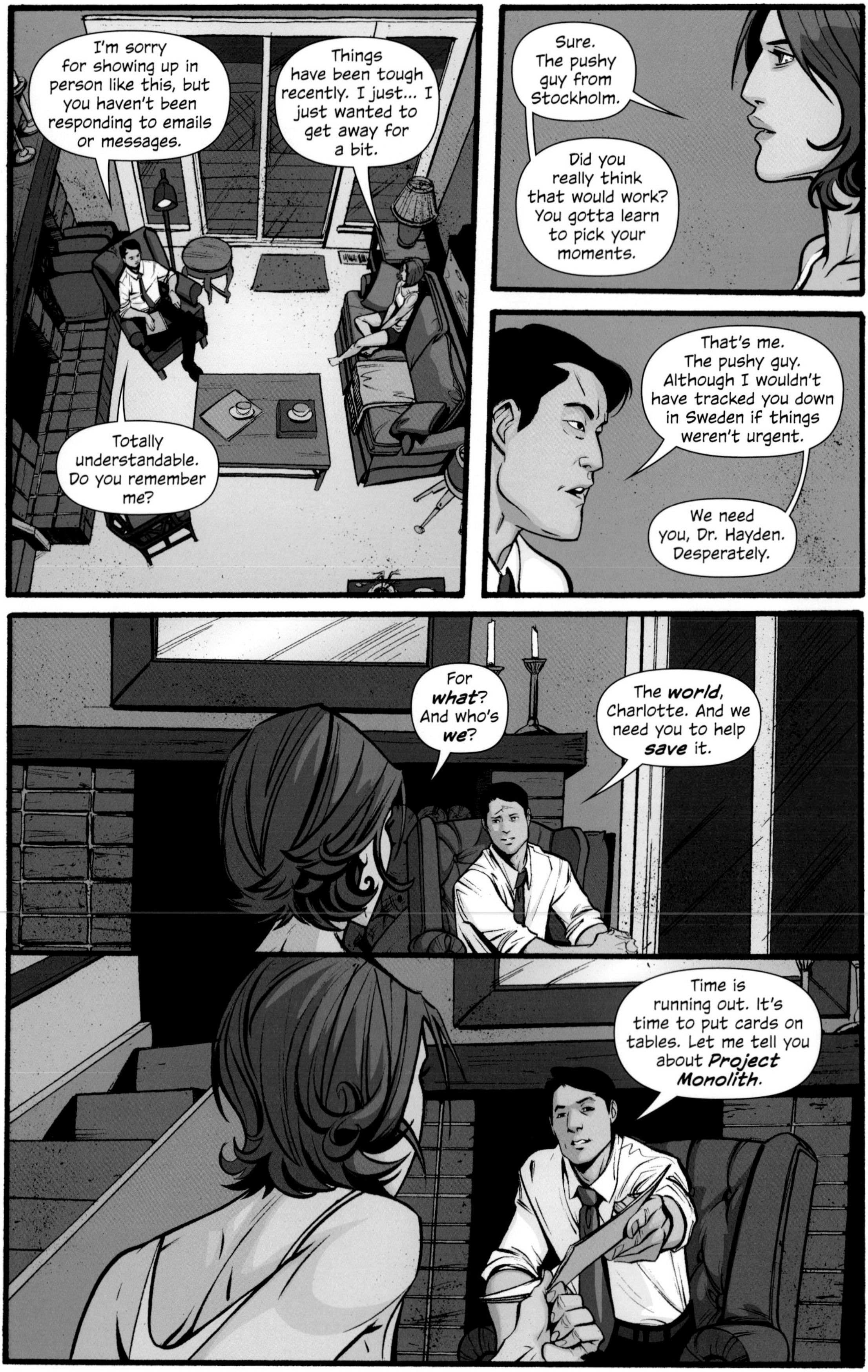
I'm sorry for showing up in person like this, but you haven't been responding to emails or messages.
Things have been tough recently. I just... I just wanted to get away for a bit.
Totally understandable. Do you remember me?
Sure. The pushy guy from Stockholm.
Did you really think that would work? You gotta learn to pick your moments.
That's me. The pushy guy. Although I wouldn't have tracked you down in Sweden if things weren't urgent.
We need you, Dr. Hayden. Desperately.
For *what*? And who's *we*?
The *world*, Charlotte. And we need you to help *save* it.
Time is running out. It's time to put cards on tables. Let me tell you about *Project Monolith*.

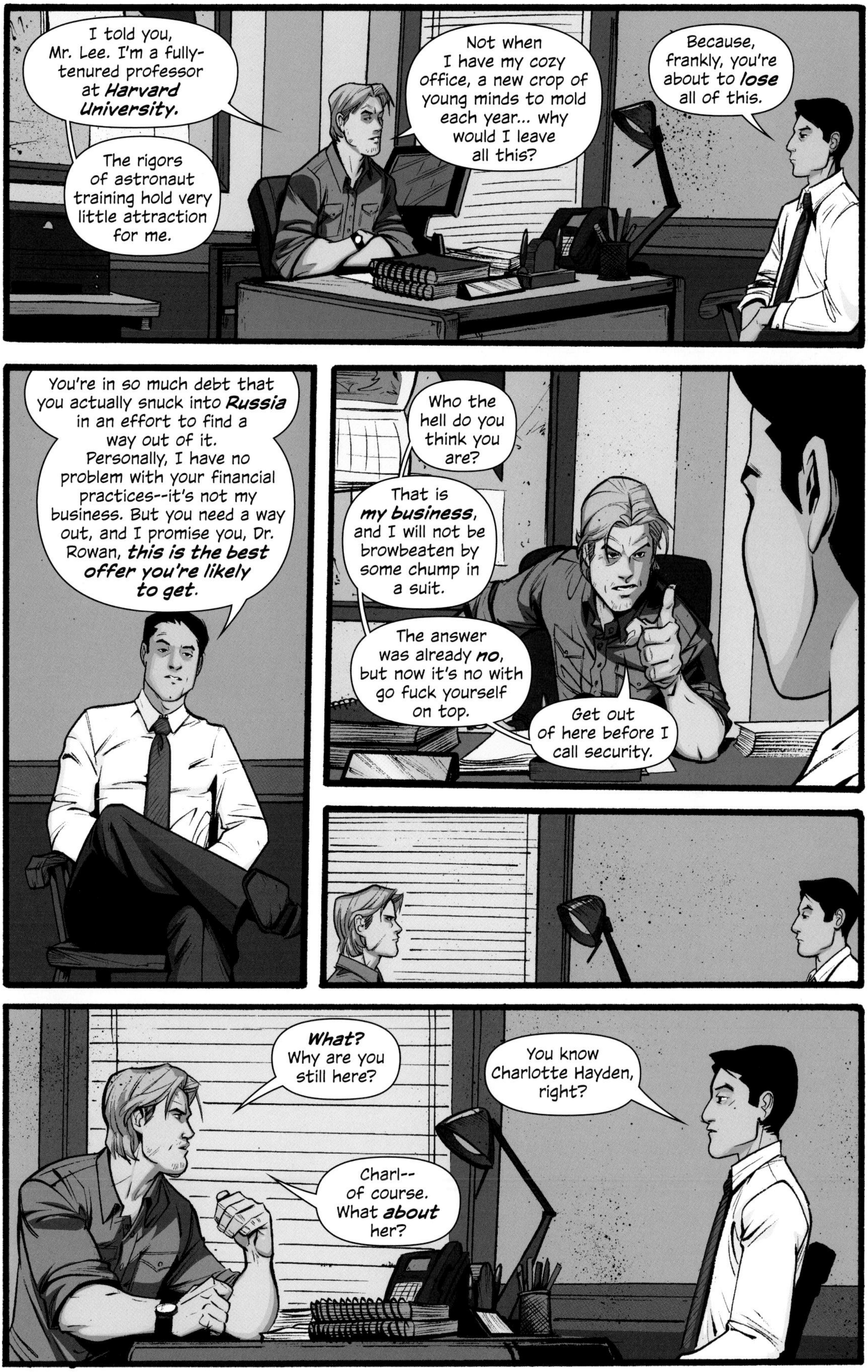
I told you, Mr. Lee. I'm a fully-tenured professor at *Harvard University.*
The rigors of astronaut training hold very little attraction for me.
Not when I have my cozy office, a new crop of young minds to mold each year... why would I leave all this?
Because, frankly, you're about to *lose* all of this.
You're in so much debt that you actually snuck into *Russia* in an effort to find a way out of it. Personally, I have no problem with your financial practices--it's not my business. But you need a way out, and I promise you, Dr. Rowan, ***this is the best offer you're likely to get***.
Who the hell do you think you are?
That is ***my business***, and I will not be browbeaten by some chump in a suit.
The answer was already ***no***, but now it's no with go fuck yourself on top.
Get out of here before I call security.
What? Why are you still here?
You know Charlotte Hayden, right?
Charl-- of course. What ***about*** her?

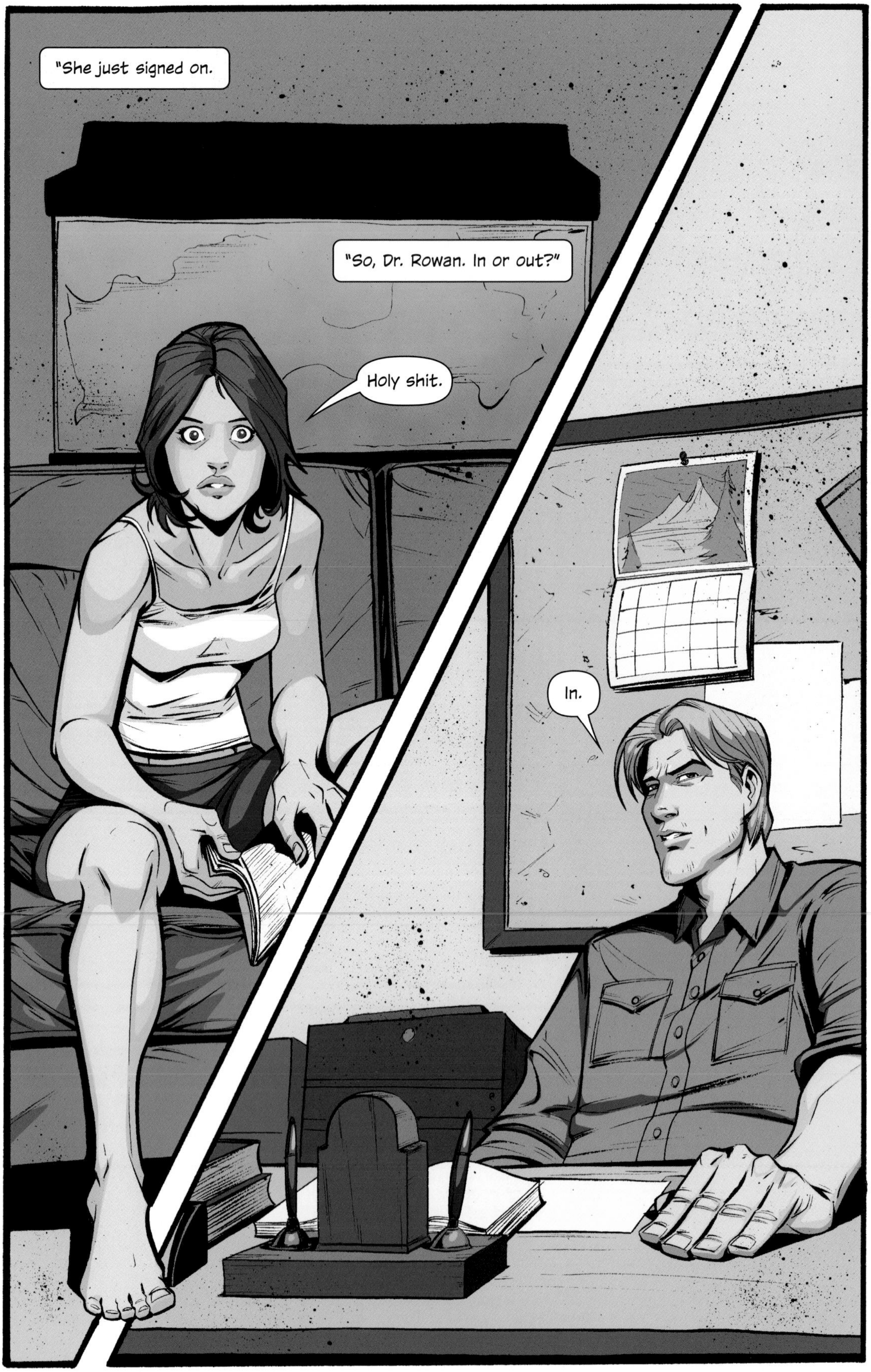
"She just signed on.
"So, Dr. Rowan. In or out?"
Holy shit.
In.

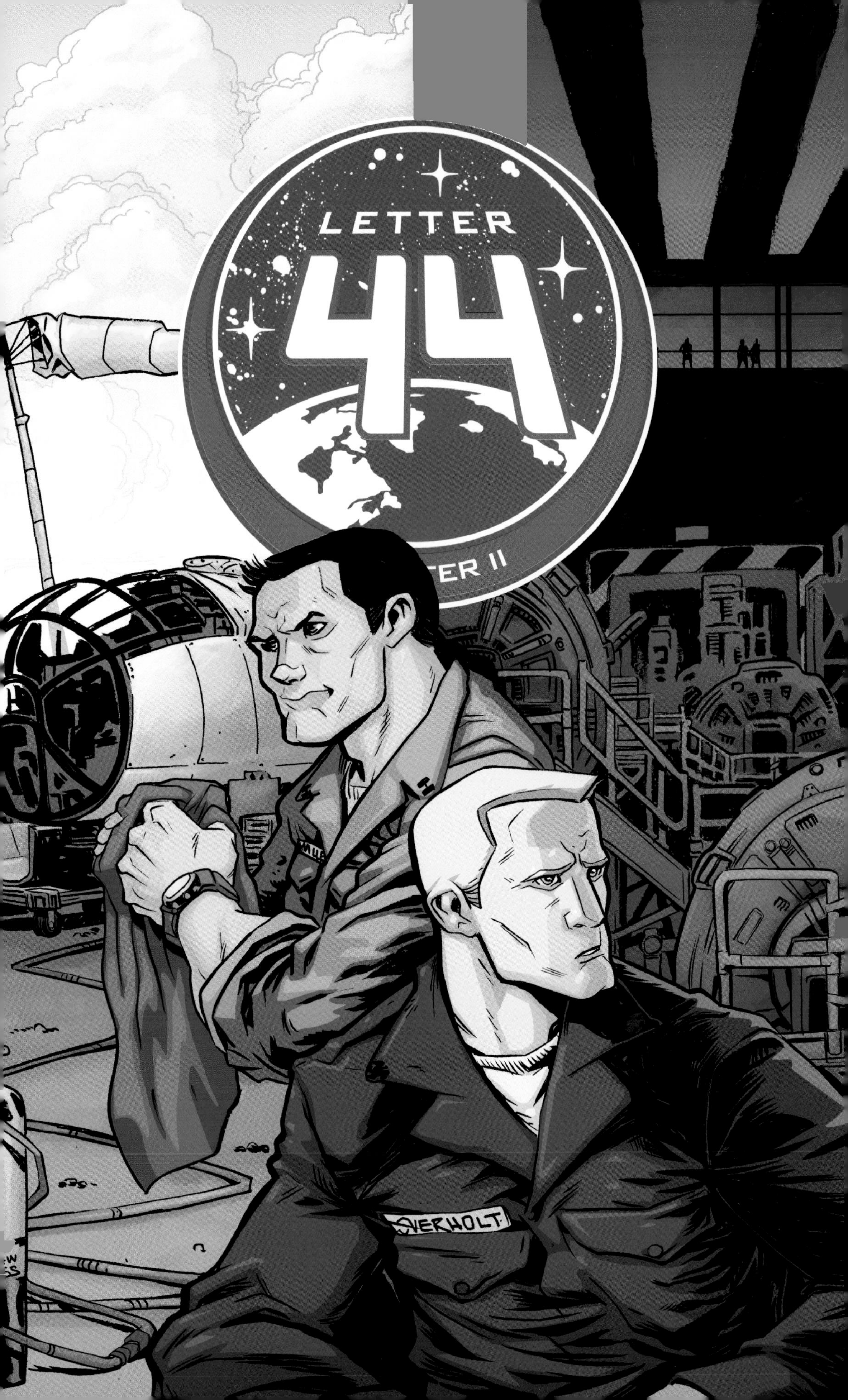
LETTER
44

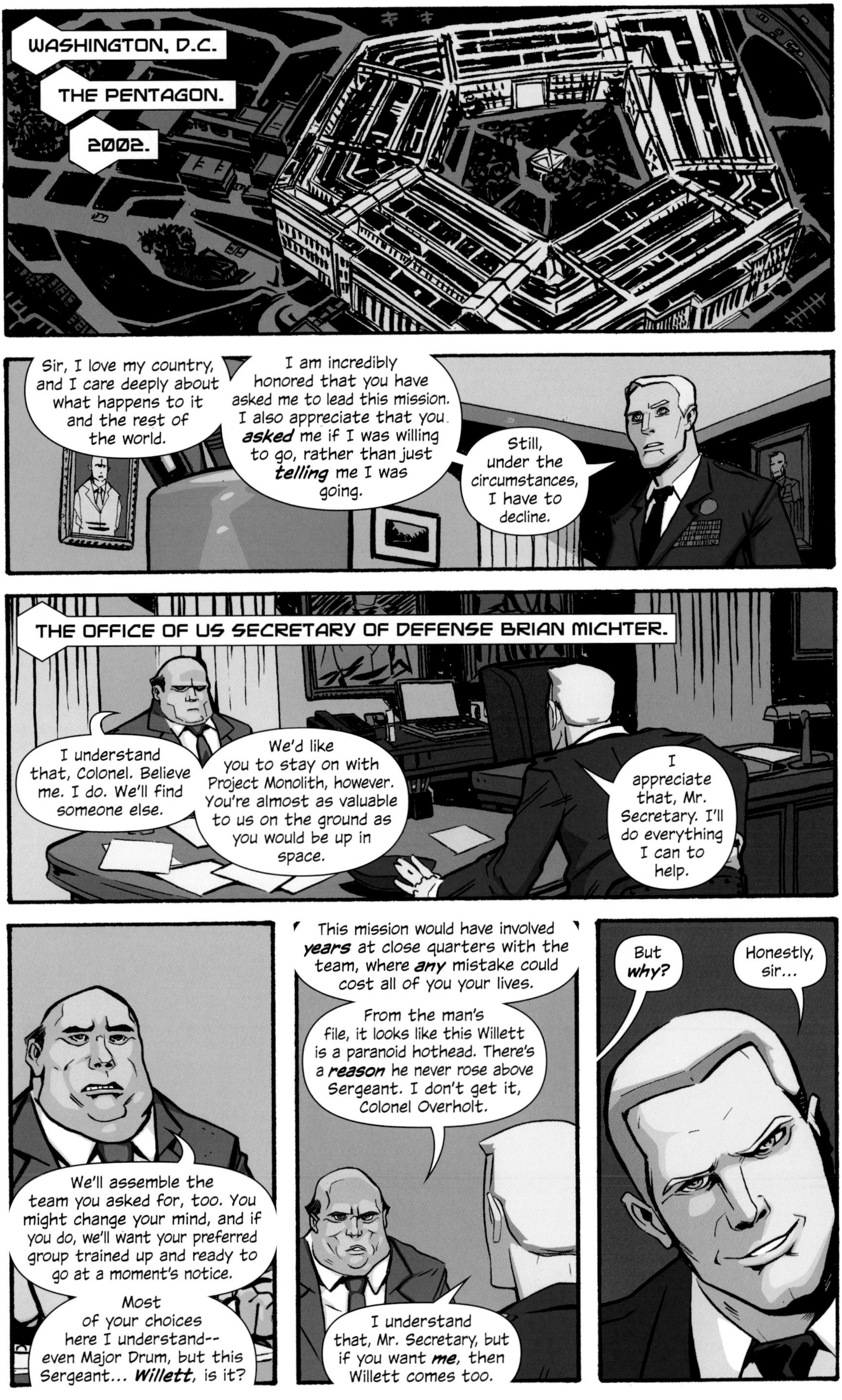
WASHINGTON, D.C.
THE PENTAGON.
2002.
Sir, I love my country, and I care deeply about what happens to it and the rest of the world.
I am incredibly honored that you have asked me to lead this mission. I also appreciate that you **asked** me if I was willing to go, rather than just **telling** me I was going.
Still, under the circumstances, I have to decline.
THE OFFICE OF US SECRETARY OF DEFENSE BRIAN MICHTER.
I understand that, Colonel. Believe me. I do. We'll find someone else.
We'd like you to stay on with Project Monolith, however. You're almost as valuable to us on the ground as you would be up in space.
I appreciate that, Mr. Secretary. I'll do everything I can to help.
We'll assemble the team you asked for, too. You might change your mind, and if you do, we'll want your preferred group trained up and ready to go at a moment's notice.
Most of your choices here I understand-- even Major Drum, but this Sergeant... **Willett**, is it?
This mission would have involved **years** at close quarters with the team, where **any** mistake could cost all of you your lives.
From the man's file, it looks like this Willett is a paranoid hothead. There's a **reason** he never rose above Sergeant. I don't get it, Colonel Overholt.
I understand that, Mr. Secretary, but if you want **me**, then Willett comes too.
But **why?**
Honestly, sir...

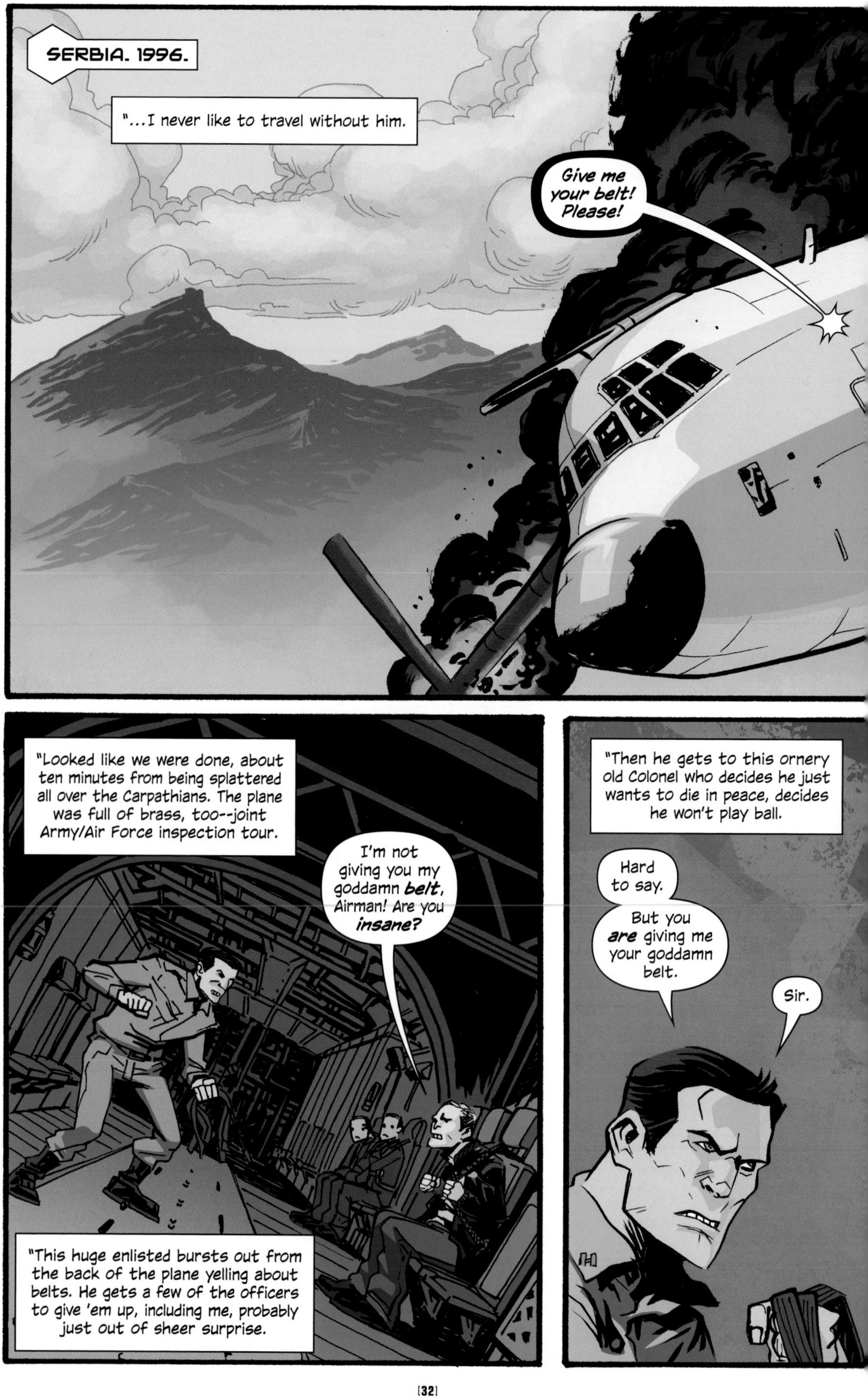
SERBIA. 1996.
"...I never like to travel without him.
Give me your belt! Please!
"Looked like we were done, about ten minutes from being splattered all over the Carpathians. The plane was full of brass, too--joint Army/Air Force inspection tour.
I'm not giving you my goddamn belt, Airman! Are you insane?
"This huge enlisted bursts out from the back of the plane yelling about belts. He gets a few of the officers to give 'em up, including me, probably just out of sheer surprise.
"Then he gets to this ornery old Colonel who decides he just wants to die in peace, decides he won't play ball.
Hard to say.
But you are giving me your goddamn belt.
Sir.

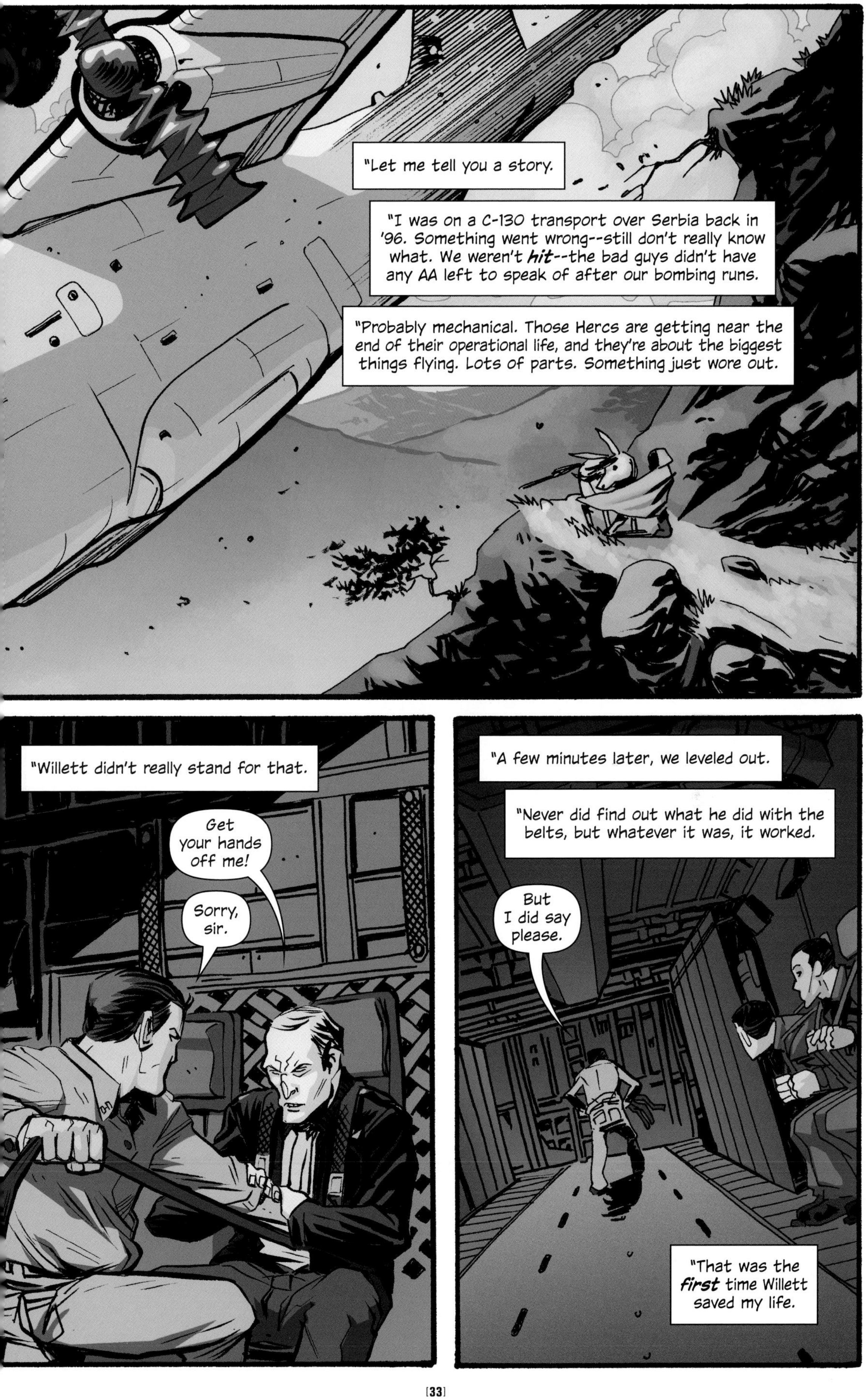
"Let me tell you a story.
"I was on a C-130 transport over Serbia back in '96. Something went wrong--still don't really know what. We weren't *hit*--the bad guys didn't have any AA left to speak of after our bombing runs.
"Probably mechanical. Those Hercs are getting near the end of their operational life, and they're about the biggest things flying. Lots of parts. Something just wore out.
"Willett didn't really stand for that.
Get your hands off me!
Sorry, sir.
"A few minutes later, we leveled out.
"Never did find out what he did with the belts, but whatever it was, it worked.
But I did say please.
"That was the *first* time Willett saved my life.

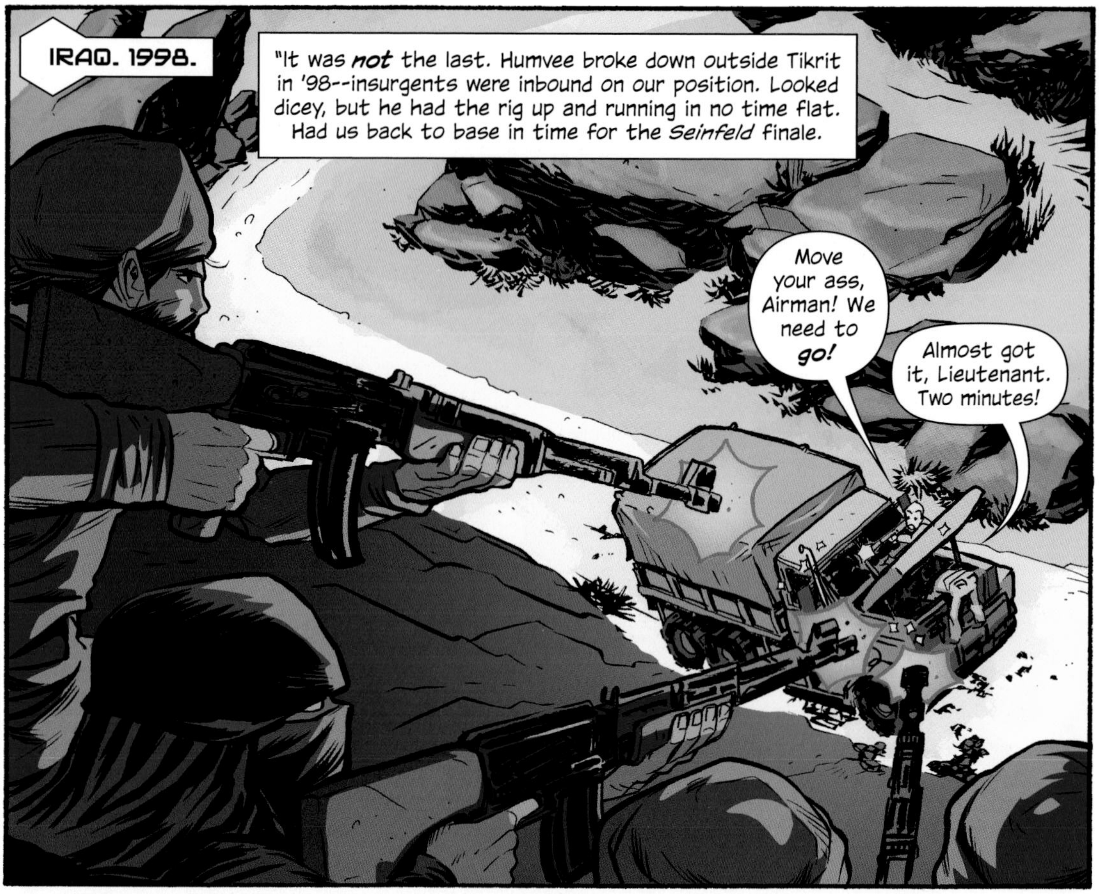
IRAQ. 1998.
"It was *not* the last. Humvee broke down outside Tikrit in '98--insurgents were inbound on our position. Looked dicey, but he had the rig up and running in no time flat. Had us back to base in time for the *Seinfeld* finale.
Move your ass, Airman! We need to *go!*
Almost got it, Lieutenant. Two minutes!

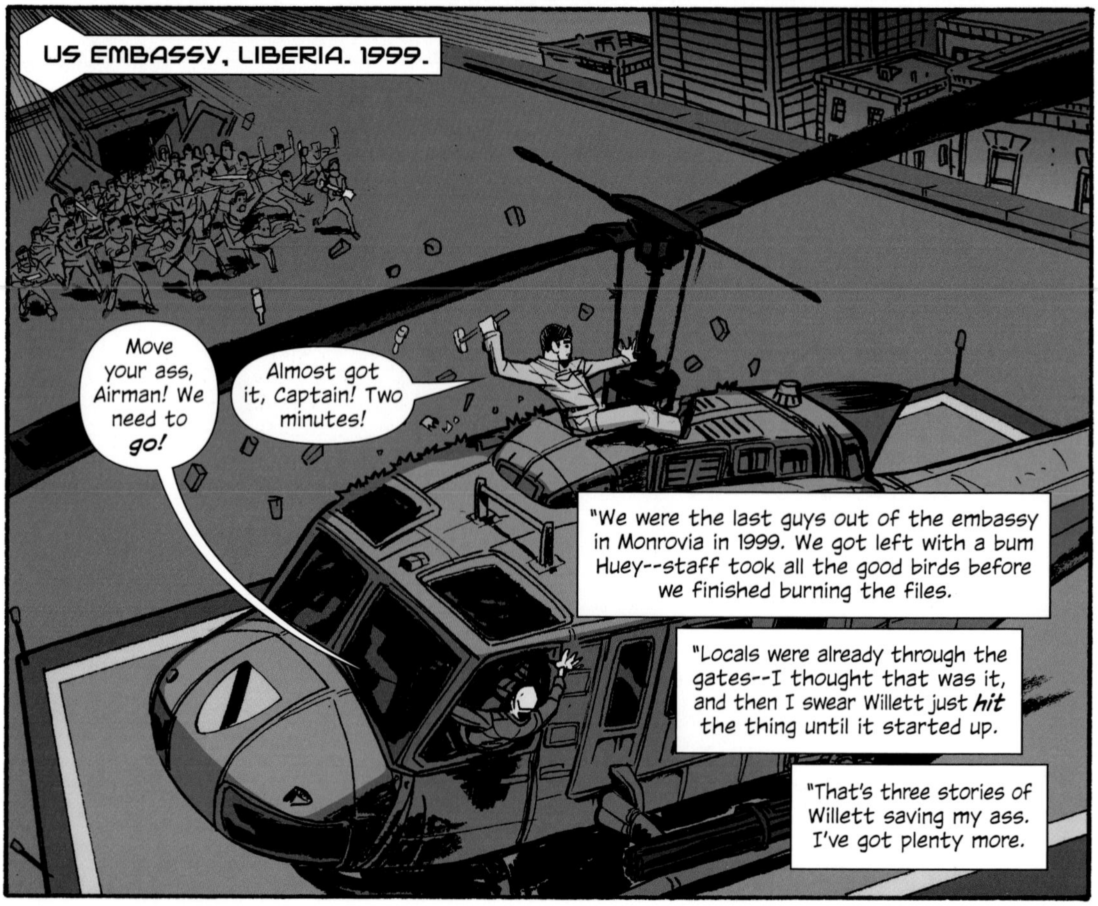
US EMBASSY, LIBERIA. 1999.
Move your ass, Airman! We need to *go!*
Almost got it, Captain! Two minutes!
"We were the last guys out of the embassy in Monrovia in 1999. We got left with a bum Huey--staff took all the good birds before we finished burning the files.
"Locals were already through the gates--I thought that was it, and then I swear Willett just *hit* the thing until it started up.
"That's three stories of Willett saving my ass. I've got plenty more.

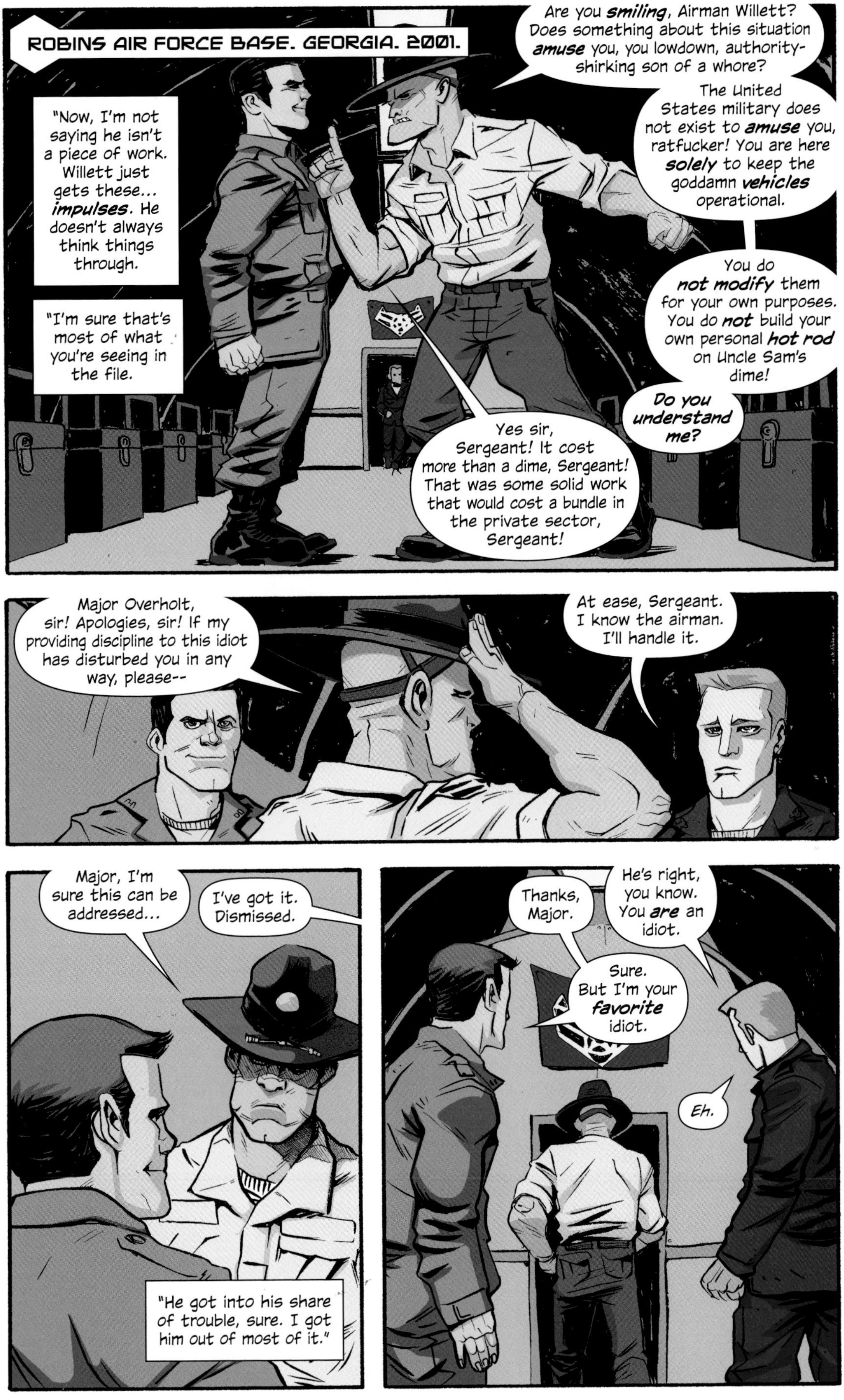
ROBINS AIR FORCE BASE. GEORGIA. 2001.
"Now, I'm not saying he isn't a piece of work. Willett just gets these... impulses. He doesn't always think things through.
"I'm sure that's most of what you're seeing in the file.
Are you smiling, Airman Willett? Does something about this situation amuse you, you lowdown, authority-shirking son of a whore?
The United States military does not exist to amuse you, ratfucker! You are here solely to keep the goddamn vehicles operational.
You do not modify them for your own purposes. You do not build your own personal hot rod on Uncle Sam's dime!
Do you understand me?
Yes sir, Sergeant! It cost more than a dime, Sergeant! That was some solid work that would cost a bundle in the private sector, Sergeant!
Major Overholt, sir! Apologies, sir! If my providing discipline to this idiot has disturbed you in any way, please--
At ease, Sergeant. I know the airman. I'll handle it.
Major, I'm sure this can be addressed...
I've got it. Dismissed.
"He got into his share of trouble, sure. I got him out of most of it."
Thanks, Major.
He's right, you know. You are an idiot.
Sure. But I'm your favorite idiot.
Eh.

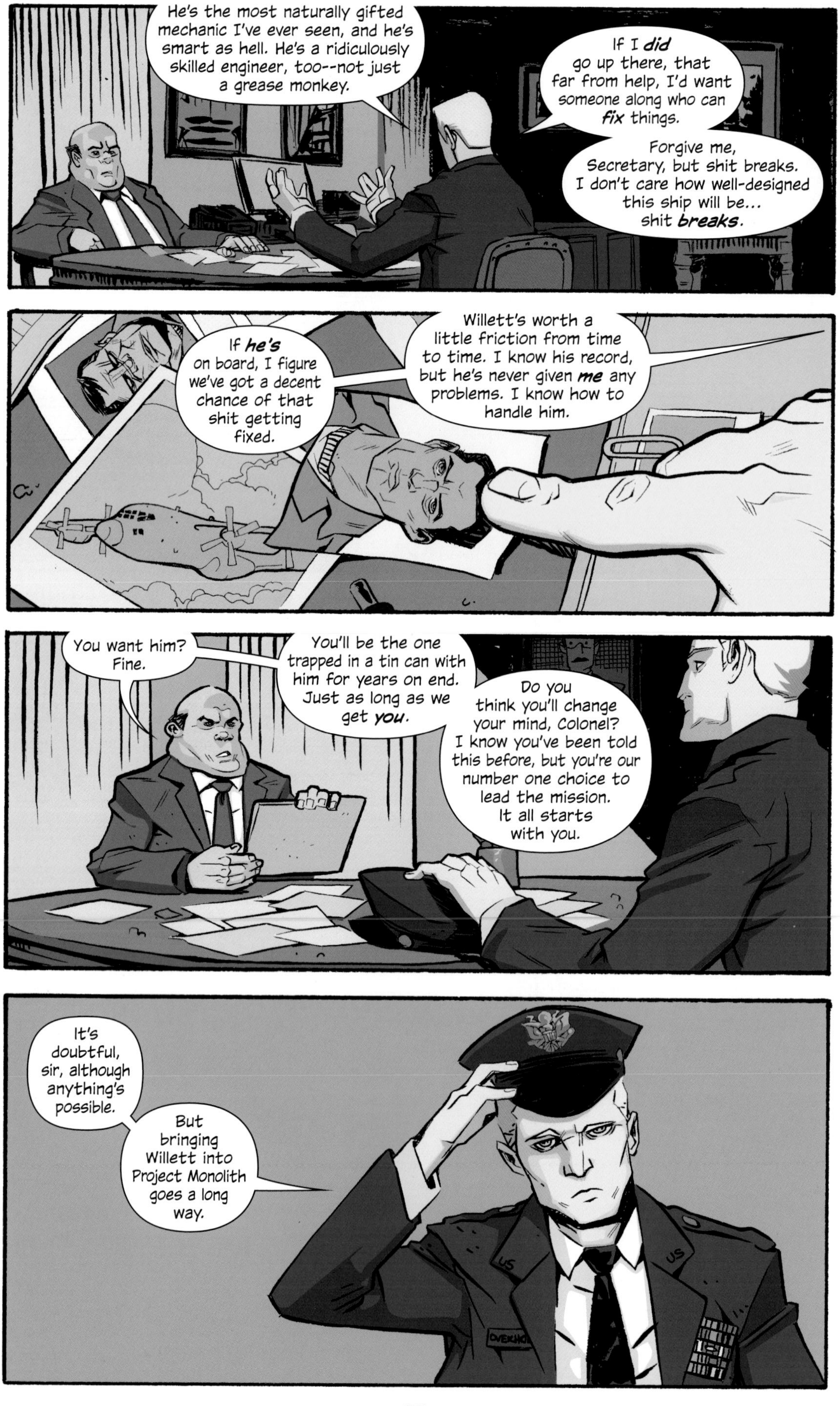
He's the most naturally gifted mechanic I've ever seen, and he's smart as hell. He's a ridiculously skilled engineer, too--not just a grease monkey.
If I *did* go up there, that far from help, I'd want someone along who can *fix* things.
Forgive me, Secretary, but shit breaks. I don't care how well-designed this ship will be... shit *breaks*.
Willett's worth a little friction from time to time. I know his record, but he's never given *me* any problems. I know how to handle him.
If *he's* on board, I figure we've got a decent chance of that shit getting fixed.
You want him? Fine.
You'll be the one trapped in a tin can with him for years on end. Just as long as we get *you*.
Do you think you'll change your mind, Colonel? I know you've been told this before, but you're our number one choice to lead the mission. It all starts with you.
It's doubtful, sir, although anything's possible.
But bringing Willett into Project Monolith goes a long way.

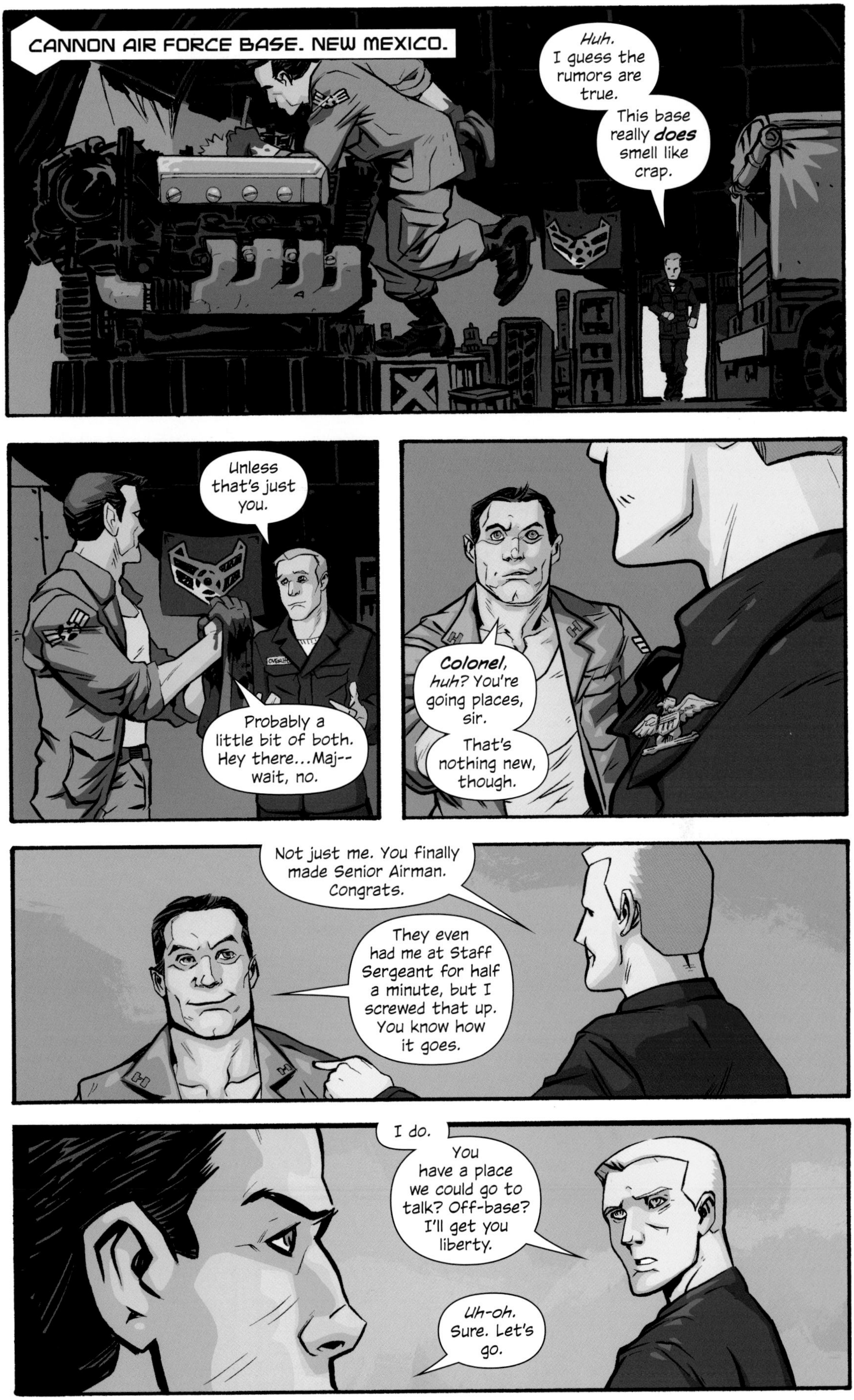
CANNON AIR FORCE BASE. NEW MEXICO.
Huh. I guess the rumors are true.
This base really does smell like crap.
Unless that's just you.
Probably a little bit of both. Hey there...Maj--wait, no.
Colonel, huh? You're going places, sir.
That's nothing new, though.
Not just me. You finally made Senior Airman. Congrats.
They even had me at Staff Sergeant for half a minute, but I screwed that up. You know how it goes.
I do.
You have a place we could go to talk? Off-base? I'll get you liberty.
Uh-oh. Sure. Let's go.

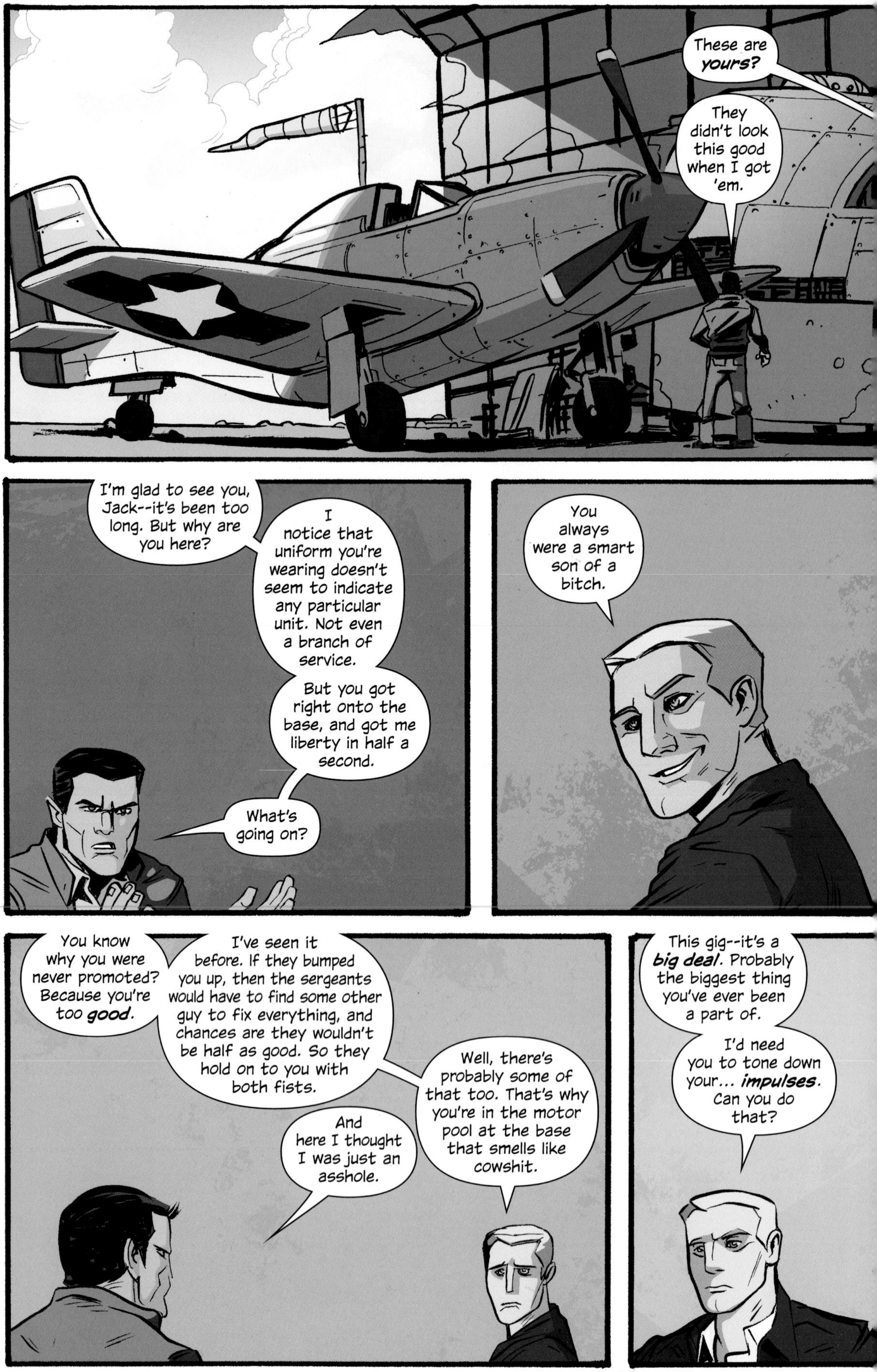
These are *yours?*
They didn't look this good when I got 'em.
I'm glad to see you, Jack--it's been too long. But why are you here?
I notice that uniform you're wearing doesn't seem to indicate any particular unit. Not even a branch of service.
But you got right onto the base, and got me liberty in half a second.
What's going on?
You always were a smart son of a bitch.
You know why you were never promoted? Because you're too *good*.
I've seen it before. If they bumped you up, then the sergeants would have to find some other guy to fix everything, and chances are they wouldn't be half as good. So they hold on to you with both fists.
And here I thought I was just an asshole.
Well, there's probably some of that too. That's why you're in the motor pool at the base that smells like cowshit.
This gig--it's a *big deal*. Probably the biggest thing you've ever been a part of.
I'd need you to tone down your... *impulses*. Can you do that?

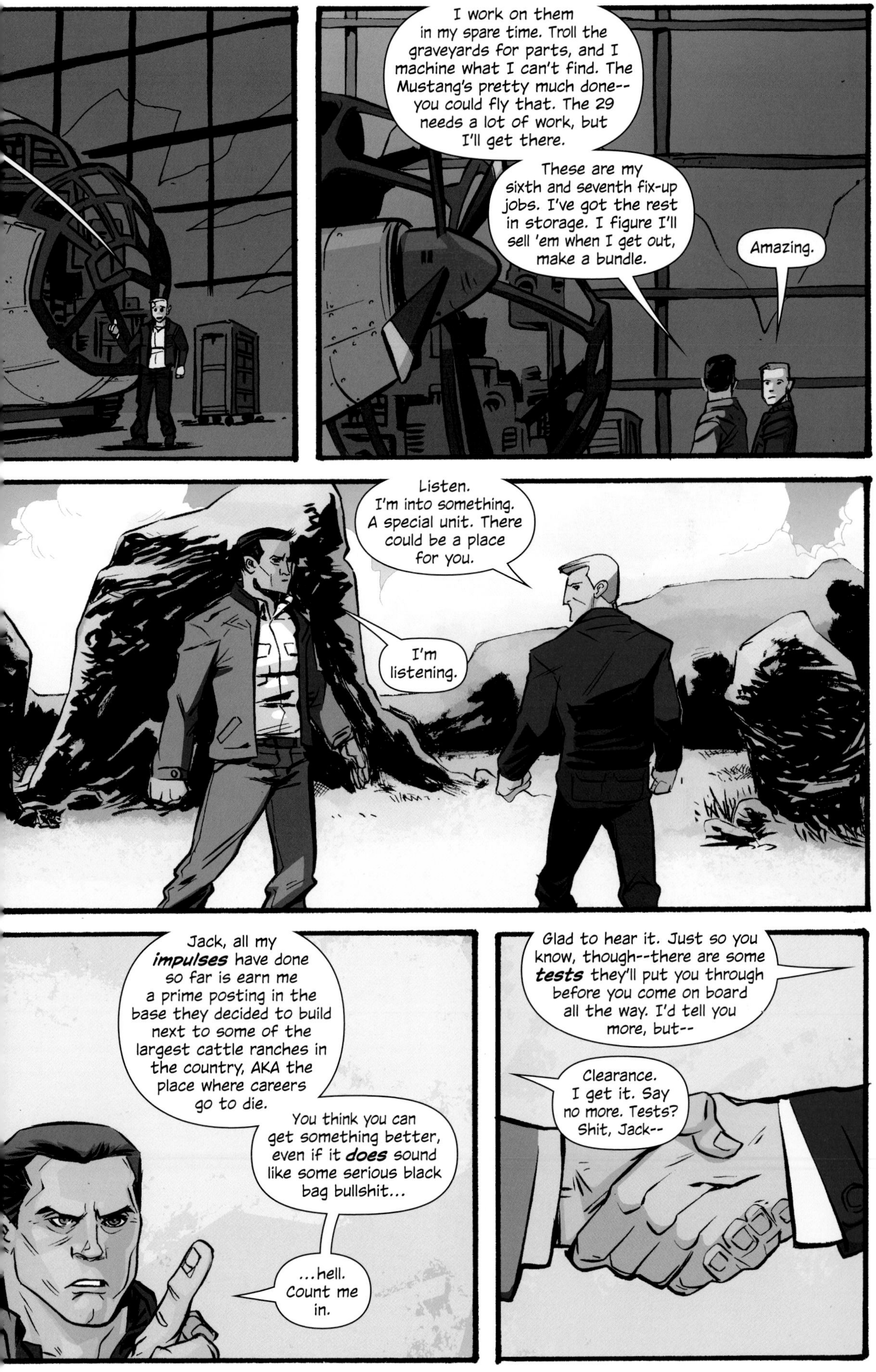
I work on them in my spare time. Troll the graveyards for parts, and I machine what I can't find. The Mustang's pretty much done--you could fly that. The 29 needs a lot of work, but I'll get there.
These are my sixth and seventh fix-up jobs. I've got the rest in storage. I figure I'll sell 'em when I get out, make a bundle.
Amazing.
Listen. I'm into something. A special unit. There could be a place for you.
I'm listening.
Jack, all my ***impulses*** have done so far is earn me a prime posting in the base they decided to build next to some of the largest cattle ranches in the country, AKA the place where careers go to die.
You think you can get something better, even if it ***does*** sound like some serious black bag bullshit...
...hell. Count me in.
Glad to hear it. Just so you know, though--there are some ***tests*** they'll put you through before you come on board all the way. I'd tell you more, but--
Clearance. I get it. Say no more. Tests? Shit, Jack--

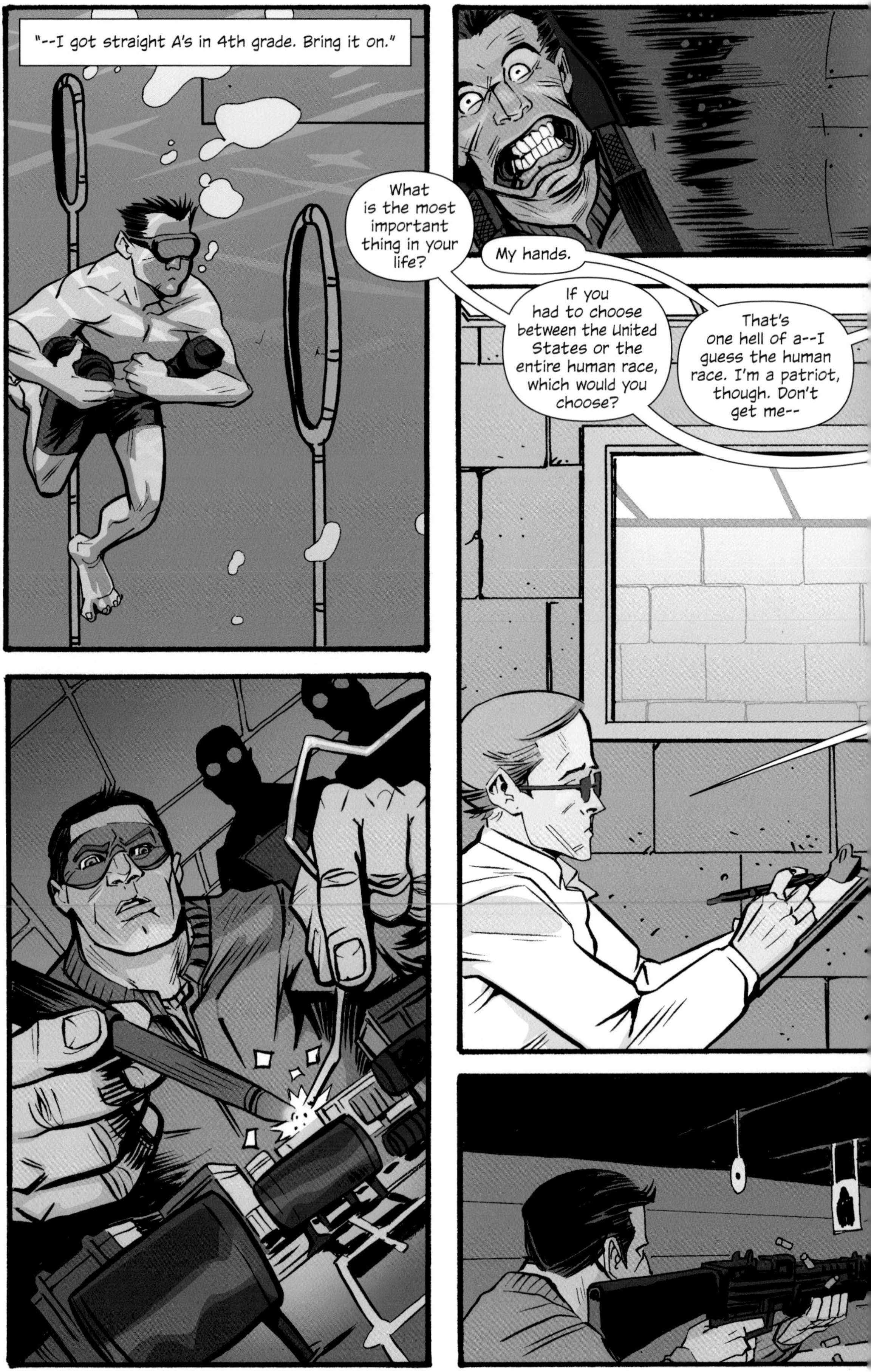
"--I got straight A's in 4th grade. Bring it on."
What is the most important thing in your life?
My hands.
If you had to choose between the United States or the entire human race, which would you choose?
That's one hell of a--I guess the human race. I'm a patriot, though. Don't get me--

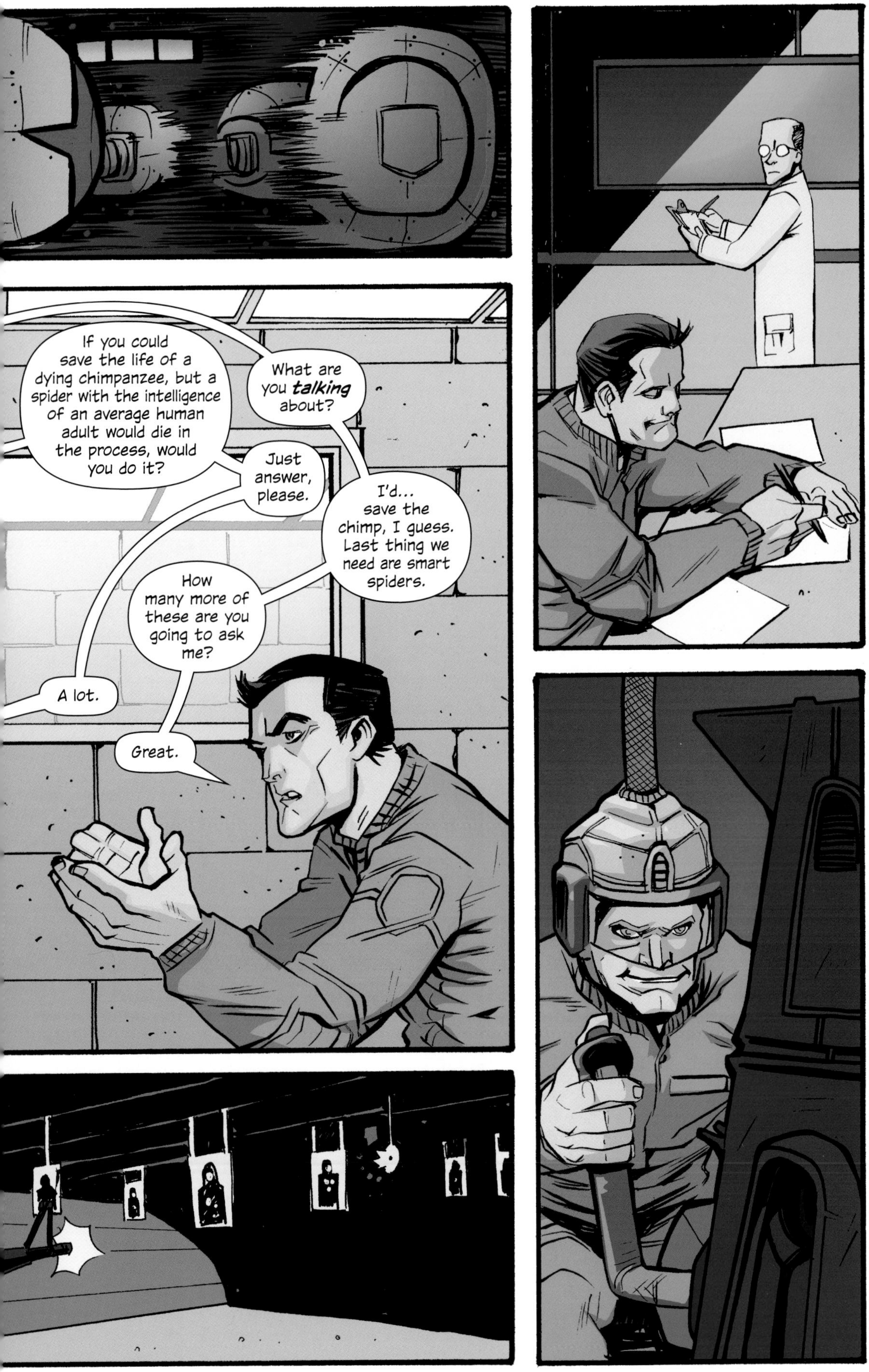
If you could save the life of a dying chimpanzee, but a spider with the intelligence of an average human adult would die in the process, would you do it?
What are you *talking* about?
Just answer, please.
I'd... save the chimp, I guess. Last thing we need are smart spiders.
How many more of these are you going to ask me?
A lot.
Great.

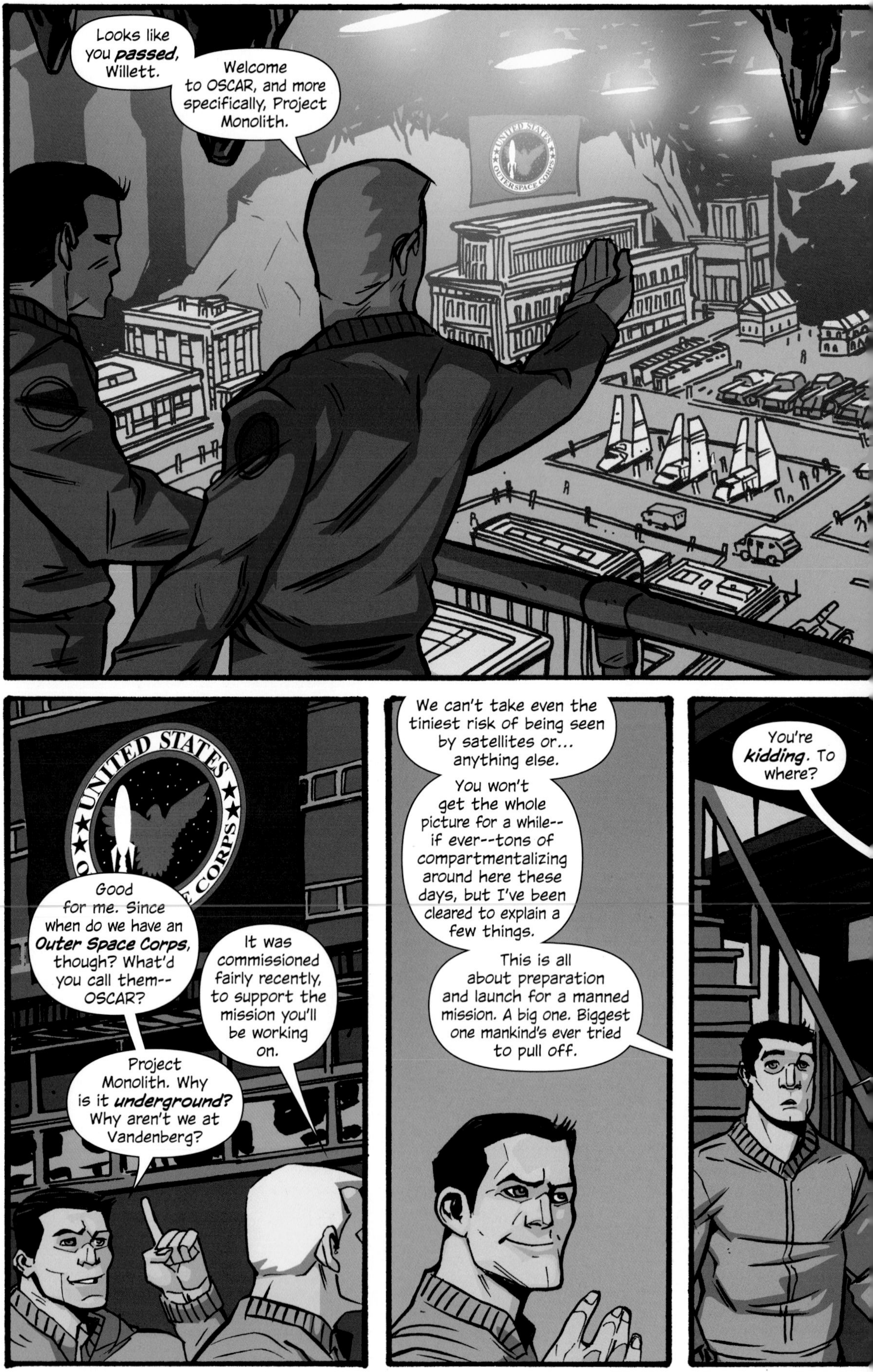
Looks like you **passed**, Willett.
Welcome to OSCAR, and more specifically, Project Monolith.
UNITED STATES
Good for me. Since when do we have an ***Outer Space Corps***, though? What'd you call them--OSCAR?
It was commissioned fairly recently, to support the mission you'll be working on.
Project Monolith. Why is it ***underground?*** Why aren't we at Vandenberg?
We can't take even the tiniest risk of being seen by satellites or... anything else.
You won't get the whole picture for a while--if ever--tons of compartmentalizing around here these days, but I've been cleared to explain a few things.
This is all about preparation and launch for a manned mission. A big one. Biggest one mankind's ever tried to pull off.
You're ***kidding***. To where?

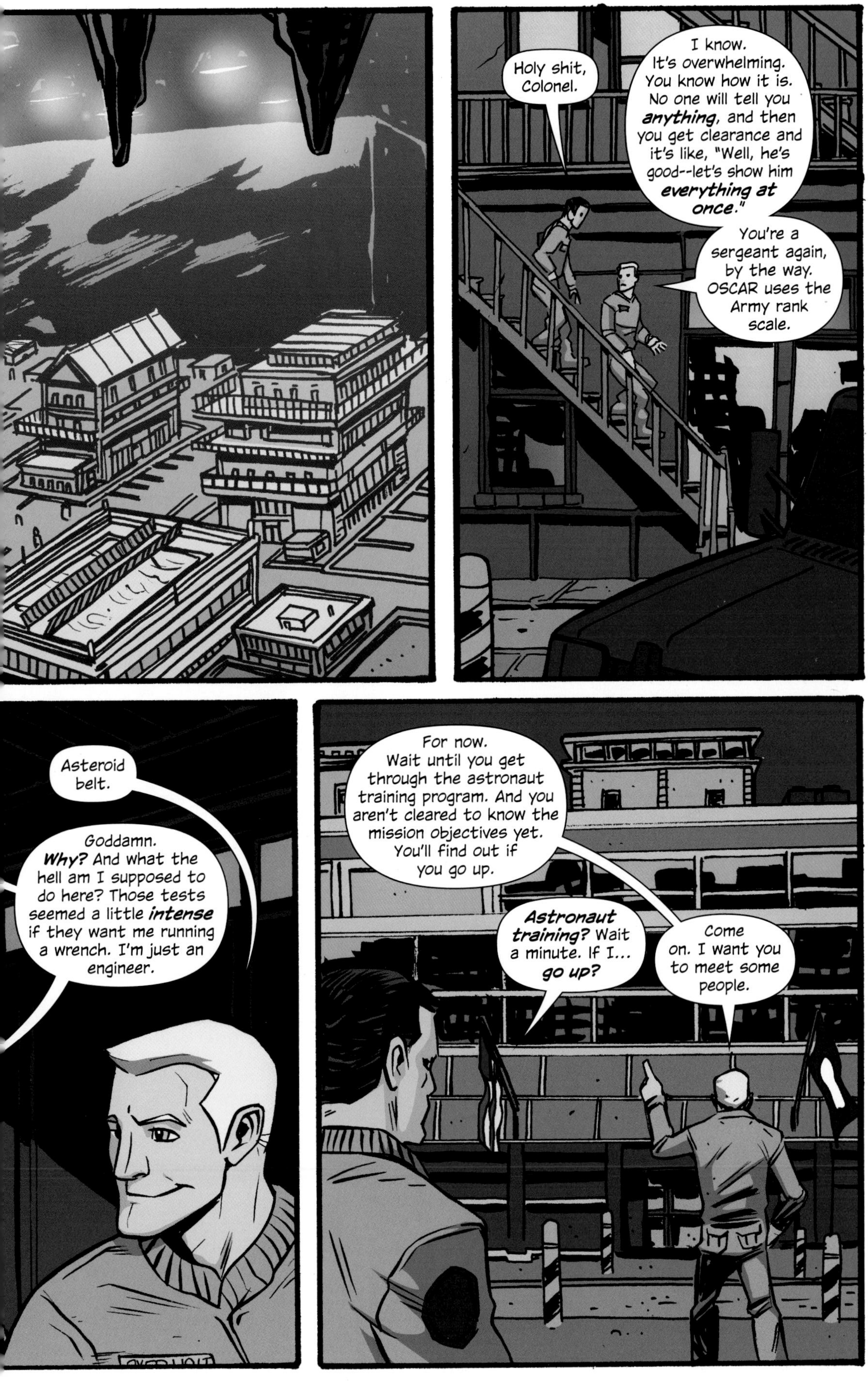
Holy shit, Colonel.
I know. It's overwhelming. You know how it is. No one will tell you *anything*, and then you get clearance and it's like, "Well, he's good--let's show him *everything at once*."
You're a sergeant again, by the way. OSCAR uses the Army rank scale.
Asteroid belt.
Goddamn. *Why?* And what the hell am I supposed to do here? Those tests seemed a little *intense* if they want me running a wrench. I'm just an engineer.
For now. Wait until you get through the astronaut training program. And you aren't cleared to know the mission objectives yet. You'll find out if you go up.
Astronaut training? Wait a minute. If I... *go up?*
Come on. I want you to meet some people.

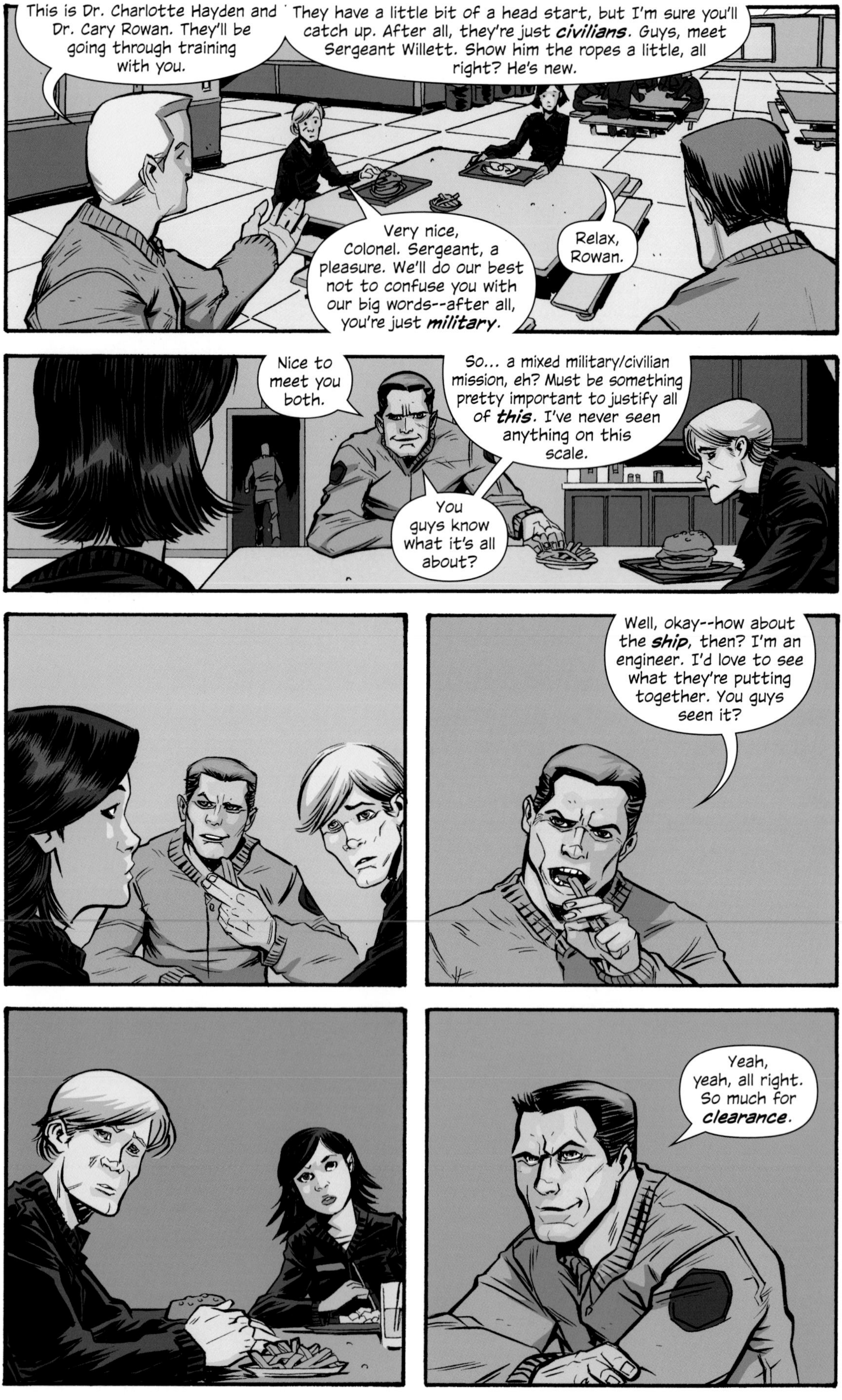
This is Dr. Charlotte Hayden and Dr. Cary Rowan. They'll be going through training with you.
They have a little bit of a head start, but I'm sure you'll catch up. After all, they're just *civilians*. Guys, meet Sergeant Willett. Show him the ropes a little, all right? He's new.
Very nice, Colonel. Sergeant, a pleasure. We'll do our best not to confuse you with our big words--after all, you're just *military*.
Relax, Rowan.
Nice to meet you both.
So... a mixed military/civilian mission, eh? Must be something pretty important to justify all of *this*. I've never seen anything on this scale.
You guys know what it's all about?
Well, okay--how about the *ship*, then? I'm an engineer. I'd love to see what they're putting together. You guys seen it?
Yeah, yeah, all right. So much for *clearance*.

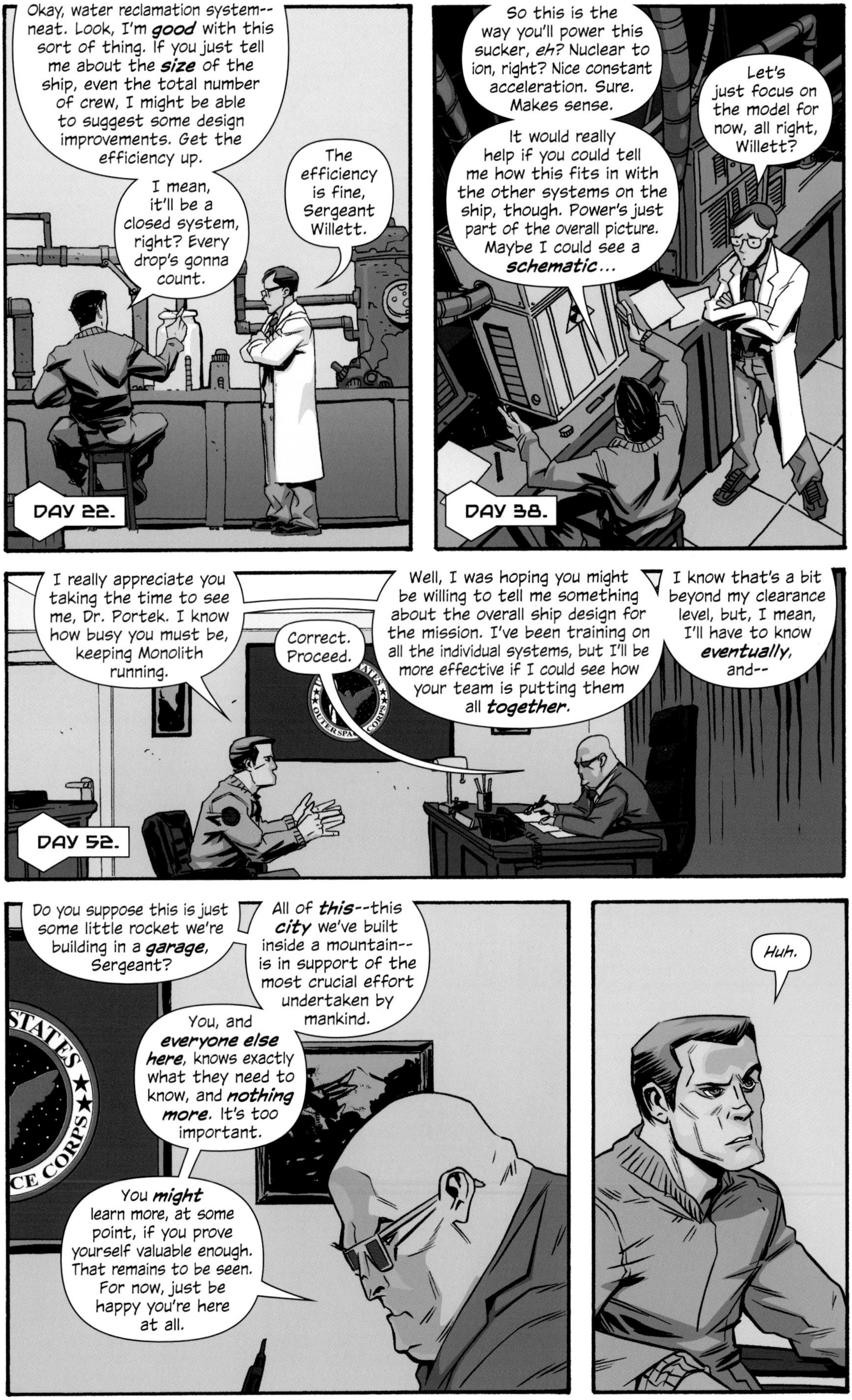
Okay, water reclamation system--neat. Look, I'm good with this sort of thing. If you just tell me about the size of the ship, even the total number of crew, I might be able to suggest some design improvements. Get the efficiency up.
I mean, it'll be a closed system, right? Every drop's gonna count.
The efficiency is fine, Sergeant Willett.
DAY 22.
So this is the way you'll power this sucker, eh? Nuclear to ion, right? Nice constant acceleration. Sure. Makes sense.
It would really help if you could tell me how this fits in with the other systems on the ship, though. Power's just part of the overall picture. Maybe I could see a schematic...
Let's just focus on the model for now, all right, Willett?
DAY 38.
I really appreciate you taking the time to see me, Dr. Portek. I know how busy you must be, keeping Monolith running.
Correct. Proceed.
Well, I was hoping you might be willing to tell me something about the overall ship design for the mission. I've been training on all the individual systems, but I'll be more effective if I could see how your team is putting them all together.
I know that's a bit beyond my clearance level, but, I mean, I'll have to know eventually, and--
DAY 52.
Do you suppose this is just some little rocket we're building in a garage, Sergeant?
All of this--this city we've built inside a mountain--is in support of the most crucial effort undertaken by mankind.
You, and everyone else here, knows exactly what they need to know, and nothing more. It's too important.
You might learn more, at some point, if you prove yourself valuable enough. That remains to be seen. For now, just be happy you're here at all.
Huh.

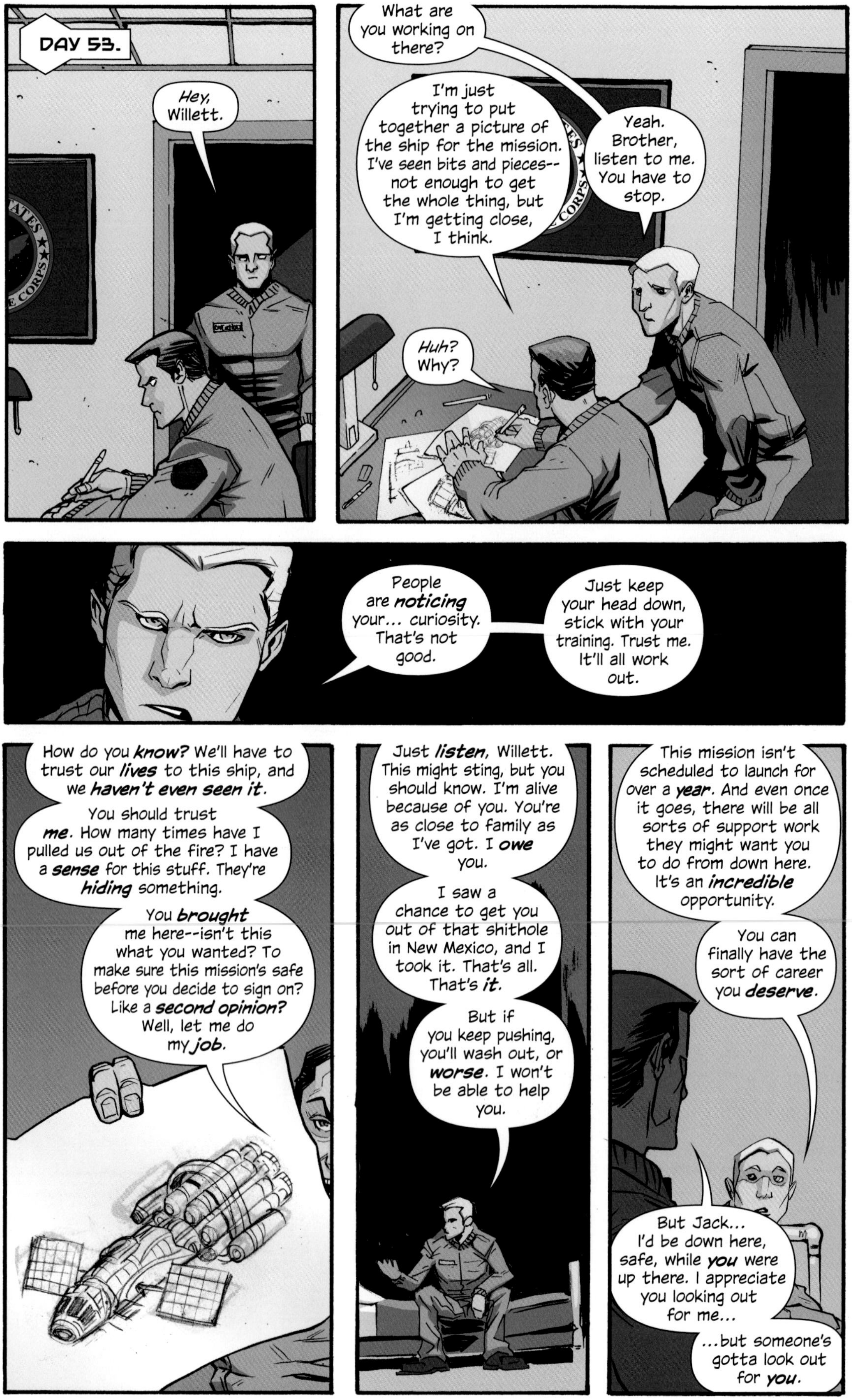
DAY 53.
Hey, Willett.
What are you working on there?
I'm just trying to put together a picture of the ship for the mission. I've seen bits and pieces--not enough to get the whole thing, but I'm getting close, I think.
Yeah. Brother, listen to me. You have to stop.
Huh? Why?
People are noticing your... curiosity. That's not good.
Just keep your head down, stick with your training. Trust me. It'll all work out.
How do you know? We'll have to trust our lives to this ship, and we haven't even seen it.
You should trust me. How many times have I pulled us out of the fire? I have a sense for this stuff. They're hiding something.
You brought me here--isn't this what you wanted? To make sure this mission's safe before you decide to sign on? Like a second opinion? Well, let me do my job.
Just listen, Willett. This might sting, but you should know. I'm alive because of you. You're as close to family as I've got. I owe you.
I saw a chance to get you out of that shithole in New Mexico, and I took it. That's all. That's it.
But if you keep pushing, you'll wash out, or worse. I won't be able to help you.
This mission isn't scheduled to launch for over a year. And even once it goes, there will be all sorts of support work they might want you to do from down here. It's an incredible opportunity.
You can finally have the sort of career you deserve.
But Jack... I'd be down here, safe, while you were up there. I appreciate you looking out for me...
...but someone's gotta look out for you.

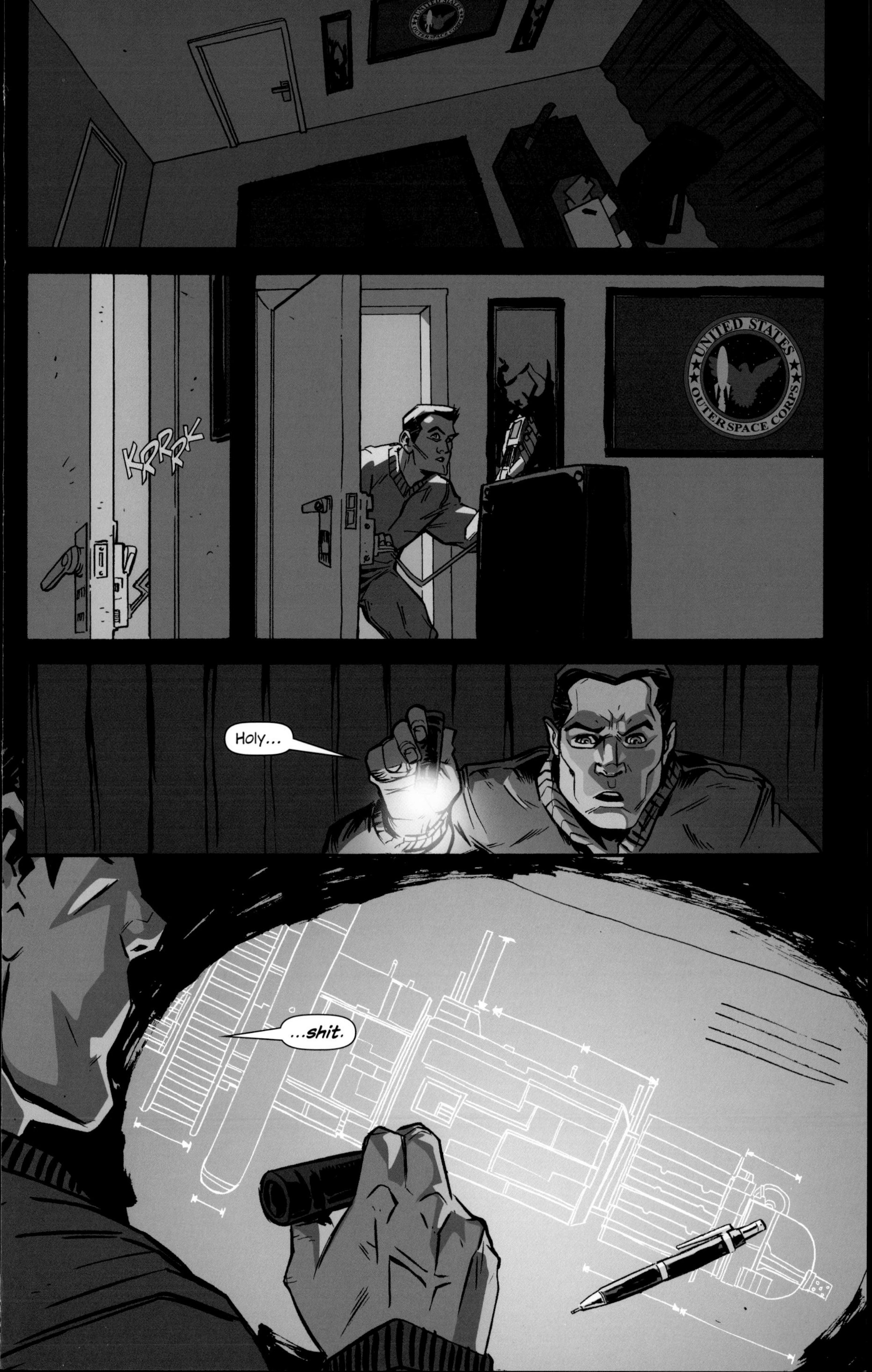
UNITED STATES OUTER SPACE CORPS
KRRRK
Holy...
...shit.

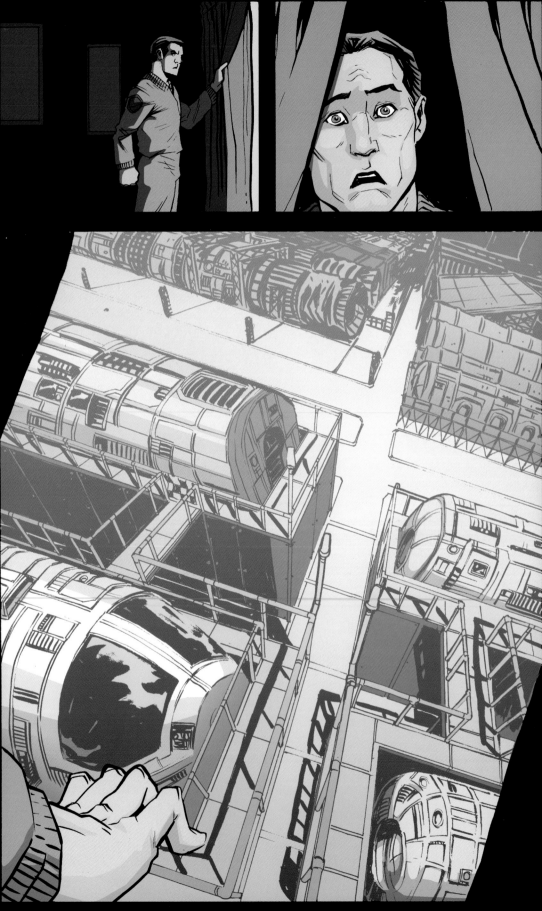

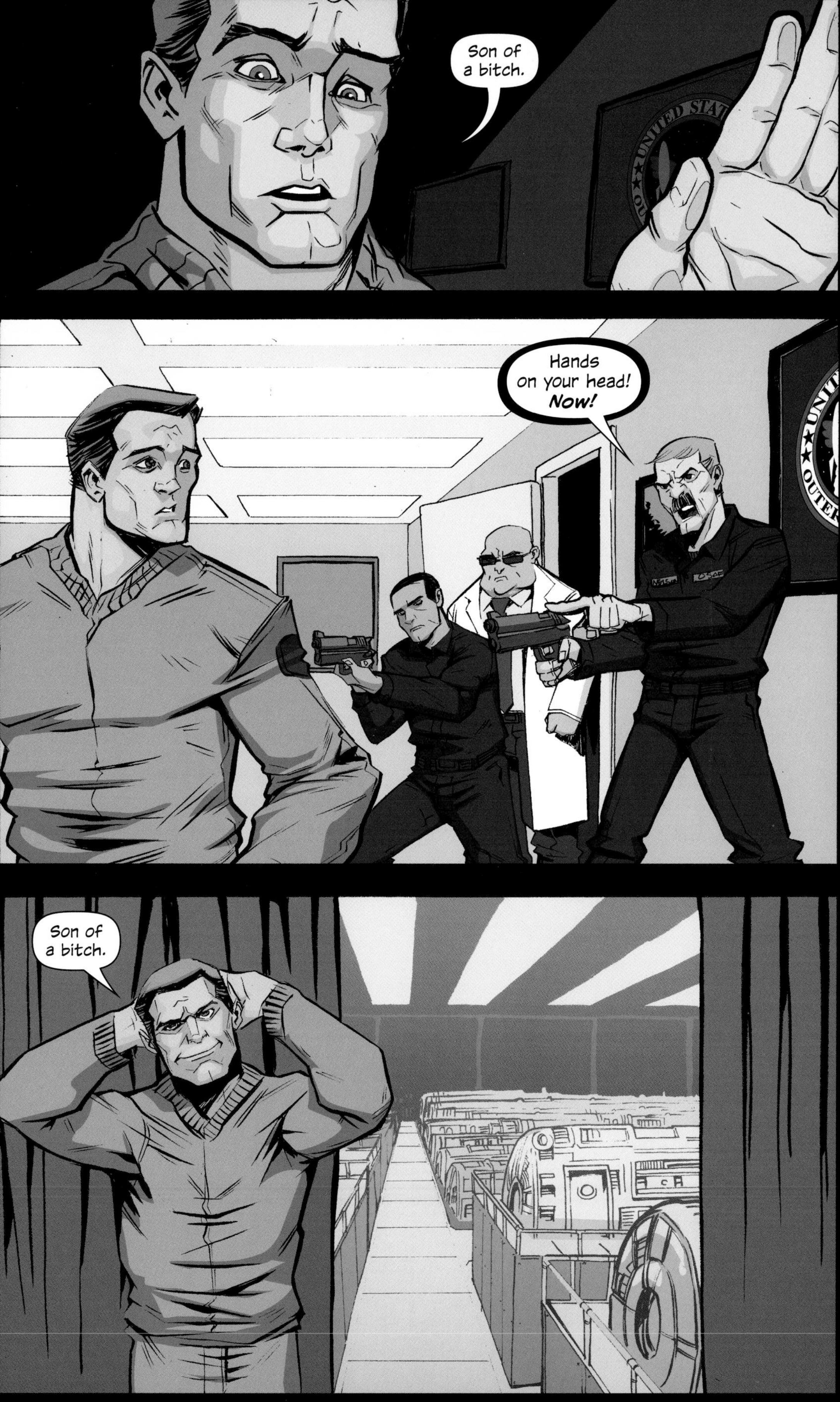
Son of
a bitch.
Hands
on your head!
Now!
Son of
a bitch.

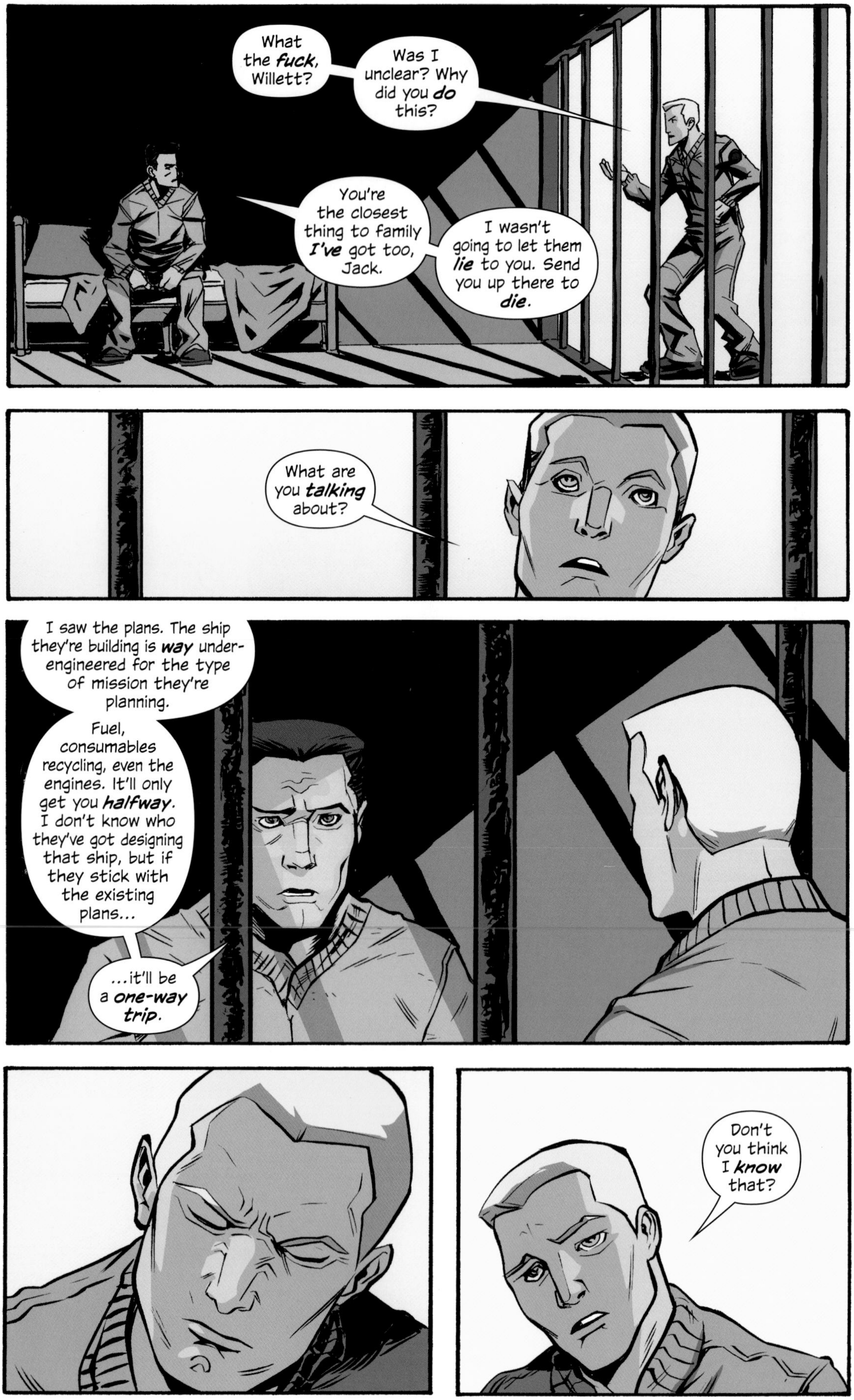
What the fuck, Willett?
Was I unclear? Why did you do this?
You're the closest thing to family I've got too, Jack.
I wasn't going to let them lie to you. Send you up there to die.
What are you talking about?
I saw the plans. The ship they're building is way under-engineered for the type of mission they're planning.
Fuel, consumables recycling, even the engines. It'll only get you halfway. I don't know who they've got designing that ship, but if they stick with the existing plans...
...it'll be a one-way trip.
Don't you think I know that?

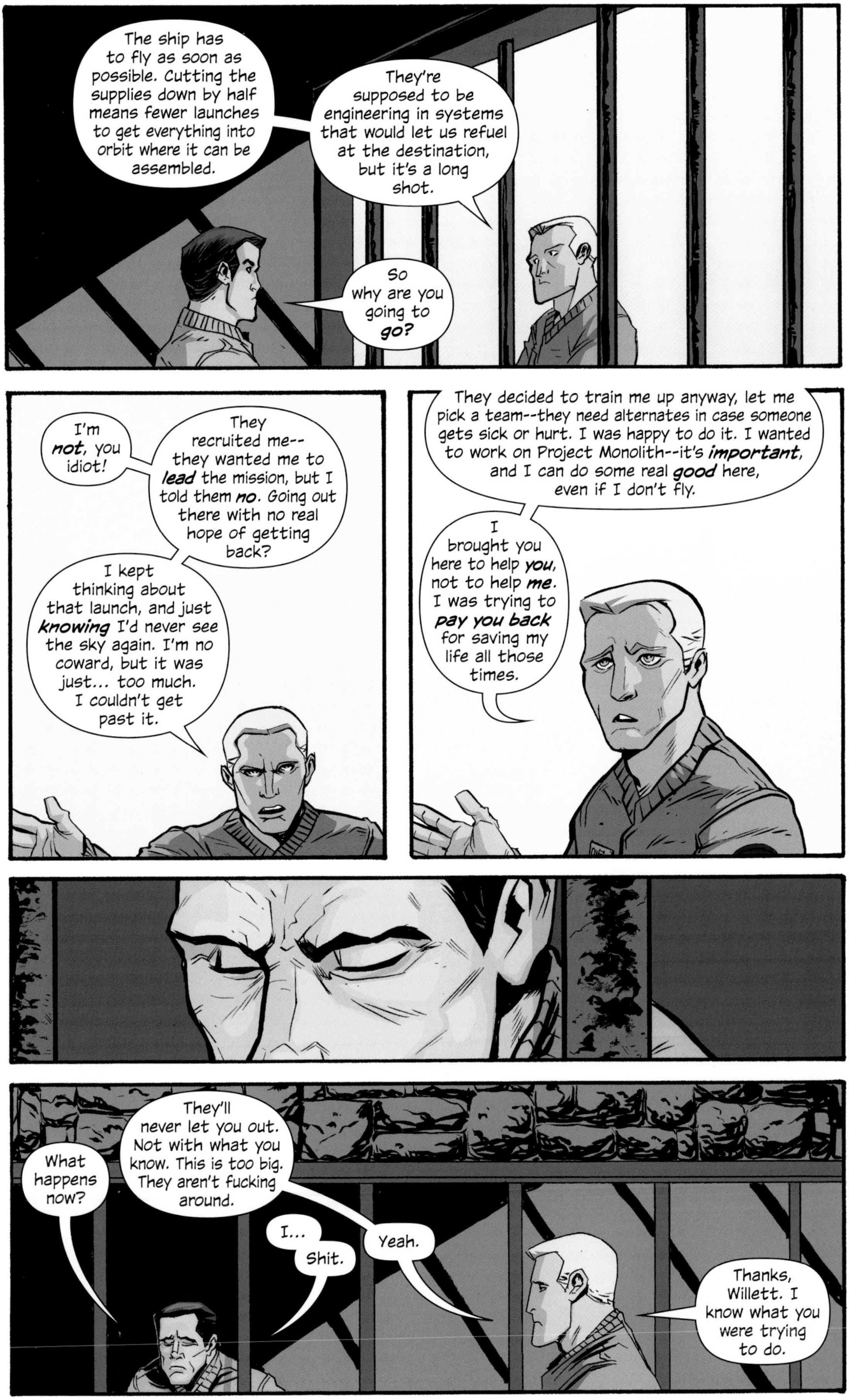
The ship has to fly as soon as possible. Cutting the supplies down by half means fewer launches to get everything into orbit where it can be assembled.
They're supposed to be engineering in systems that would let us refuel at the destination, but it's a long shot.
So why are you going to go?
I'm not, you idiot!
They recruited me--they wanted me to lead the mission, but I told them no. Going out there with no real hope of getting back?
I kept thinking about that launch, and just knowing I'd never see the sky again. I'm no coward, but it was just... too much. I couldn't get past it.
They decided to train me up anyway, let me pick a team--they need alternates in case someone gets sick or hurt. I was happy to do it. I wanted to work on Project Monolith--it's important, and I can do some real good here, even if I don't fly.
I brought you here to help you, not to help me. I was trying to pay you back for saving my life all those times.
What happens now?
They'll never let you out. Not with what you know. This is too big. They aren't fucking around.
I... Shit.
Yeah.
Thanks, Willett. I know what you were trying to do.

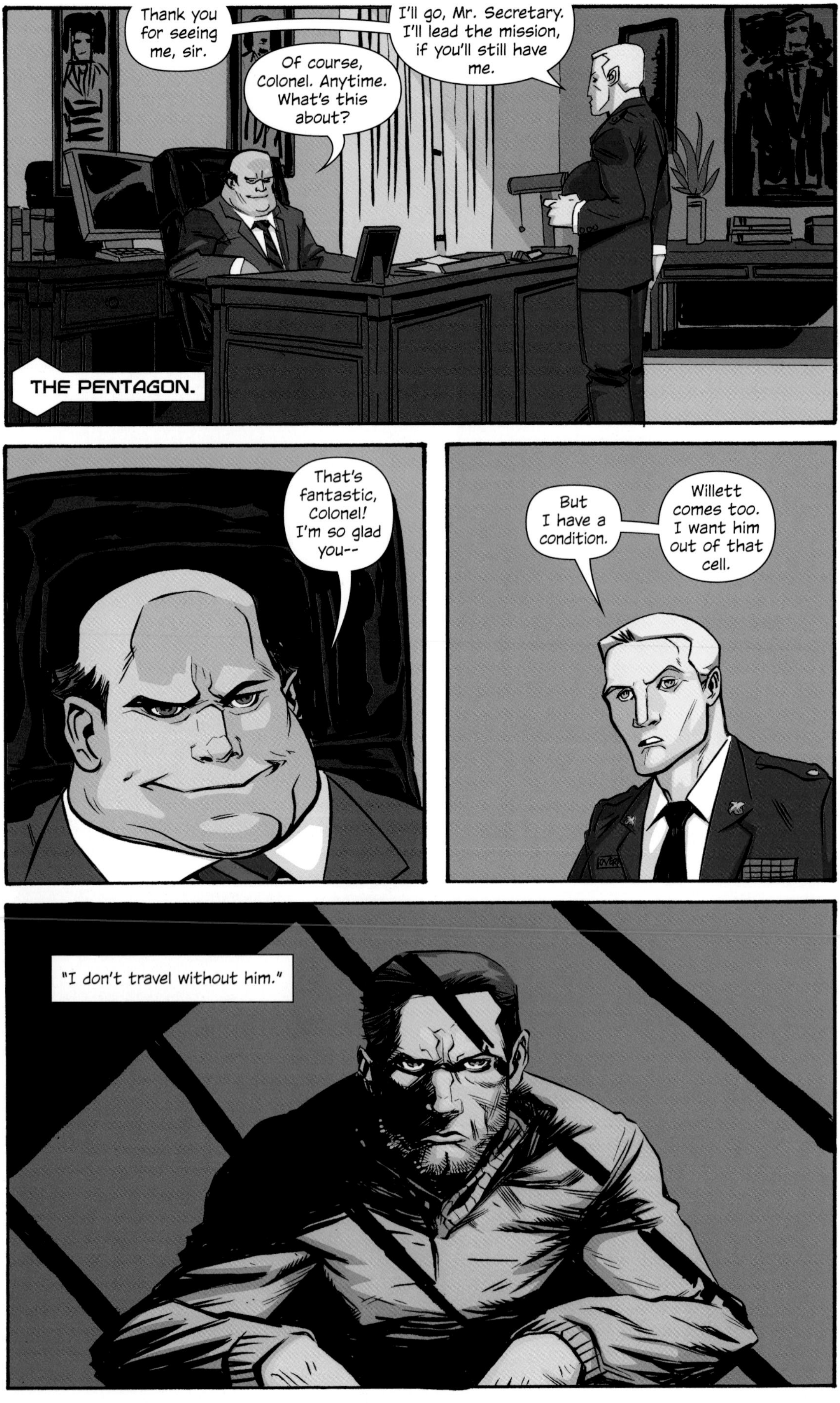
Thank you for seeing me, sir.
Of course, Colonel. Anytime. What's this about?
I'll go, Mr. Secretary. I'll lead the mission, if you'll still have me.
THE PENTAGON.
That's fantastic, Colonel! I'm so glad you--
But I have a condition.
Willett comes too. I want him out of that cell.
"I don't travel without him."

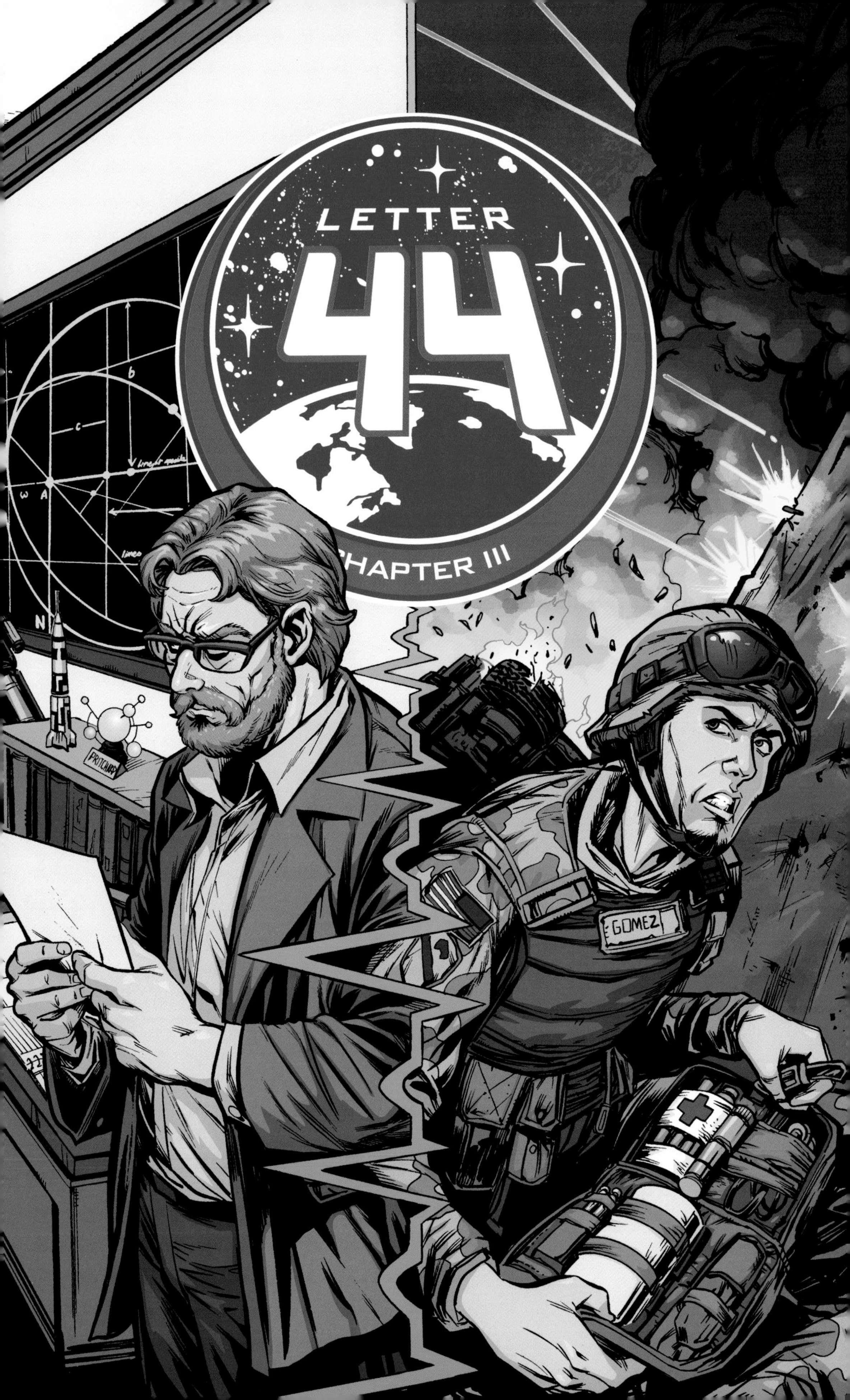
LETTER
44
CHAPTER III
PRITCHARD
GOMEZ

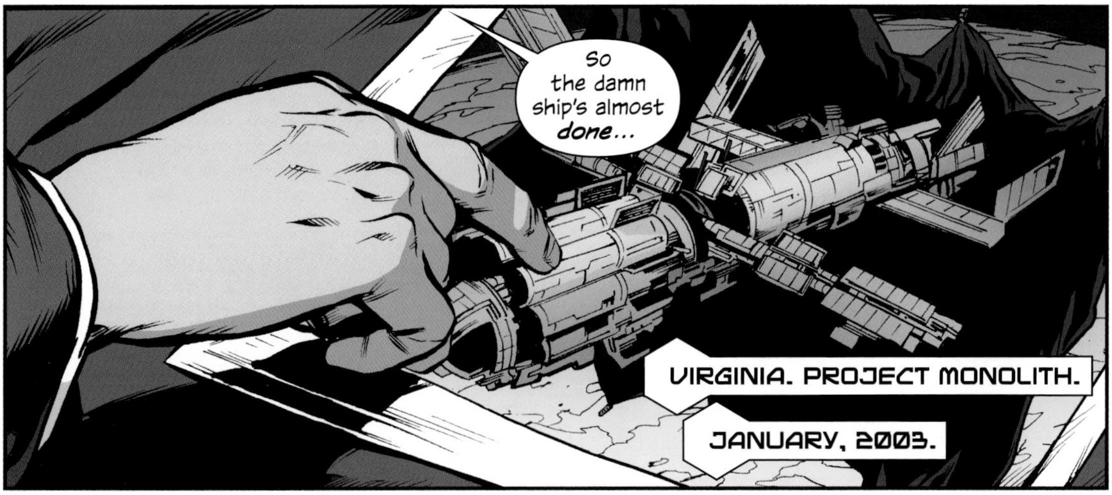
So the damn ship's almost *done*...
VIRGINIA. PROJECT MONOLITH.
JANUARY, 2003.

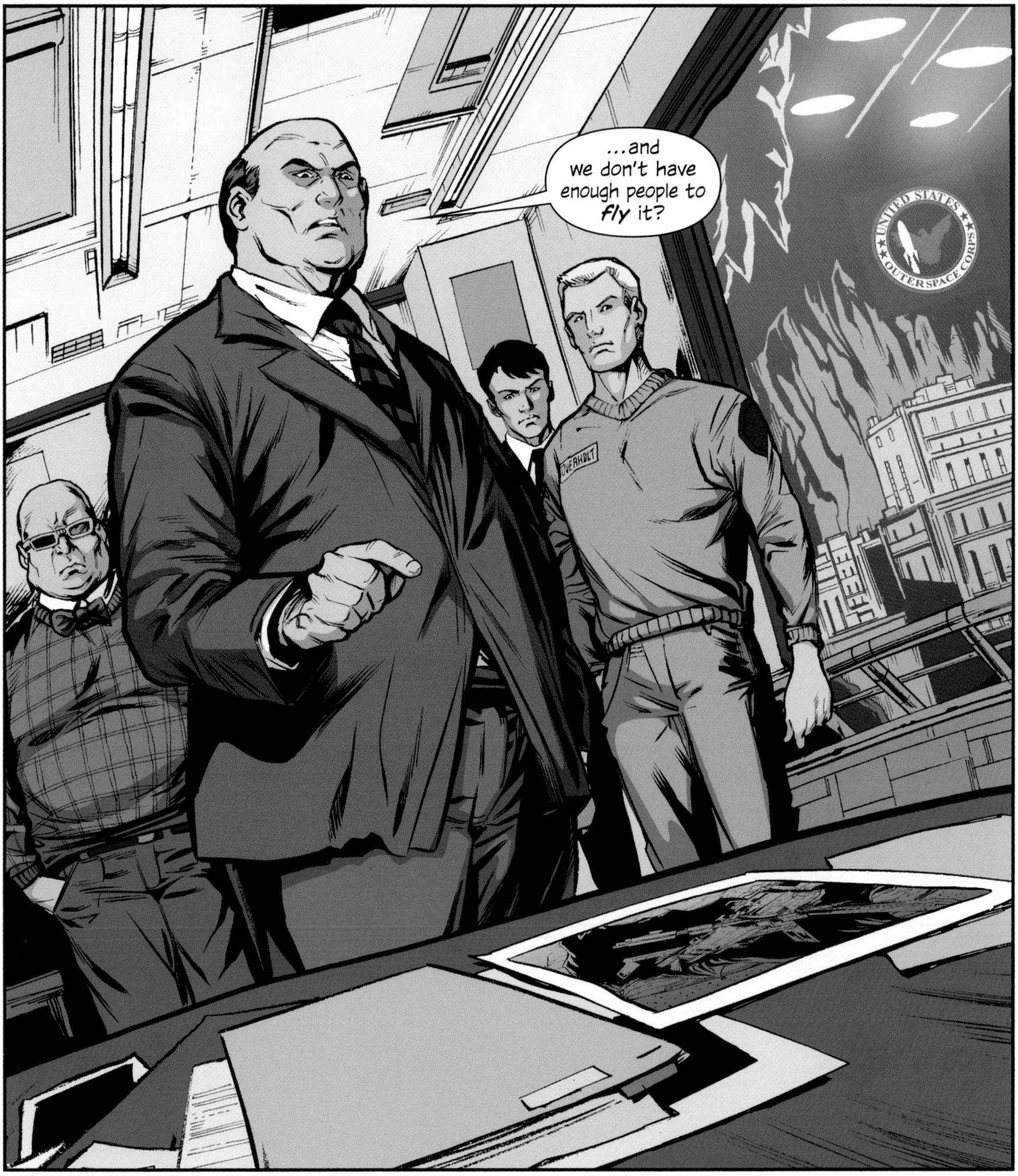
...and we don't have enough people to *fly* it?
UNITED STATES
OUTER SPACE CORPS

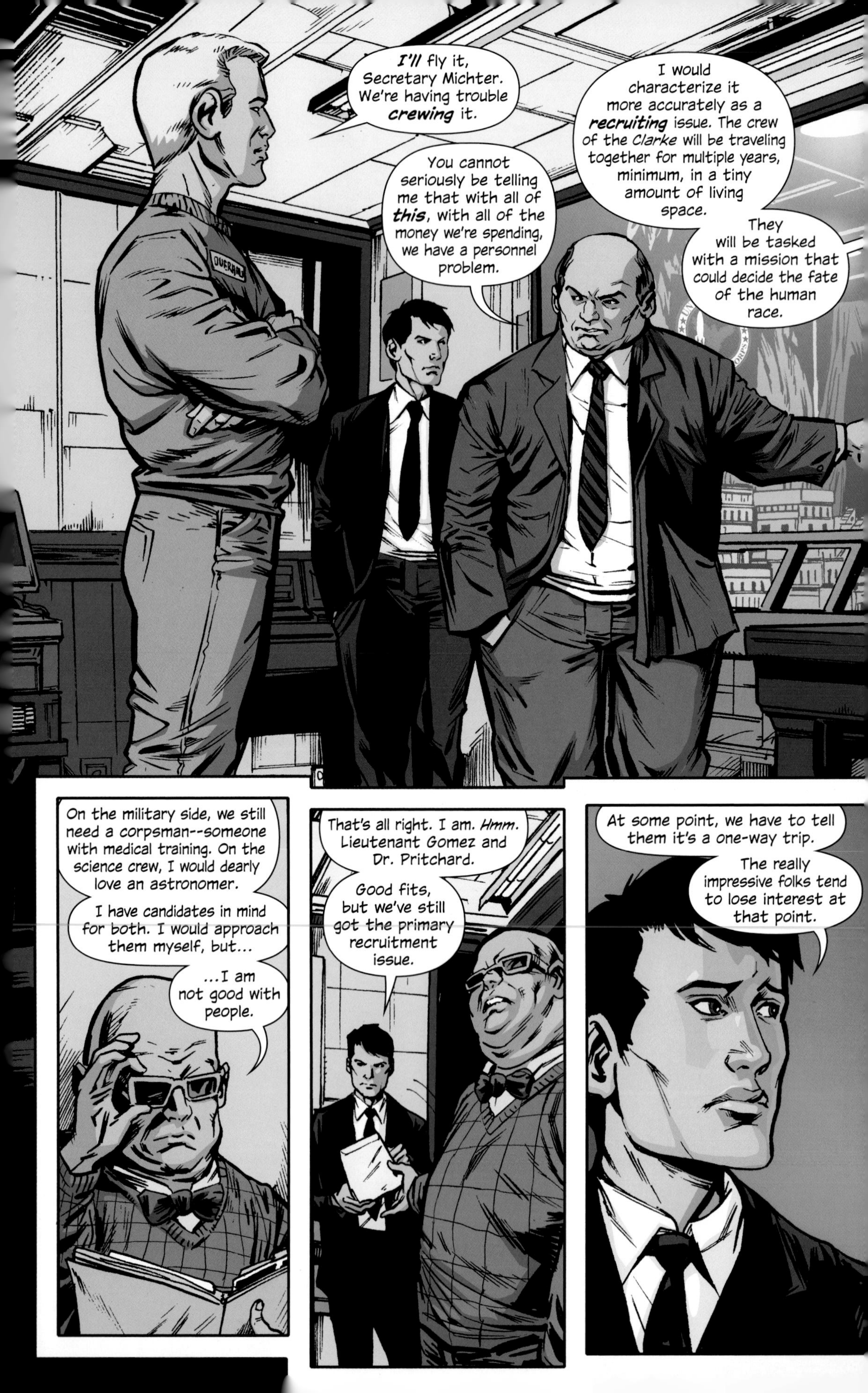
I'll fly it, Secretary Michter. We're having trouble crewing it.
You cannot seriously be telling me that with all of this, with all of the money we're spending, we have a personnel problem.
I would characterize it more accurately as a recruiting issue. The crew of the Clarke will be traveling together for multiple years, minimum, in a tiny amount of living space.
They will be tasked with a mission that could decide the fate of the human race.
On the military side, we still need a corpsman--someone with medical training. On the science crew, I would dearly love an astronomer.
I have candidates in mind for both. I would approach them myself, but...
...I am not good with people.
That's all right. I am. Hmm. Lieutenant Gomez and Dr. Pritchard.
Good fits, but we've still got the primary recruitment issue.
At some point, we have to tell them it's a one-way trip.
The really impressive folks tend to lose interest at that point.

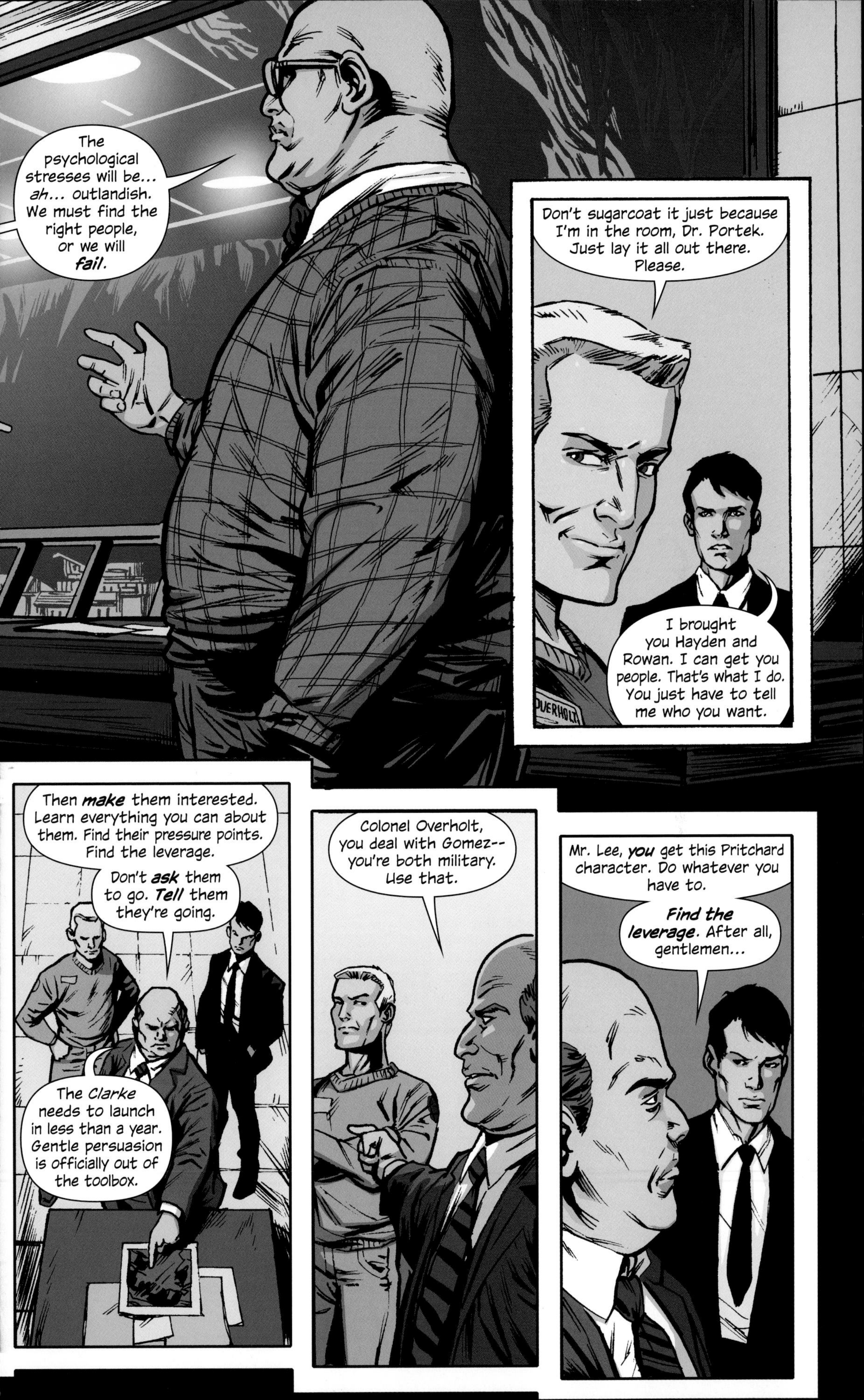
The psychological stresses will be... ah... outlandish. We must find the right people, or we will fail.
Don't sugarcoat it just because I'm in the room, Dr. Portek. Just lay it all out there. Please.
I brought you Hayden and Rowan. I can get you people. That's what I do. You just have to tell me who you want.
OVERHOLT
Then make them interested. Learn everything you can about them. Find their pressure points. Find the leverage.
Don't ask them to go. Tell them they're going.
The Clarke needs to launch in less than a year. Gentle persuasion is officially out of the toolbox.
Colonel Overholt, you deal with Gomez-- you're both military. Use that.
Mr. Lee, you get this Pritchard character. Do whatever you have to.
Find the leverage. After all, gentlemen...

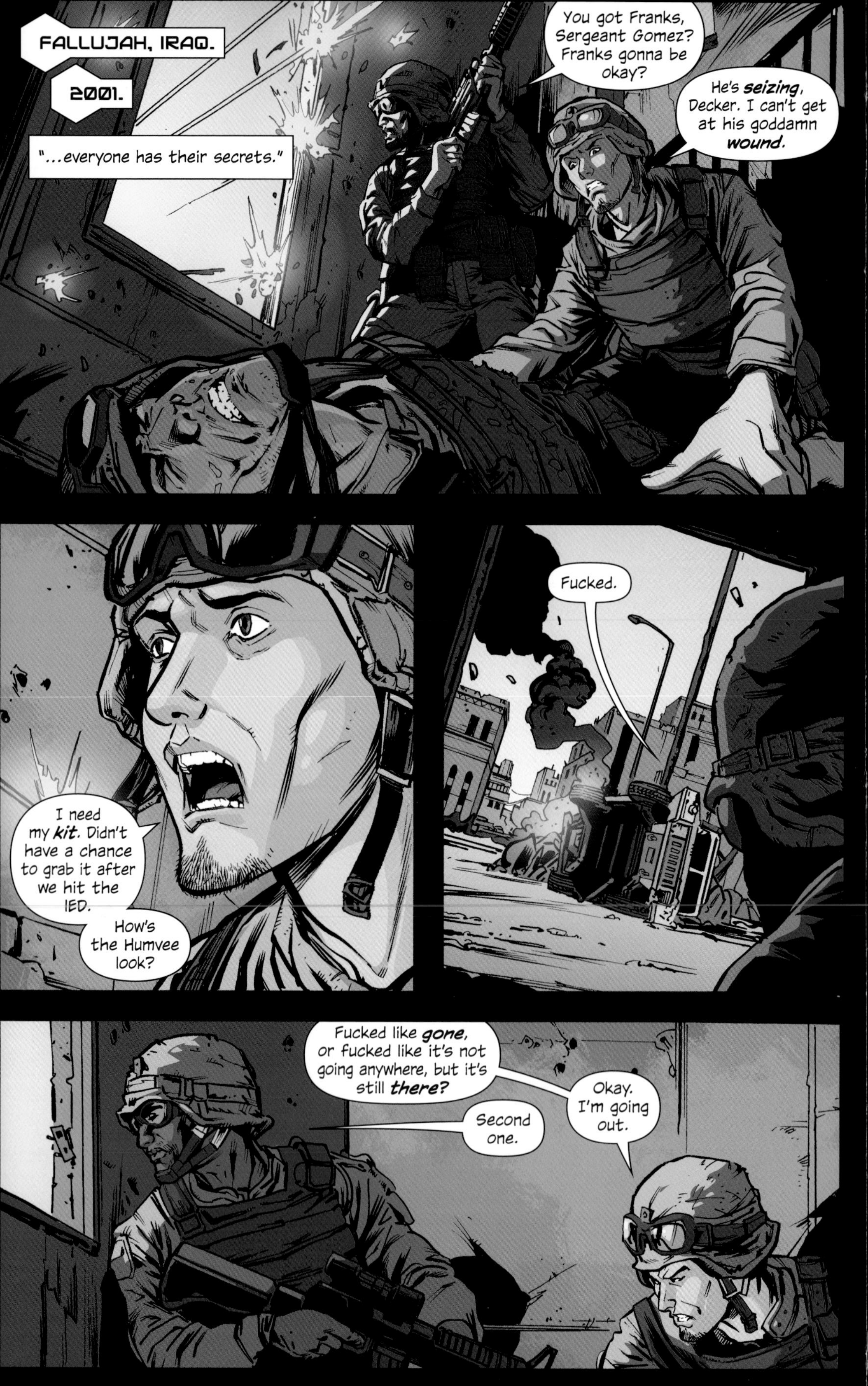
FALLUJAH, IRAQ.
2001.
"...everyone has their secrets."
You got Franks, Sergeant Gomez? Franks gonna be okay?
He's *seizing*, Decker. I can't get at his goddamn *wound*.
I need my *kit*. Didn't have a chance to grab it after we hit the IED.
How's the Humvee look?
Fucked.
Fucked like *gone*, or fucked like it's not going anywhere, but it's still *there?*
Second one.
Okay. I'm going out.

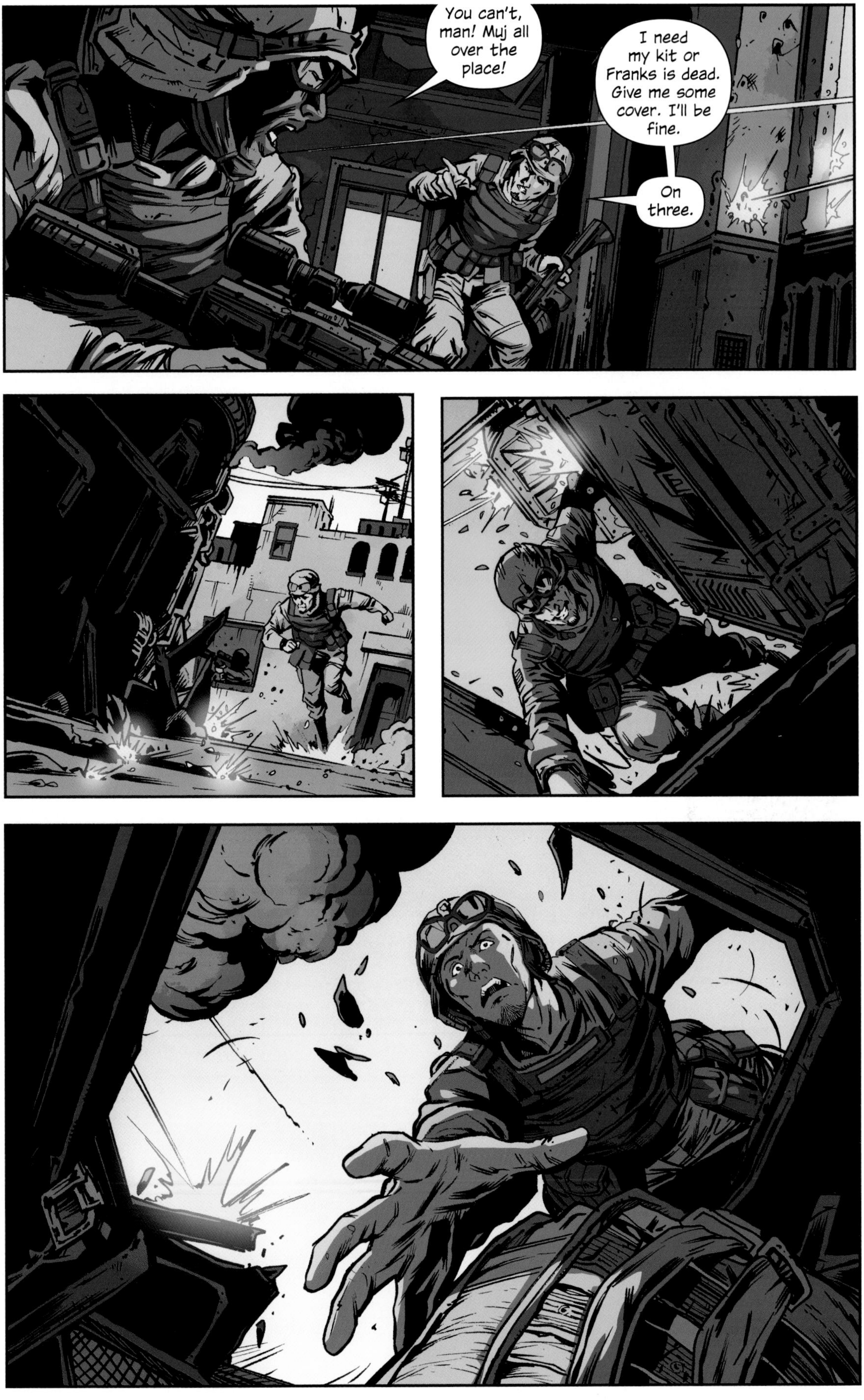
You can't, man! Muj all over the place!
I need my kit or Franks is dead. Give me some cover. I'll be fine.
On three.

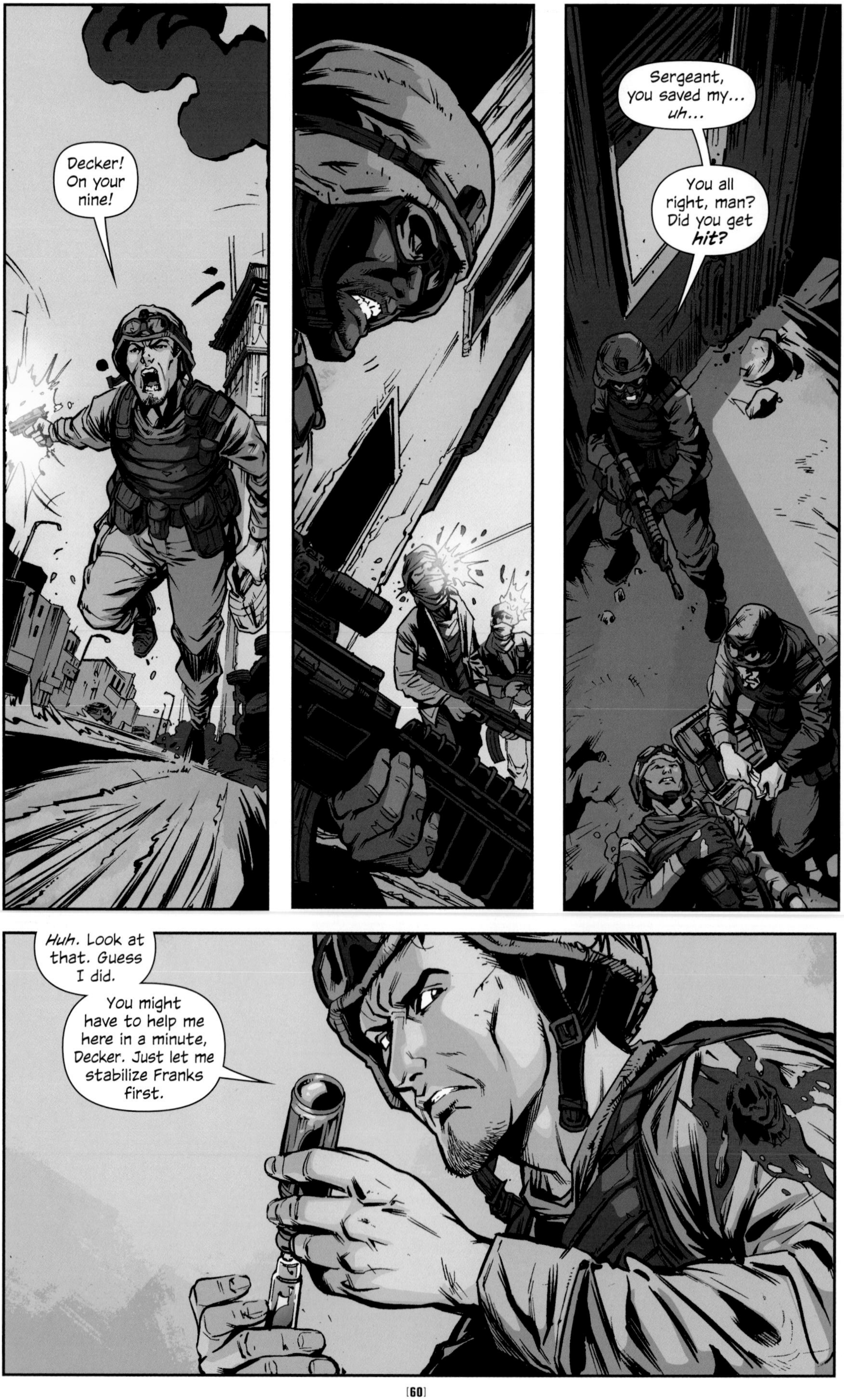
Decker! On your nine!
Sergeant, you saved my... uh...
You all right, man? Did you get *hit?*
Huh. Look at that. Guess I did.
You might have to help me here in a minute, Decker. Just let me stabilize Franks first.

BAGHDAD. THE GREEN ZONE.

2003.

"So that's how it happened."

You know, I find this a little... I mean, that's a Bronze Star, at least. Maybe even a Silver.

Uh-huh. He wouldn't let me bring it up in any official way. And since he outranked me... but I told the story, and word got around. Guess that's how you heard about it.

Now, I want to ask *you* a question.

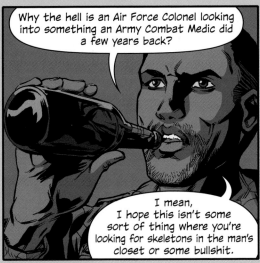

Why the hell is an Air Force Colonel looking into something an Army Combat Medic did a few years back?

I mean, I hope this isn't some sort of thing where you're looking for skeletons in the man's closet or some bullshit.

Sergeant Gomez is the best man I know. You keep poking around, that's all you're gonna hear.

I've noticed. You're not the first guy I've talked to, Corporal. I've got ten stories as good as yours or better.

Damn right. Now, you want to tell me why you're asking? *Sir?*

Not really.

Enjoy your beer. Ice cold Bud, all the way out here in the desert.

God bless America.

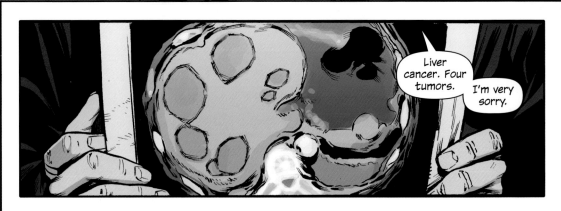

Liver cancer. Four tumors.
I'm very sorry.
CALIFORNIA INSTITUTE OF TECHNOLOGY.
CAHILL CENTER FOR ASTRONOMY AND ASTROPHYSICS.
How the fuck did you get this? And who the fuck are you?
Those are the wrong questions, Dr. Pritchard.
Here's the right one:
How the fuck do I get a new liver?

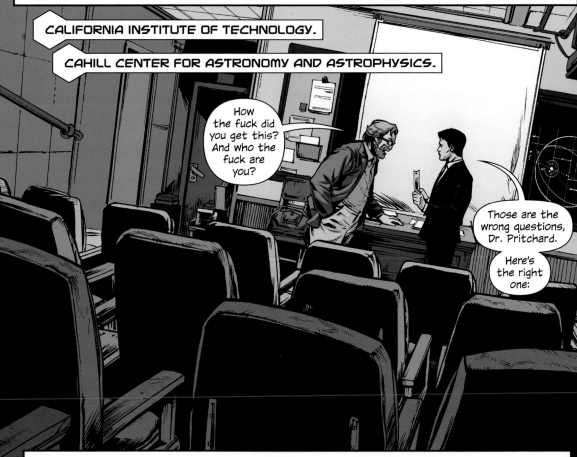

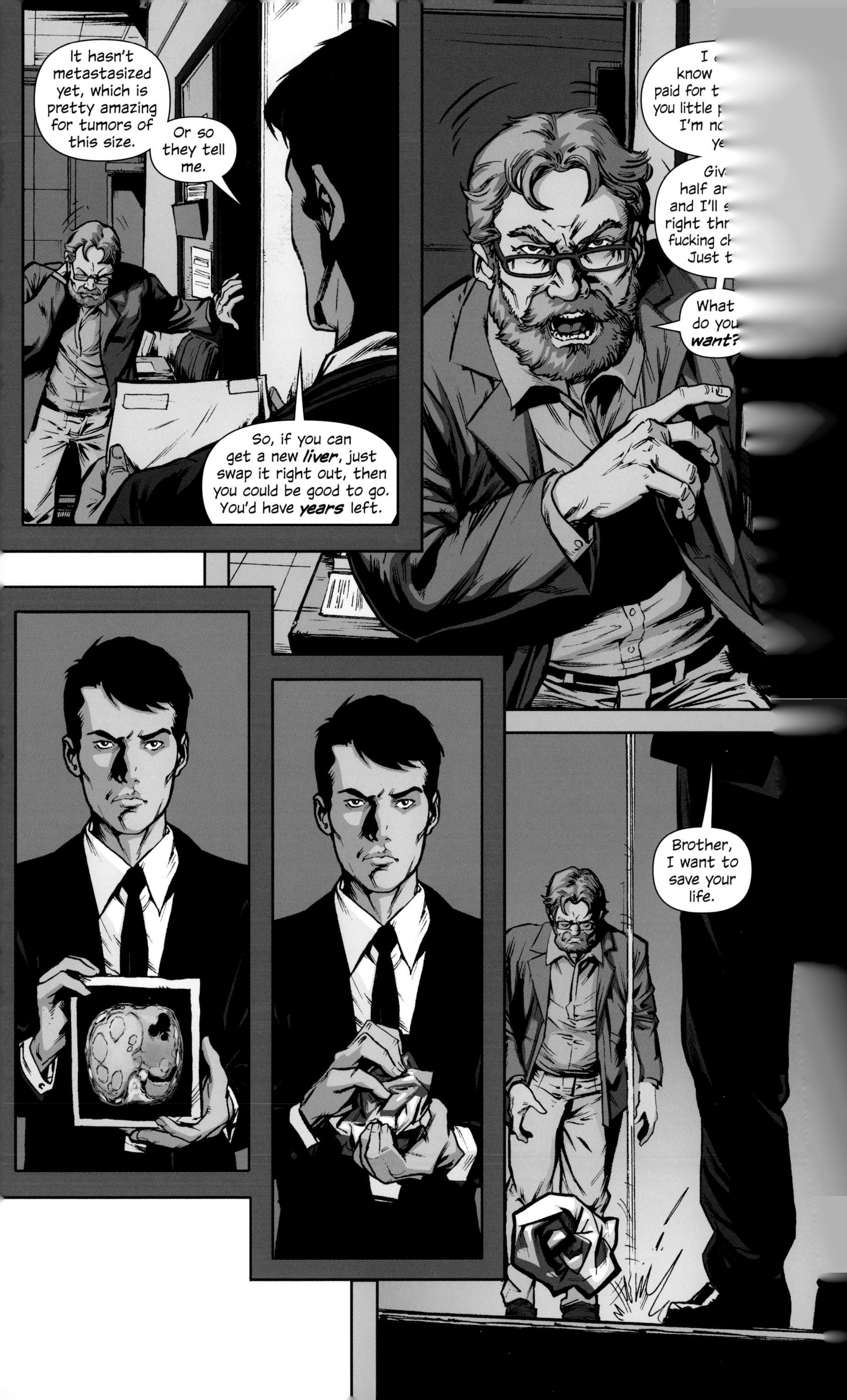
It hasn't metastasized yet, which is pretty amazing for tumors of this size.
Or so they tell me.
So, if you can get a new *liver*, just swap it right out, then you could be good to go. You'd have *years* left.
know paid for you little I'm
half and I'll right fucking Just
What do you *want?*
Brother, I want to save your life.

Here. Look at this. It's not everything-- not even most of it--but it will give you a sense of the playing field.

This... this isn't real. It can't be. In... in the *asteroid belt?* That *close?* How did we *miss* them?

I mean... this can't be *real*.

I assure you, Dr. Pritchard. It's legit.

And you... you want me to help somehow? Of course. It's not even a question. I would be honored.

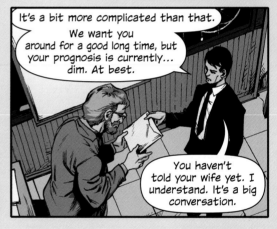

It's a bit more complicated than that.

We want you around for a good long time, but your prognosis is currently... dim. At best.

You haven't told your wife yet. I understand. It's a big conversation.

How do you... Who *are* you?

I told you. The man who wants to save your life.

We can get you a transplant, but you'd need to disappear.

You go in for surgery, as far as your wife knows, you die on the table.

Brutal. I know. But put it this way--unless you and I keep talking...

...you're there anyway in two months. Three, tops.

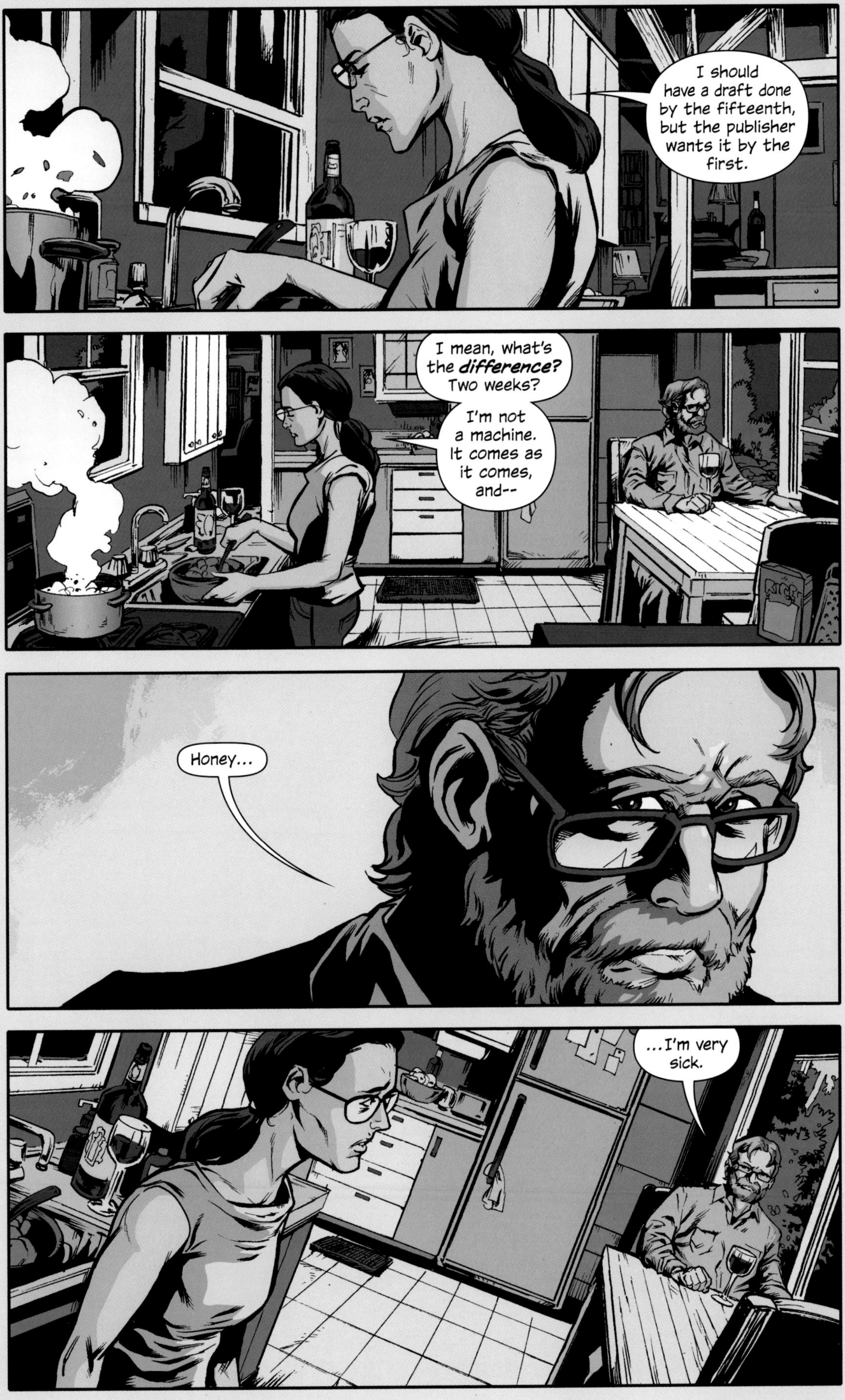
I should have a draft done by the fifteenth, but the publisher wants it by the first.
I mean, what's the *difference?* Two weeks?
I'm not a machine. It comes as it comes, and--
Honey...
...I'm very sick.

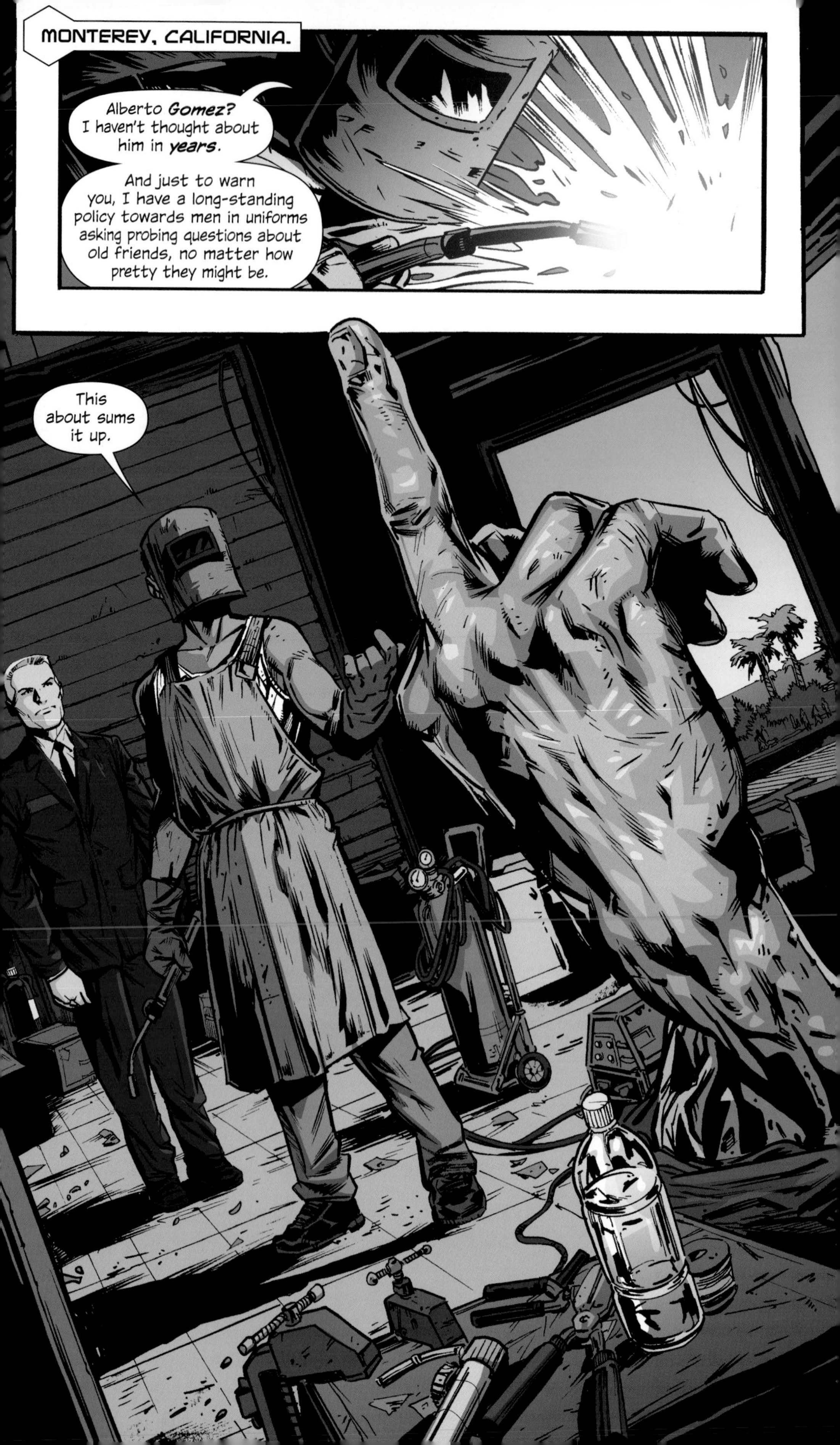
MONTEREY, CALIFORNIA.
Alberto **Gomez?** I haven't thought about him in ***years.***
And just to warn you, I have a long-standing policy towards men in uniforms asking probing questions about old friends, no matter how pretty they might be.
This about sums it up.

You mind turning off that torch, Mr. Dar? It's loud as hell.

I suppose.

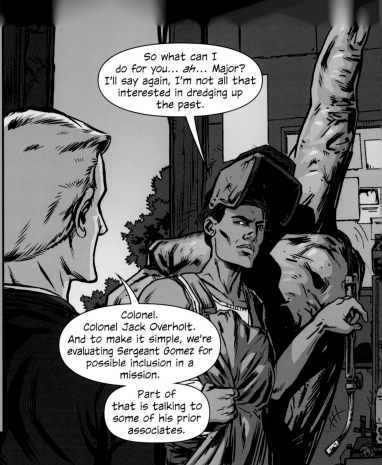

So what can I do for you... ah... Major? I'll say again, I'm not all that interested in dredging up the past.

Colonel. Colonel Jack Overholt. And to make it simple, we're evaluating Sergeant Gomez for possible inclusion in a mission.

Part of that is talking to some of his prior associates.

You knew him while he was training up at Camp Hunter-Liggett. So, we--

I may be an artist, but I'm not an idiot. Colonel.

Excuse me? I'm not sure I--

You and your awful, oppressive organization are curious about the nature of my friendship with Alberto. Some sort of witch hunt, I'm sure.

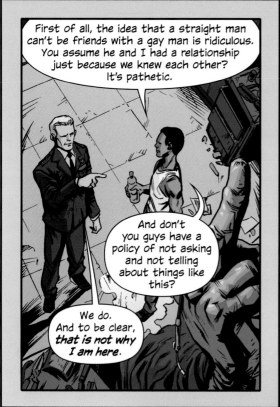

First of all, the idea that a straight man can't be friends with a gay man is ridiculous. You assume he and I had a relationship just because we knew each other? It's pathetic.

And don't you guys have a policy of not asking and not telling about things like this?

We do. And to be clear, **that is not why I am here.**

I've been looking into Sergeant Gomez for some time now, and I'm not sure I've ever seen a man who inspires more loyalty and trust.

Believe me. I am not here to cause any trouble for your friend. His free time is not my business.

At this point, I have exactly one question for you.

Why does Gomez serve?

...

We actually talked about this fairly often. Argued, really. It's one of the reasons we stopped being... close.

Part of it is a little bit of this.

But mostly, it's because Alberto **wants to help**, Colonel.

Selflessness is **always** hard. And if... **hypothetically**... it's a little harder for him? Well, so what?

Life is sacrifice. He said that a lot. You give up things to get what you want. Your time. Your money. Your opportunities for love.

Sergeant Alberto Gomez wants to **help**. And so: sacrifice.

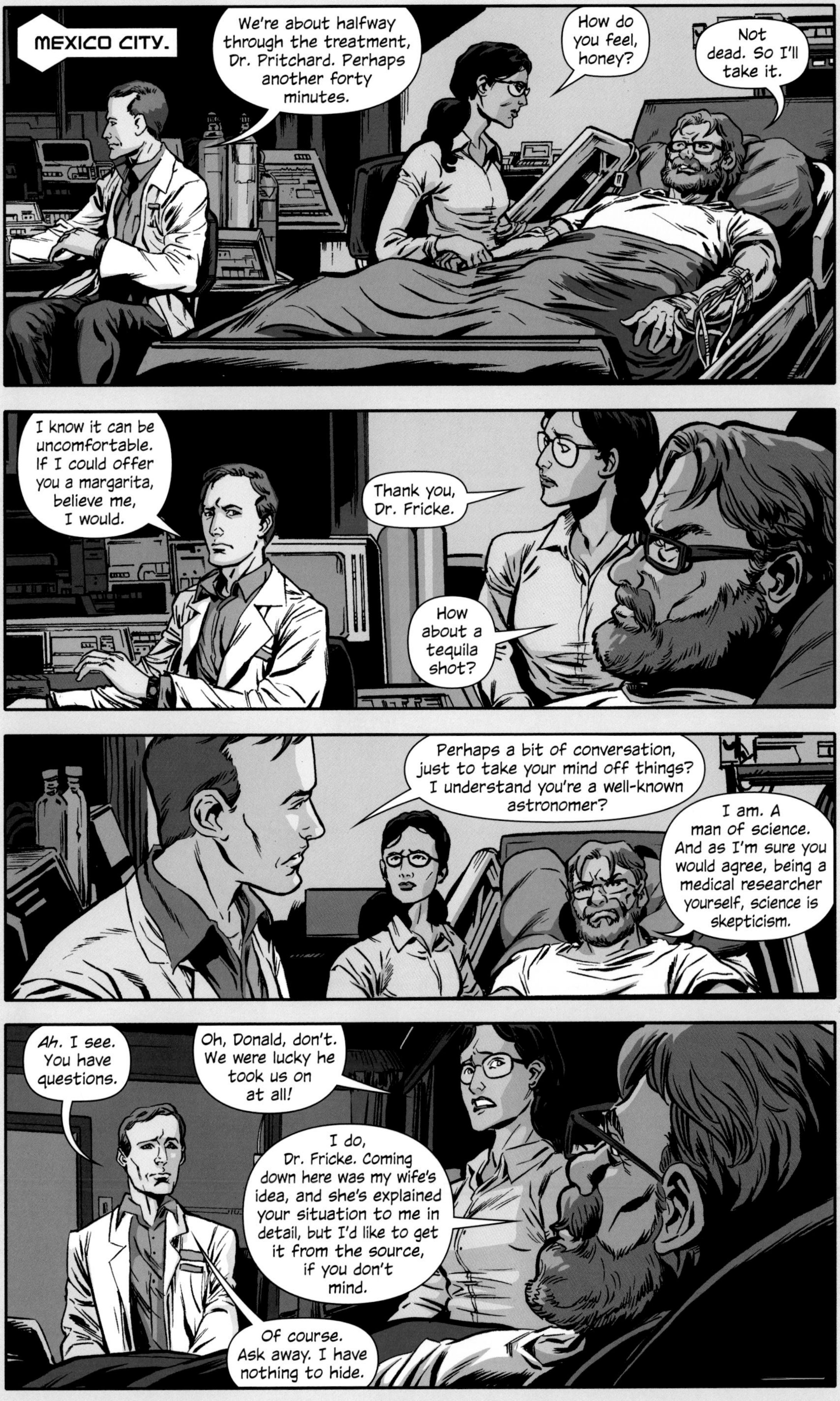
MEXICO CITY.
We're about halfway through the treatment, Dr. Pritchard. Perhaps another forty minutes.
How do you feel, honey?
Not dead. So I'll take it.
I know it can be uncomfortable. If I could offer you a margarita, believe me, I would.
Thank you, Dr. Fricke.
How about a tequila shot?
Perhaps a bit of conversation, just to take your mind off things? I understand you're a well-known astronomer?
I am. A man of science. And as I'm sure you would agree, being a medical researcher yourself, science is skepticism.
Ah. I see. You have questions.
Oh, Donald, don't. We were lucky he took us on at all!
I do, Dr. Fricke. Coming down here was my wife's idea, and she's explained your situation to me in detail, but I'd like to get it from the source, if you don't mind.
Of course. Ask away. I have nothing to hide.

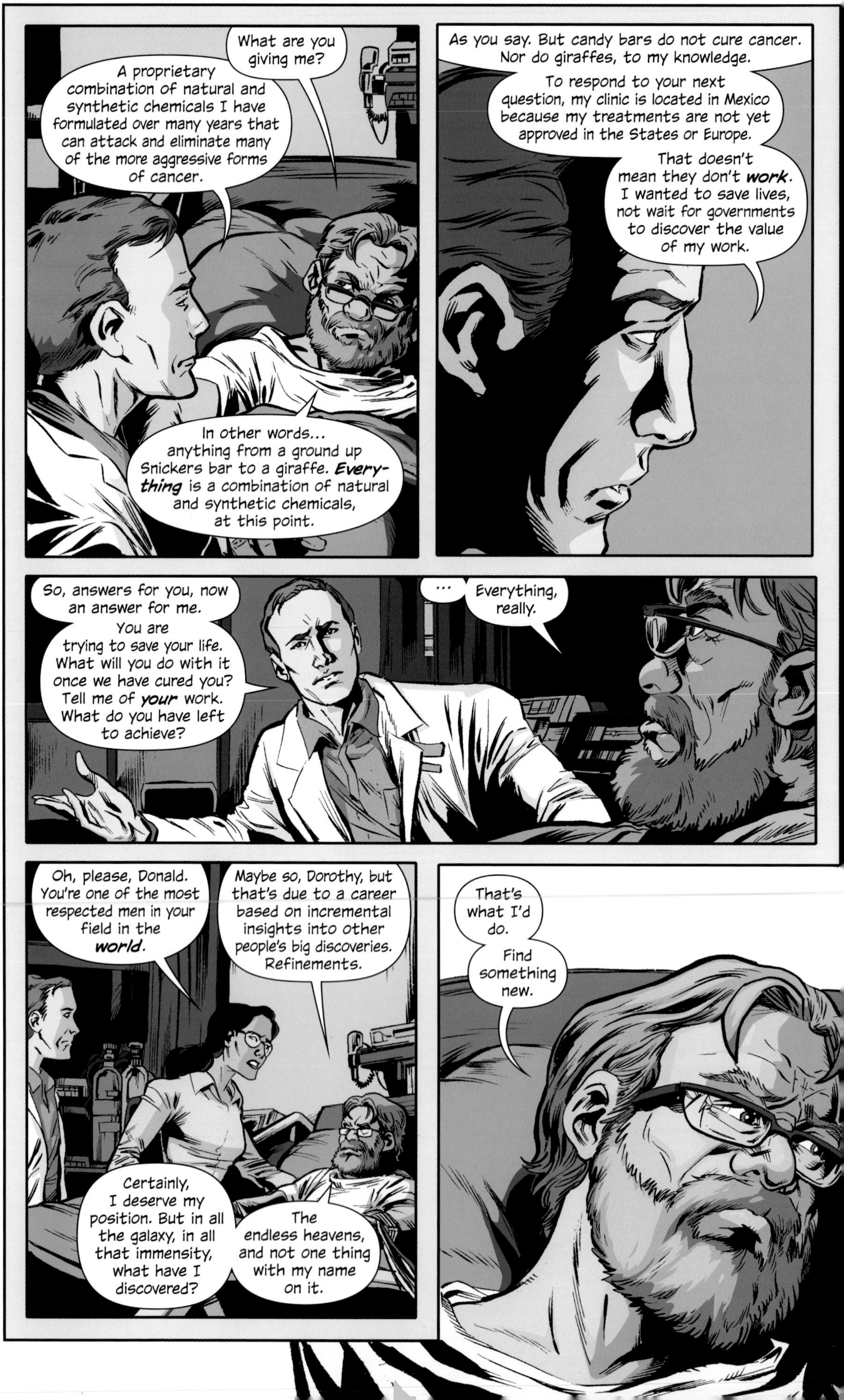
What are you giving me?
A proprietary combination of natural and synthetic chemicals I have formulated over many years that can attack and eliminate many of the more aggressive forms of cancer.
In other words... anything from a ground up Snickers bar to a giraffe. ***Everything*** is a combination of natural and synthetic chemicals, at this point.
As you say. But candy bars do not cure cancer. Nor do giraffes, to my knowledge.
To respond to your next question, my clinic is located in Mexico because my treatments are not yet approved in the States or Europe.
That doesn't mean they don't ***work***. I wanted to save lives, not wait for governments to discover the value of my work.
So, answers for you, now an answer for me.
You are trying to save your life. What will you do with it once we have cured you? Tell me of ***your*** work. What do you have left to achieve?
...
Everything, really.
Oh, please, Donald. You're one of the most respected men in your field in the ***world***.
Maybe so, Dorothy, but that's due to a career based on incremental insights into other people's big discoveries. Refinements.
Certainly, I deserve my position. But in all the galaxy, in all that immensity, what have I discovered?
The endless heavens, and not one thing with my name on it.
That's what I'd do.
Find something new.

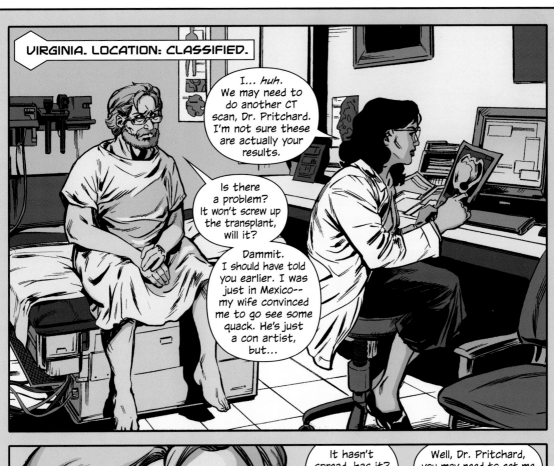

VIRGINIA. LOCATION: CLASSIFIED.

I... *huh.* We may need to do another CT scan, Dr. Pritchard. I'm not sure these are actually your results.

Is there a problem? It won't screw up the transplant, will it?

Dammit. I should have told you earlier. I was just in Mexico-- my wife convinced me to go see some quack. He's just a con artist, but...

It hasn't spread, has it? Beyond the liver? Are we too late?

Well, Dr. Pritchard, you may need to get me that con artist's name.

Because according to this...

...you're completely cured.

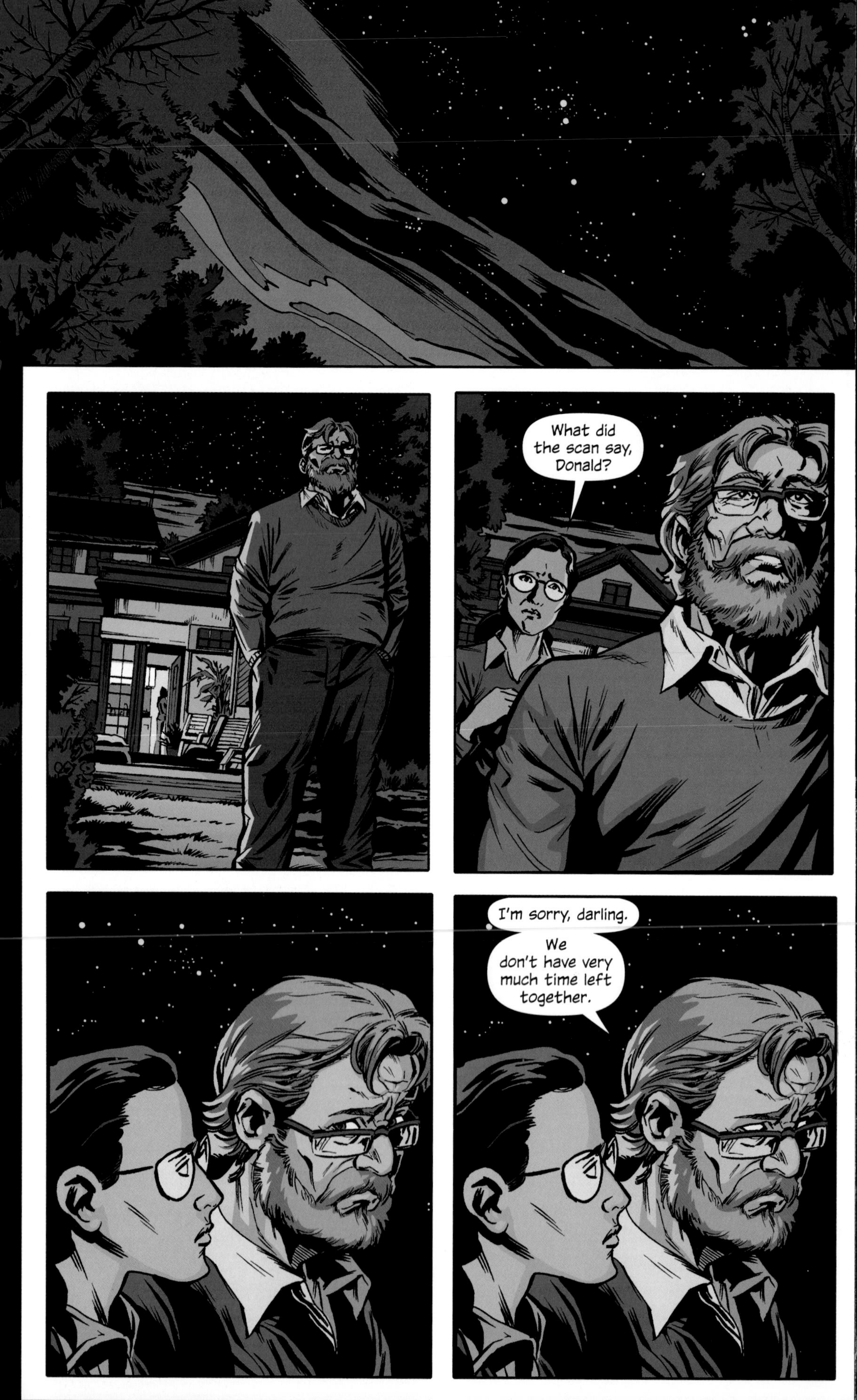
What did the scan say, Donald?
I'm sorry, darling.
We don't have very much time left together.

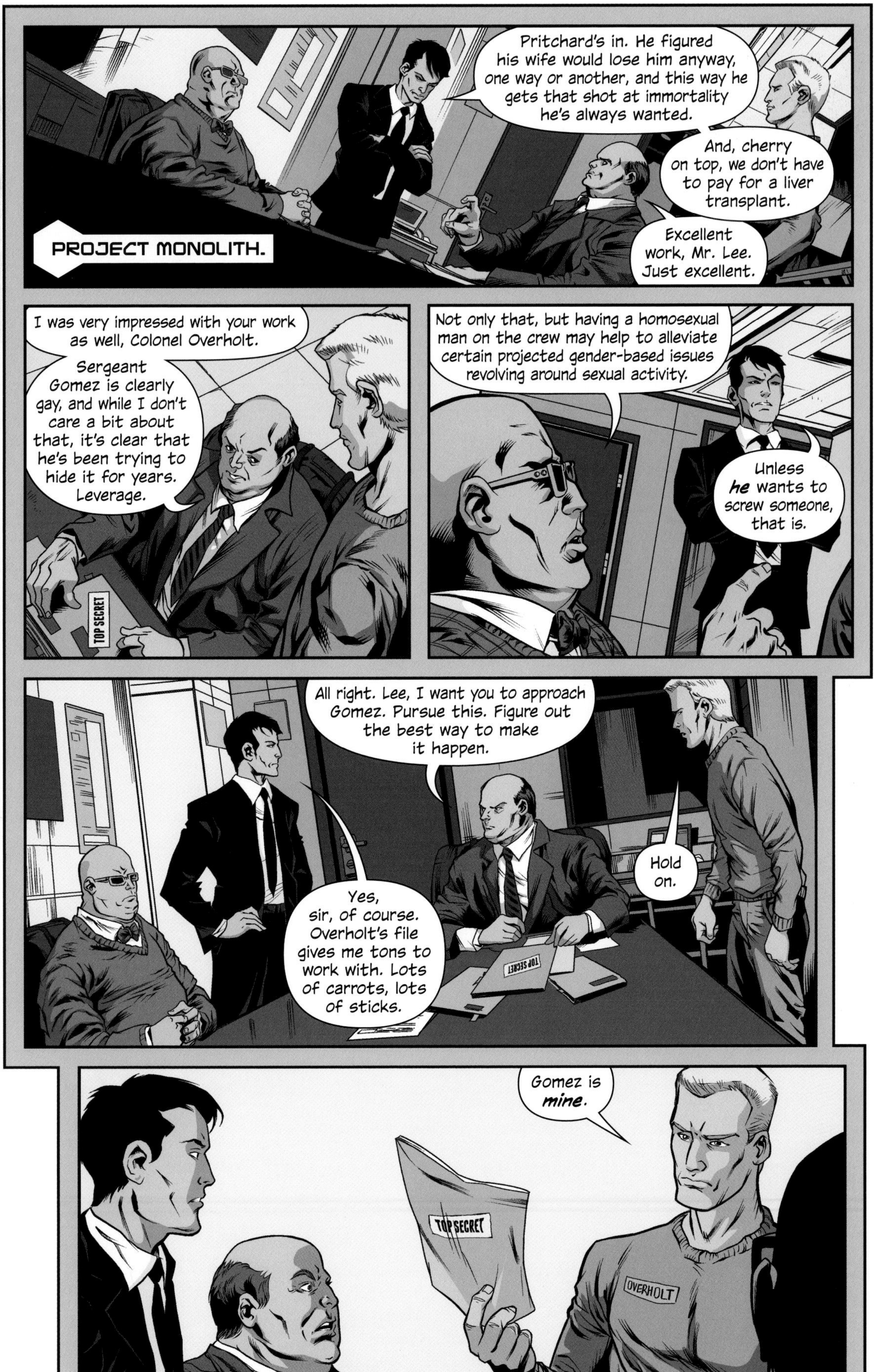
Pritchard's in. He figured his wife would lose him anyway, one way or another, and this way he gets that shot at immortality he's always wanted.
And, cherry on top, we don't have to pay for a liver transplant.
PROJECT MONOLITH.
Excellent work, Mr. Lee. Just excellent.
I was very impressed with your work as well, Colonel Overholt.
Sergeant Gomez is clearly gay, and while I don't care a bit about that, it's clear that he's been trying to hide it for years. Leverage.
TOP SECRET
Not only that, but having a homosexual man on the crew may help to alleviate certain projected gender-based issues revolving around sexual activity.
Unless *he* wants to screw someone, that is.
All right. Lee, I want you to approach Gomez. Pursue this. Figure out the best way to make it happen.
Yes, sir, of course. Overholt's file gives me tons to work with. Lots of carrots, lots of sticks.
TOP SECRET
Hold on.
Gomez is *mine*.
TOP SECRET
OVERHOLT

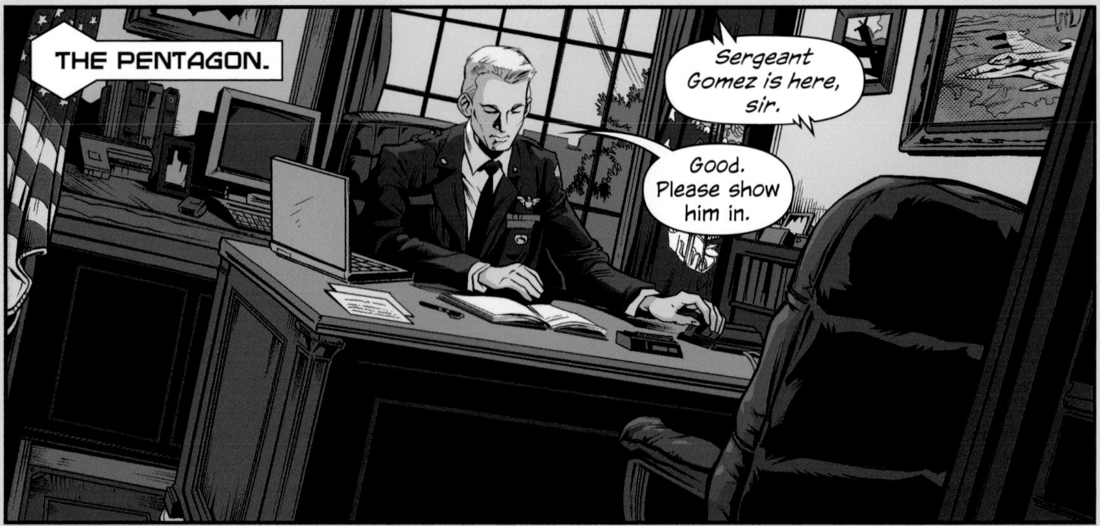
THE PENTAGON.
Sergeant Gomez is here, sir.
Good. Please show him in.

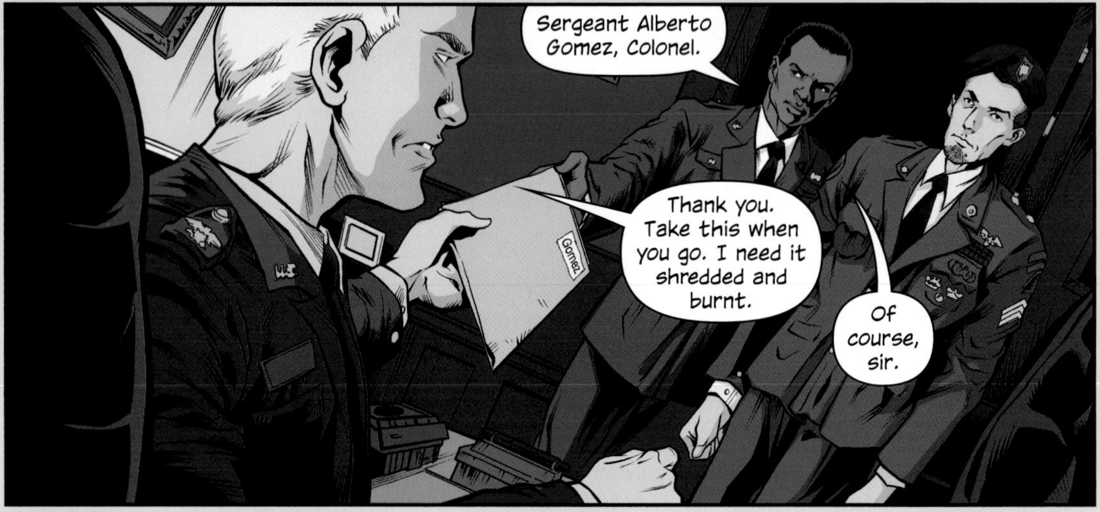
Sergeant Alberto Gomez, Colonel.
Thank you. Take this when you go. I need it shredded and burnt.
Of course, sir.
Gomez

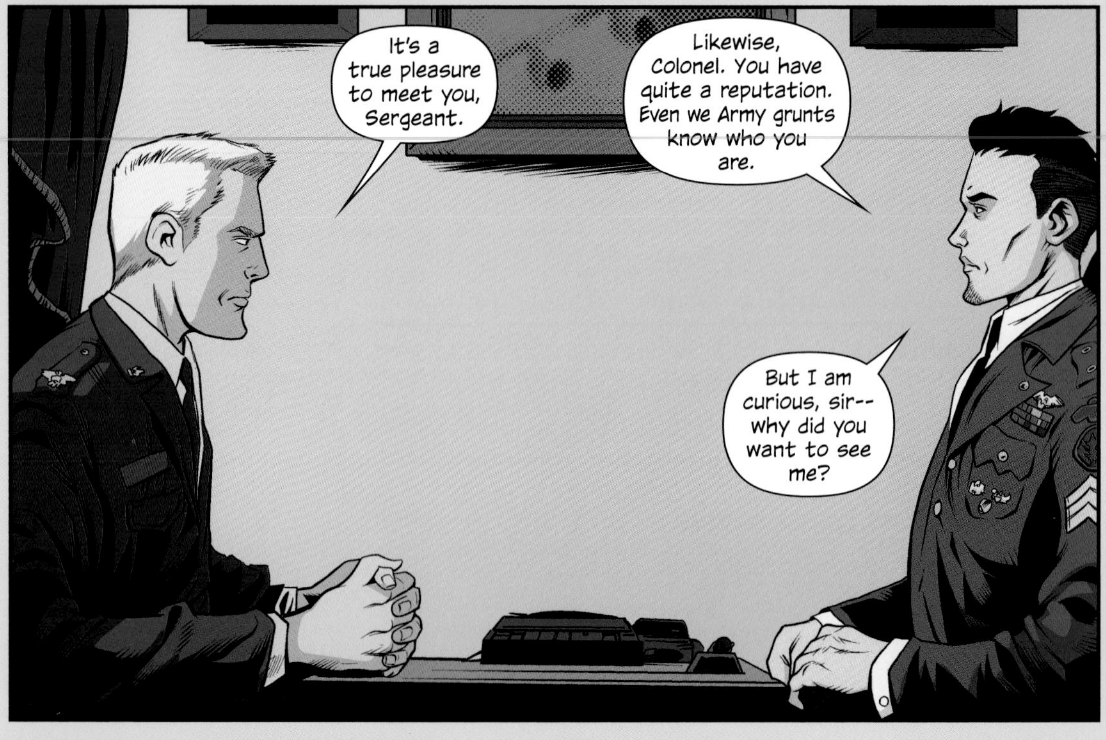
It's a true pleasure to meet you, Sergeant.
Likewise, Colonel. You have quite a reputation. Even we Army grunts know who you are.
But I am curious, sir--why did you want to see me?

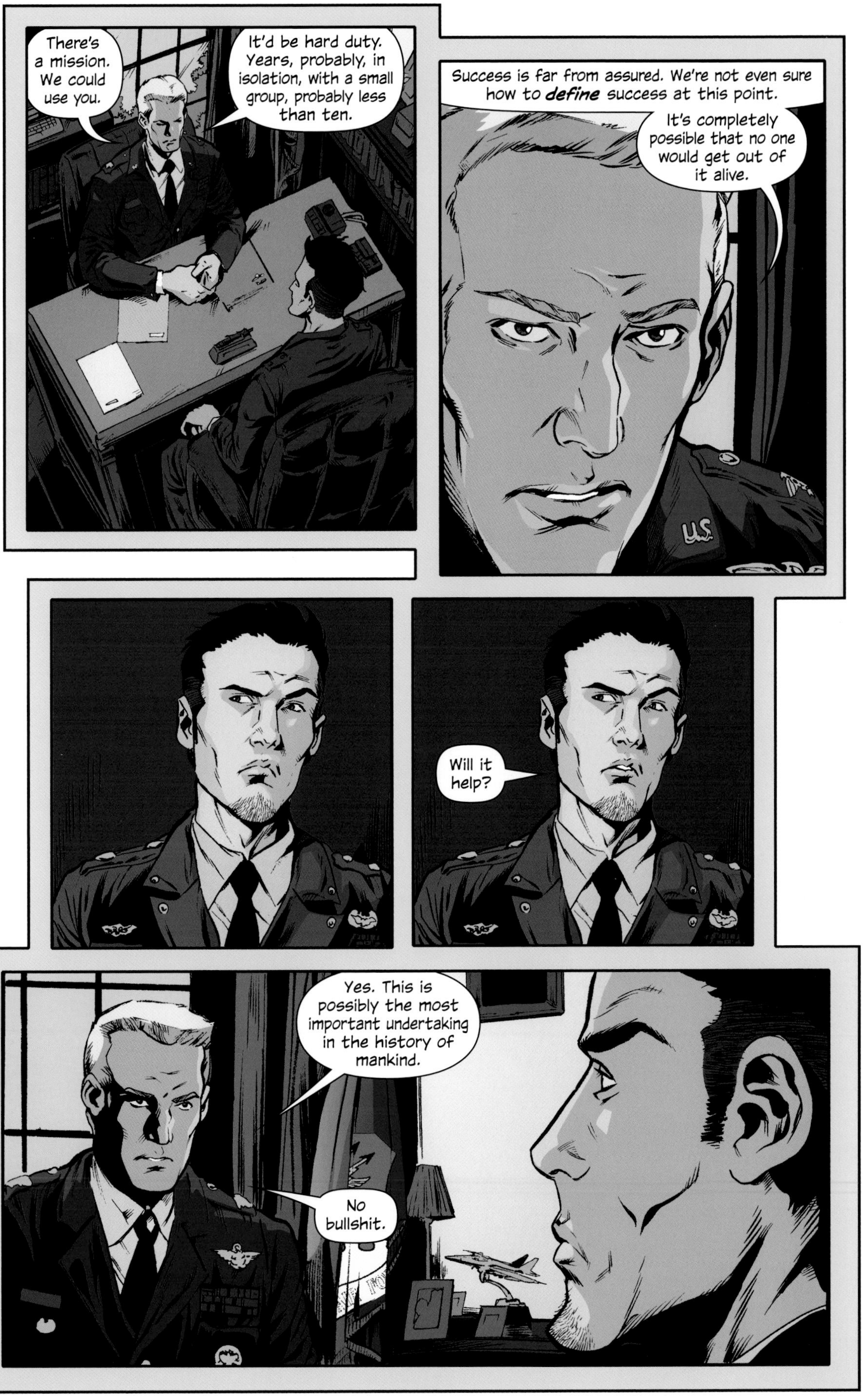
There's a mission. We could use you.
It'd be hard duty. Years, probably, in isolation, with a small group, probably less than ten.
Success is far from assured. We're not even sure how to **define** success at this point.
It's completely possible that no one would get out of it alive.
Will it help?
Yes. This is possibly the most important undertaking in the history of mankind.
No bullshit.

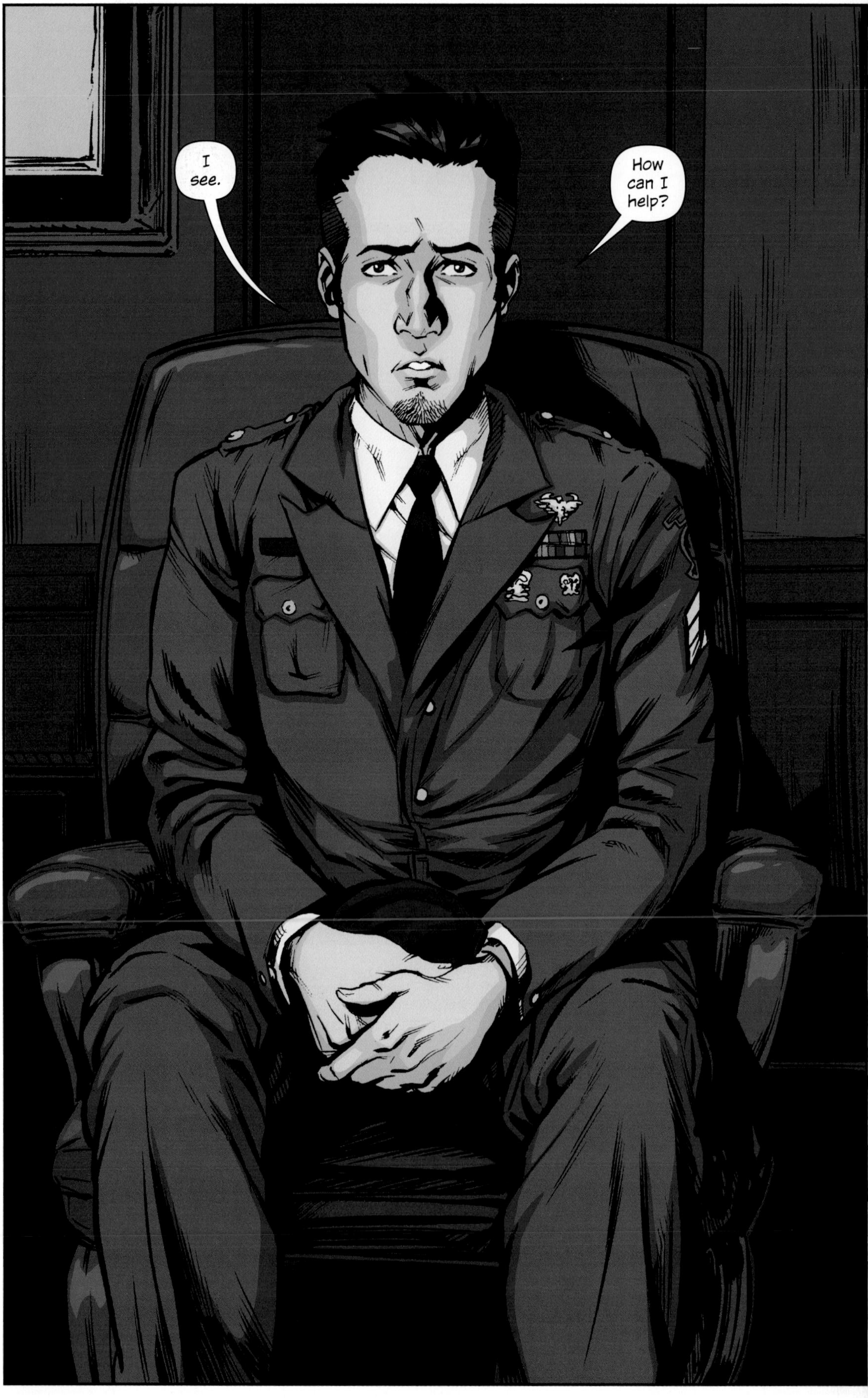
I see.
How can I help?

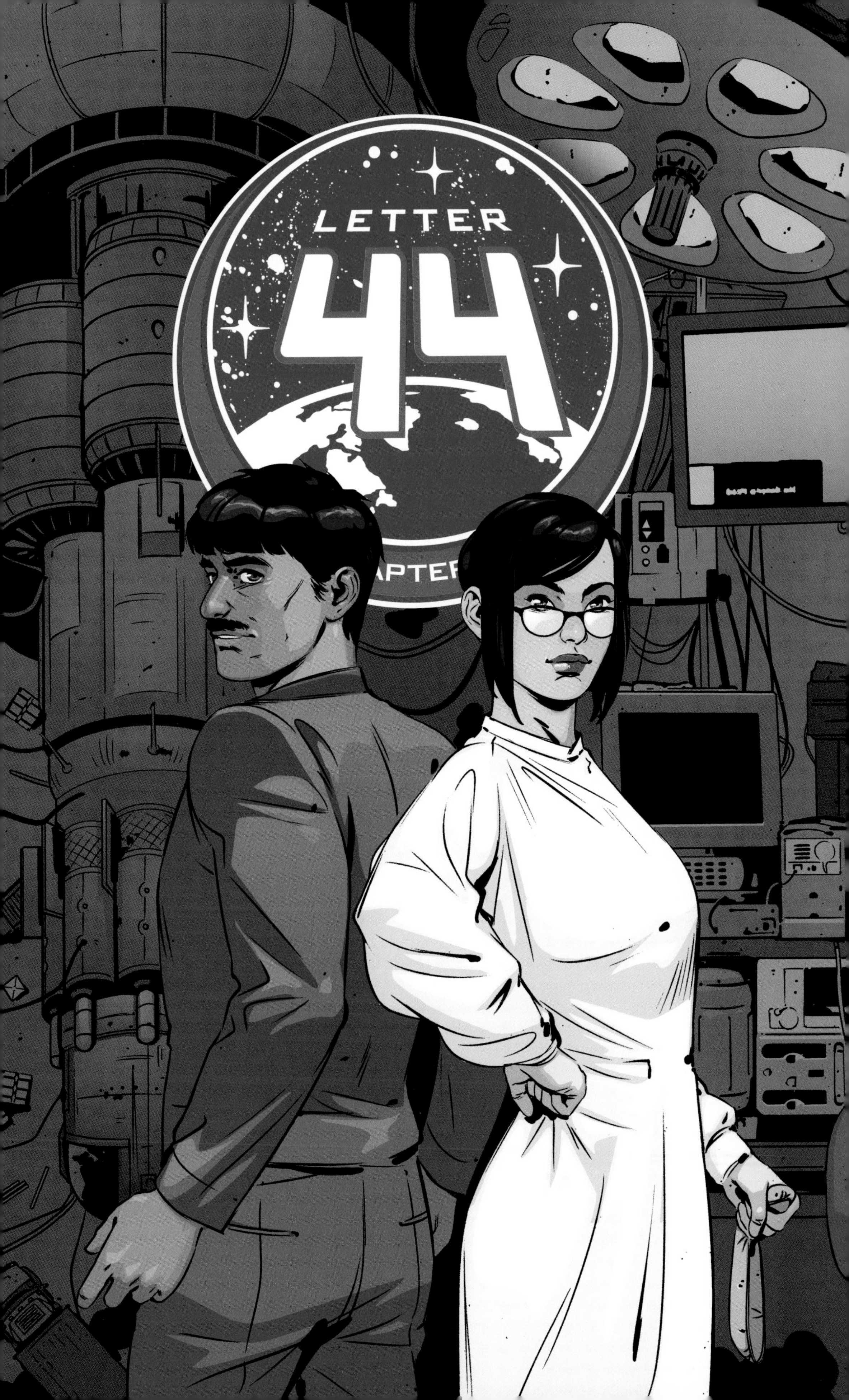
LETTER
44

THE CLARKE.

JANUARY 2003.

You know, Charlotte, this whole thing will probably go terribly wrong at some point or another.

It's inevitable-- the mission's too complex, the ship has too many parts, and worst of all, there are *human beings involved*.

Seems a little defeatist, doesn't it, Rowan?

They tried sending probes, and it didn't work. Humans have to be part of this.

No, you miss my point. We're the problem, but we're also the solution.

People are *flexible*.

When something negative happens, we can *adapt*.

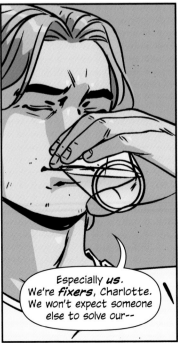

Especially *us*. We're *fixers*, Charlotte. We won't expect someone else to solve our--

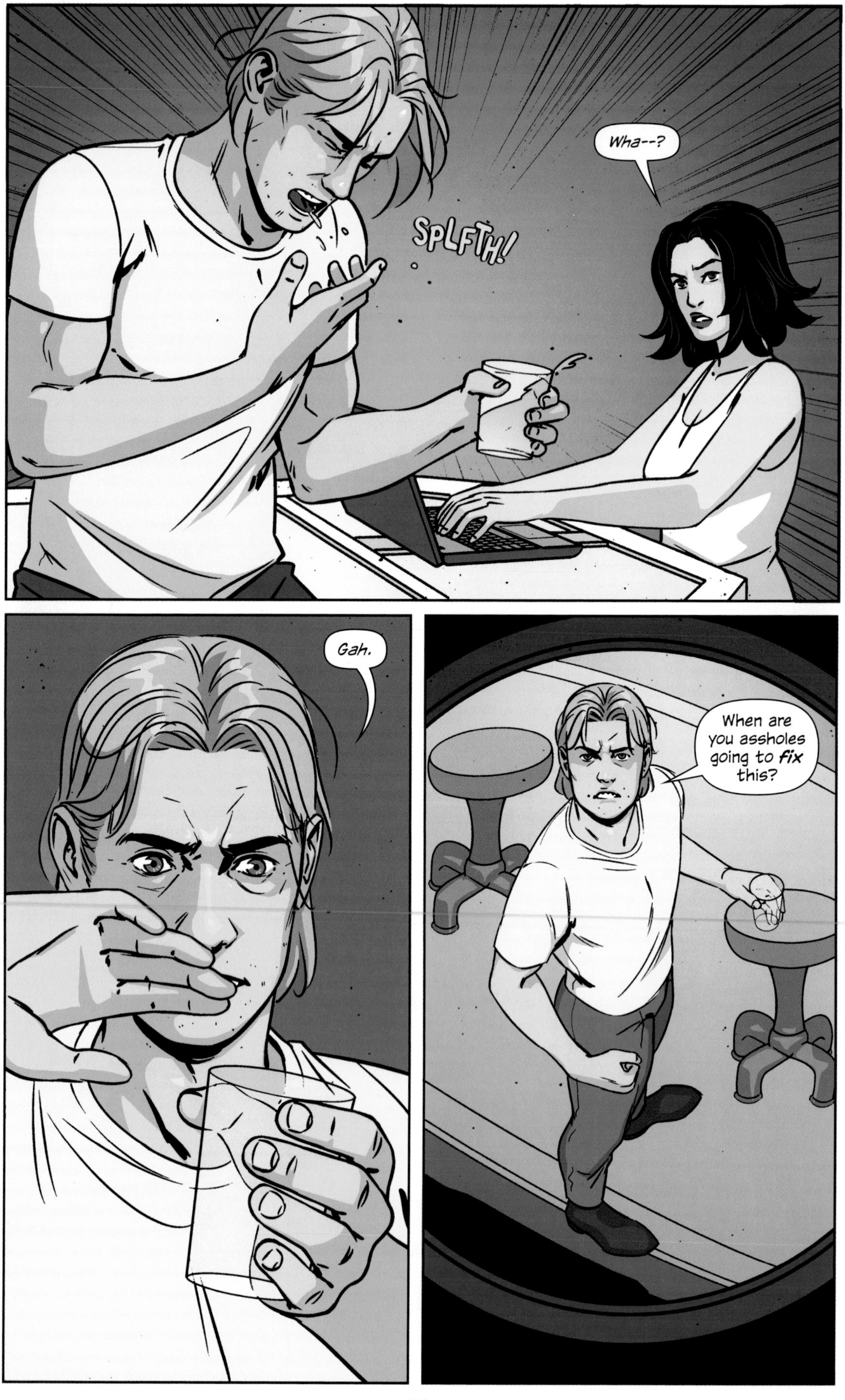
Wha--?
SPLFTH!
Gah.
When are you assholes going to *fix* this?

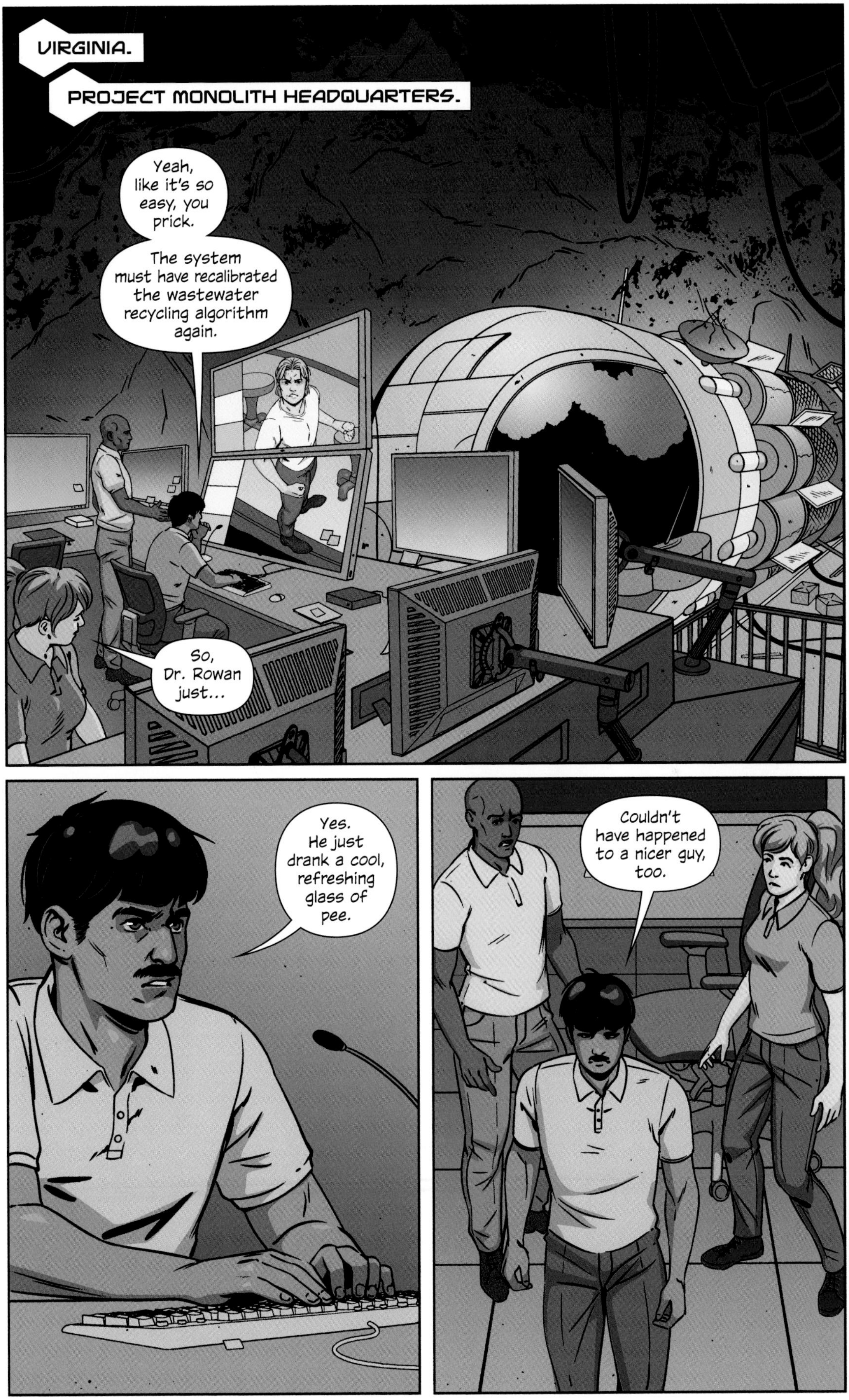
VIRGINIA.
PROJECT MONOLITH HEADQUARTERS.
Yeah, like it's so easy, you prick.
The system must have recalibrated the wastewater recycling algorithm again.
So, Dr. Rowan just...
Yes. He just drank a cool, refreshing glass of pee.
Couldn't have happened to a nicer guy, too.

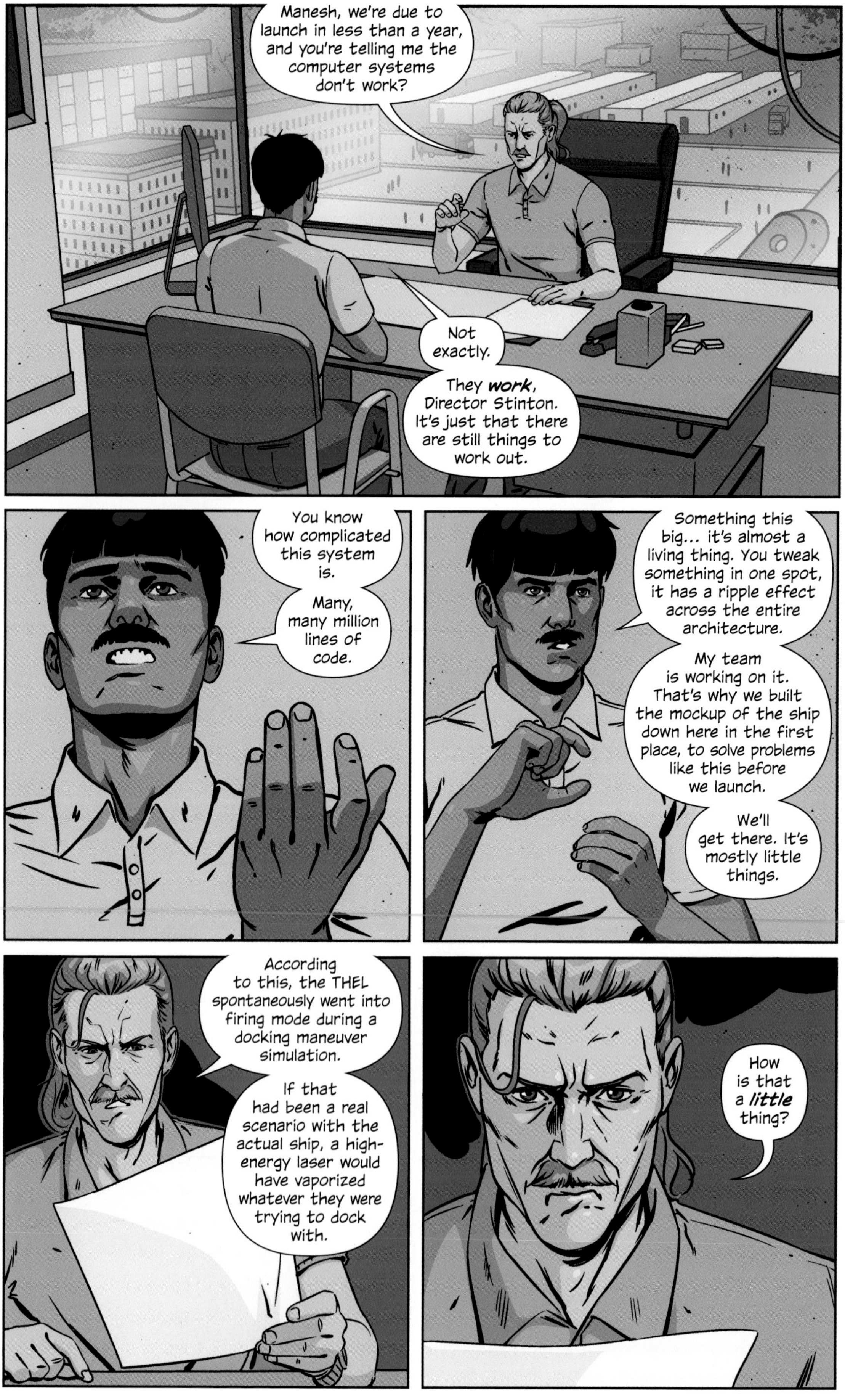
Manesh, we're due to launch in less than a year, and you're telling me the computer systems don't work?
Not exactly.
They **work**, Director Stinton. It's just that there are still things to work out.
You know how complicated this system is.
Many, many million lines of code.
Something this big... it's almost a living thing. You tweak something in one spot, it has a ripple effect across the entire architecture.
My team is working on it. That's why we built the mockup of the ship down here in the first place, to solve problems like this before we launch.
We'll get there. It's mostly little things.
According to this, the THEL spontaneously went into firing mode during a docking maneuver simulation.
If that had been a real scenario with the actual ship, a high-energy laser would have vaporized whatever they were trying to dock with.
How is that a *little* thing?

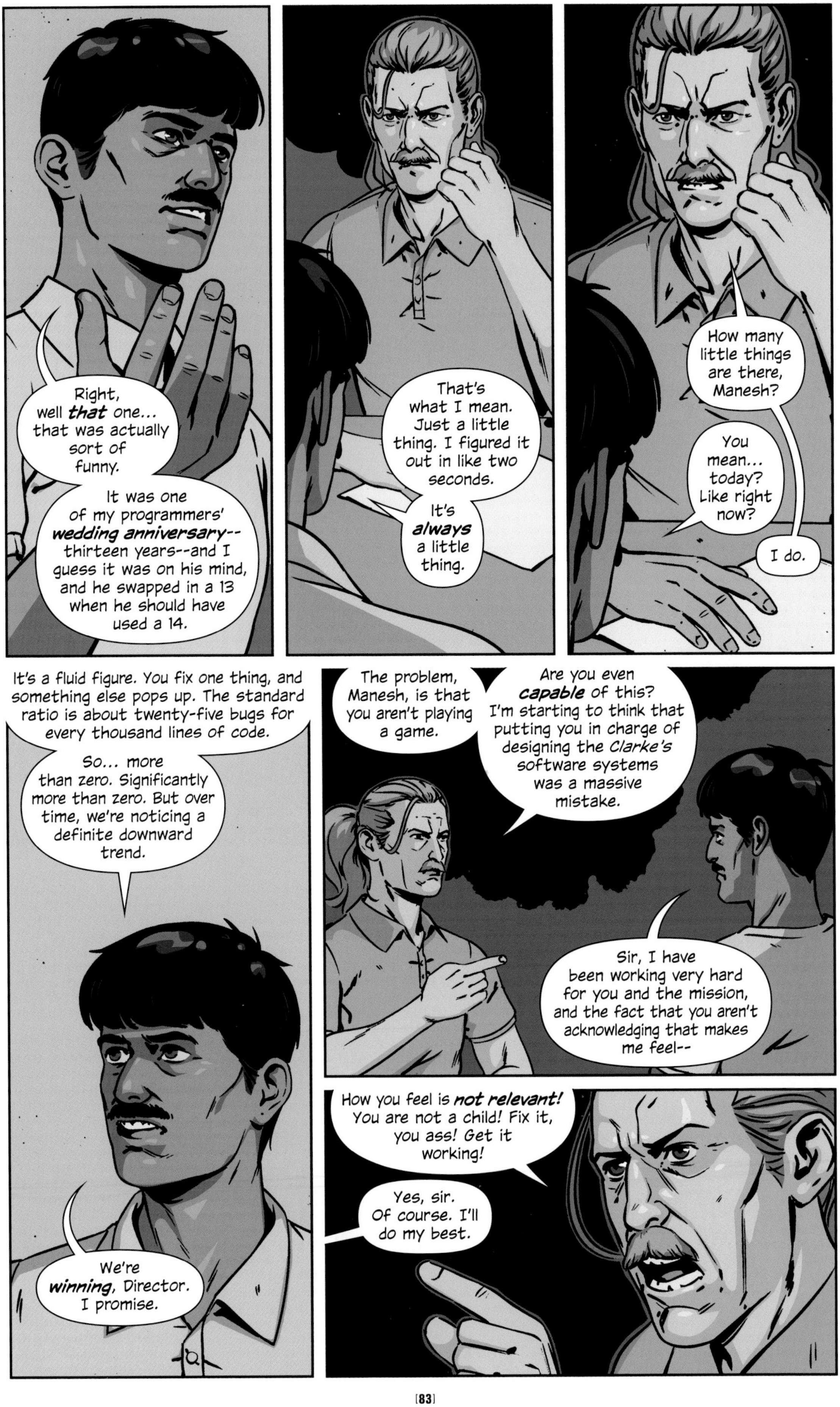
Right, well *that* one... that was actually sort of funny.
It was one of my programmers' *wedding anniversary*--thirteen years--and I guess it was on his mind, and he swapped in a 13 when he should have used a 14.
That's what I mean. Just a little thing. I figured it out in like two seconds.
It's *always* a little thing.
How many little things are there, Manesh?
You mean... today? Like right now?
I do.
It's a fluid figure. You fix one thing, and something else pops up. The standard ratio is about twenty-five bugs for every thousand lines of code.
So... more than zero. Significantly more than zero. But over time, we're noticing a definite downward trend.
We're *winning*, Director. I promise.
The problem, Manesh, is that you aren't playing a game.
Are you even *capable* of this? I'm starting to think that putting you in charge of designing the *Clarke's* software systems was a massive mistake.
Sir, I have been working very hard for you and the mission, and the fact that you aren't acknowledging that makes me feel--
How you feel is *not relevant!* You are not a child! Fix it, you ass! Get it working!
Yes, sir. Of course. I'll do my best.

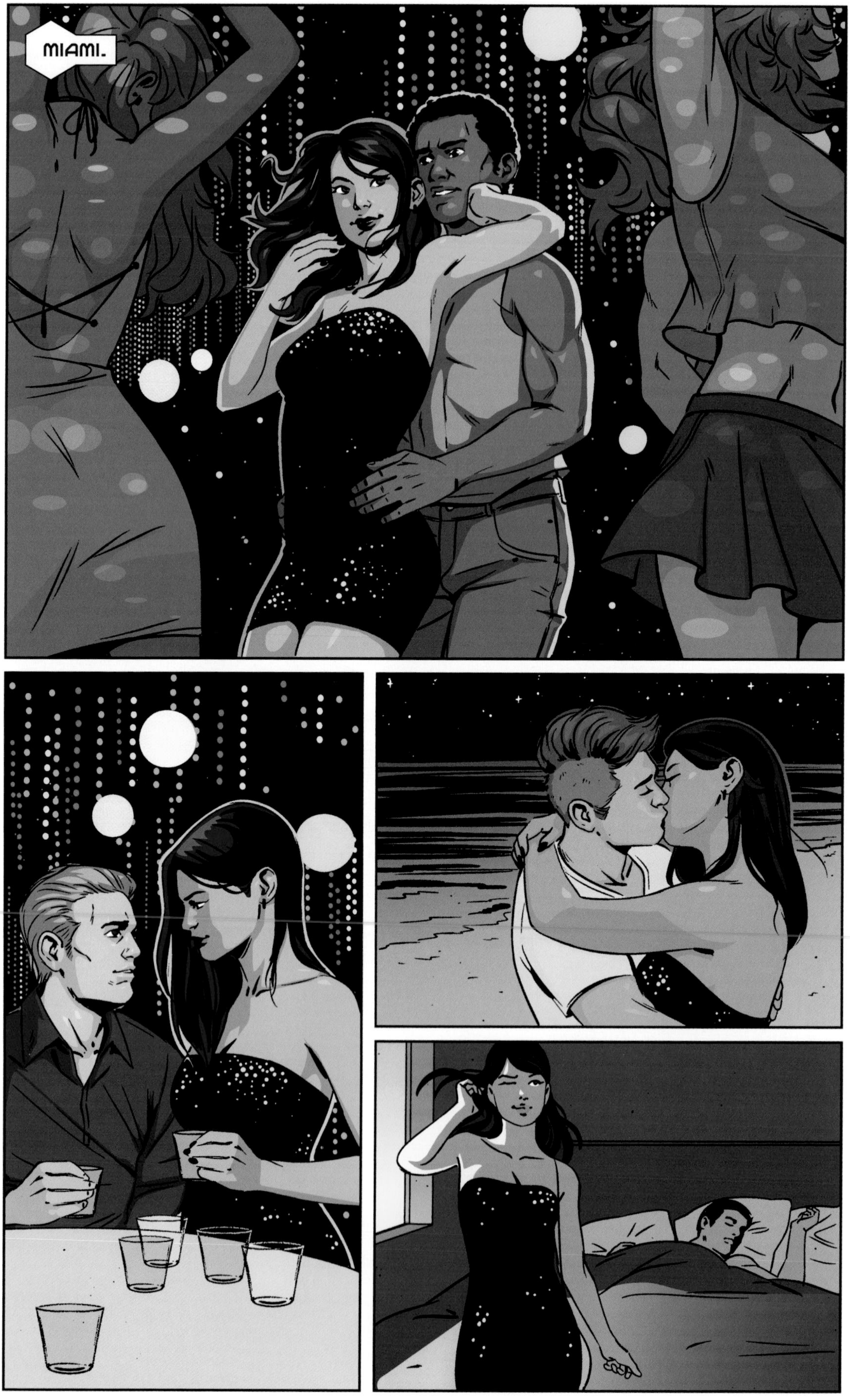
MIAMI.

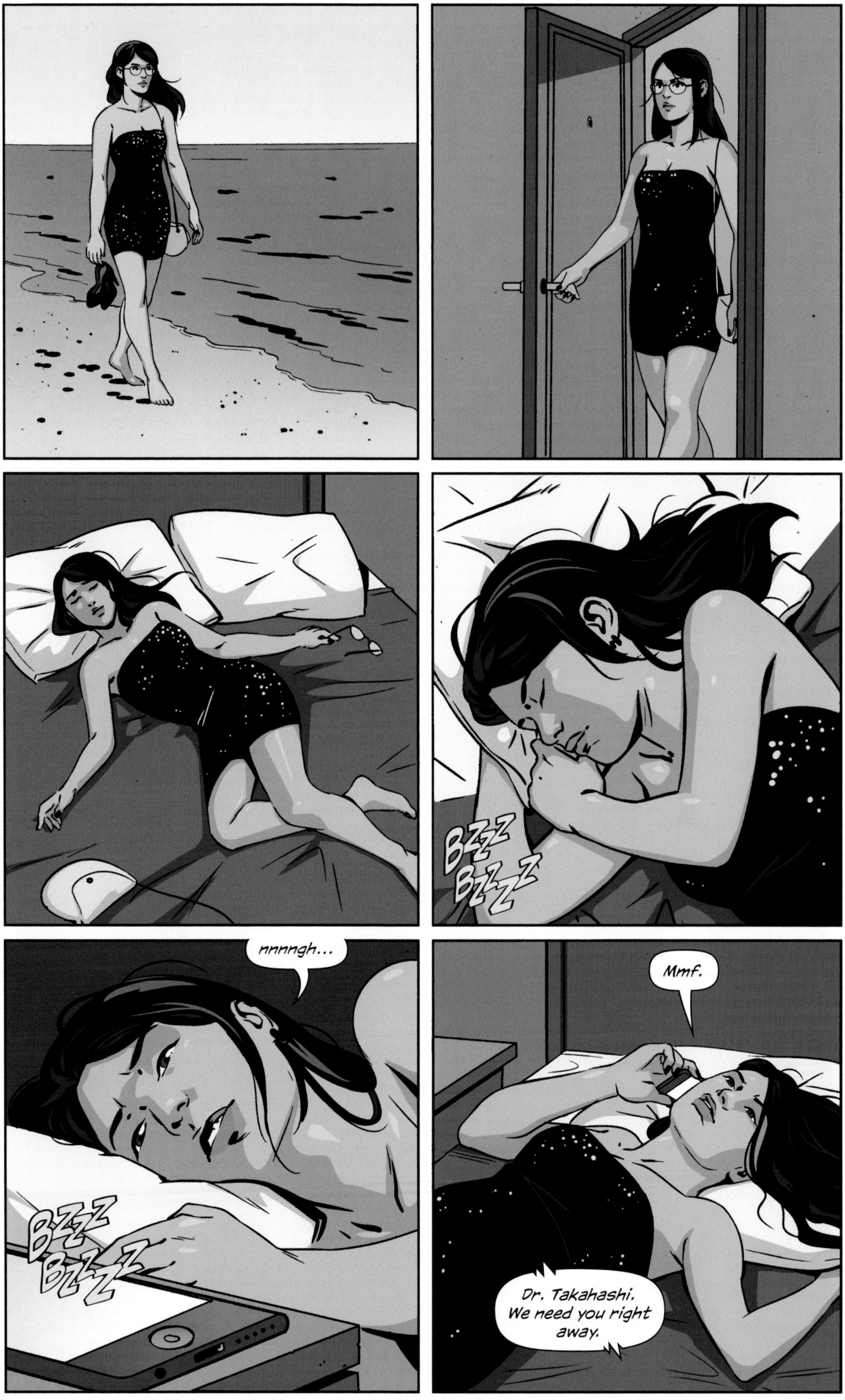
BZZZ
BZZZZ
nnnngh...
BZZZ
BZZZZ
Mmf.
Dr. Takahashi. We need you right away.

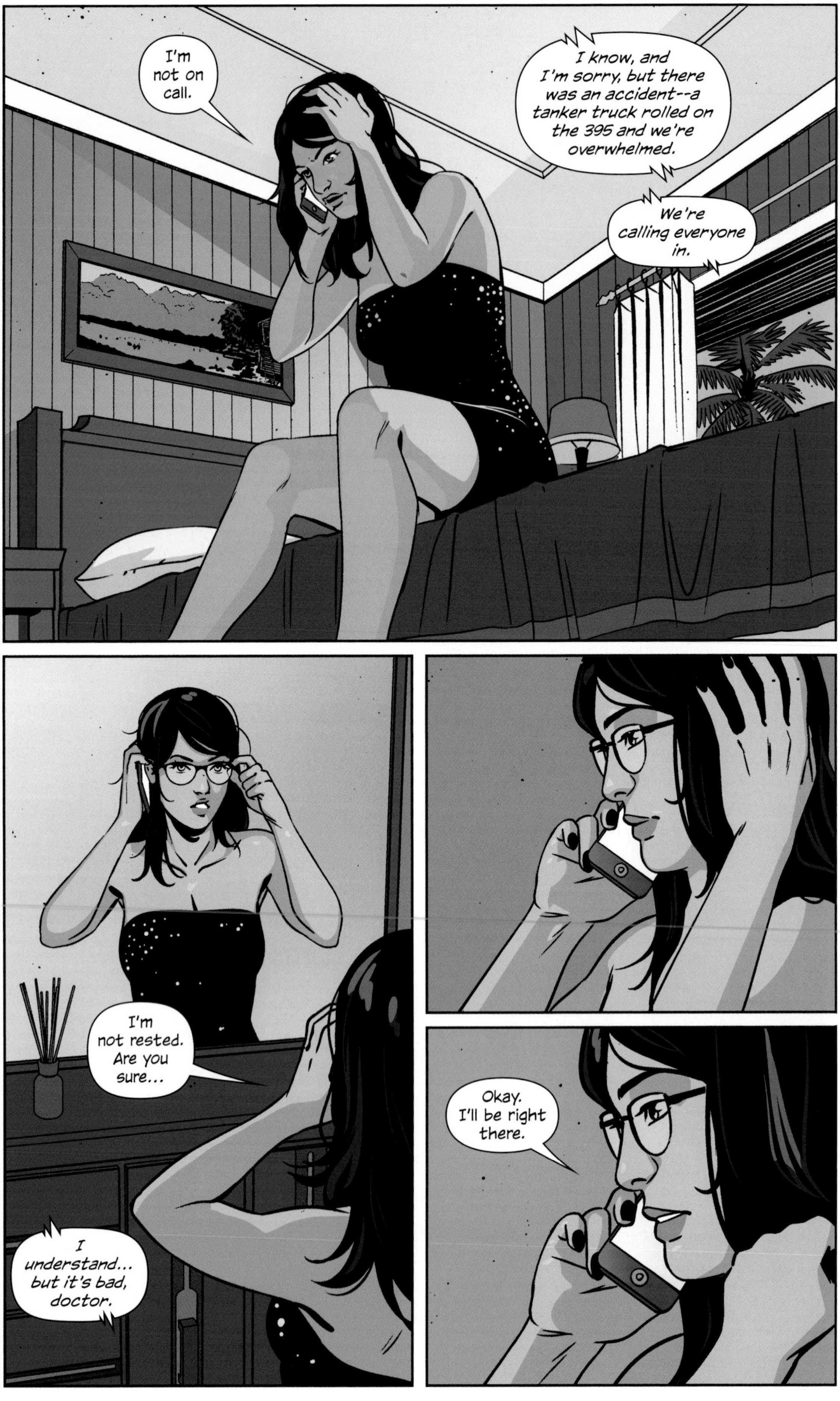
I'm not on call.
I know, and I'm sorry, but there was an accident--a tanker truck rolled on the 395 and we're overwhelmed.
We're calling everyone in.
I'm not rested. Are you sure...
I understand... but it's bad, doctor.
Okay. I'll be right there.

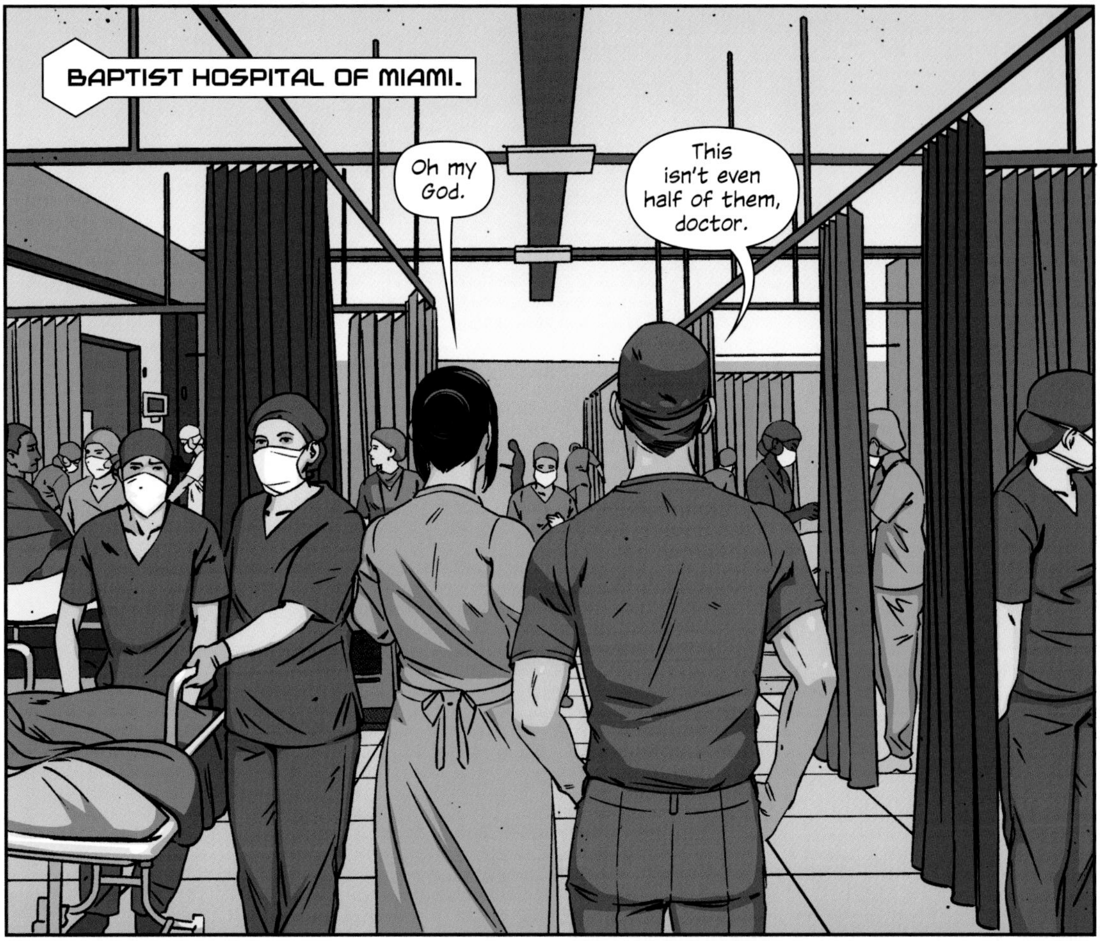
BAPTIST HOSPITAL OF MIAMI.
Oh my God.
This isn't even half of them, doctor.

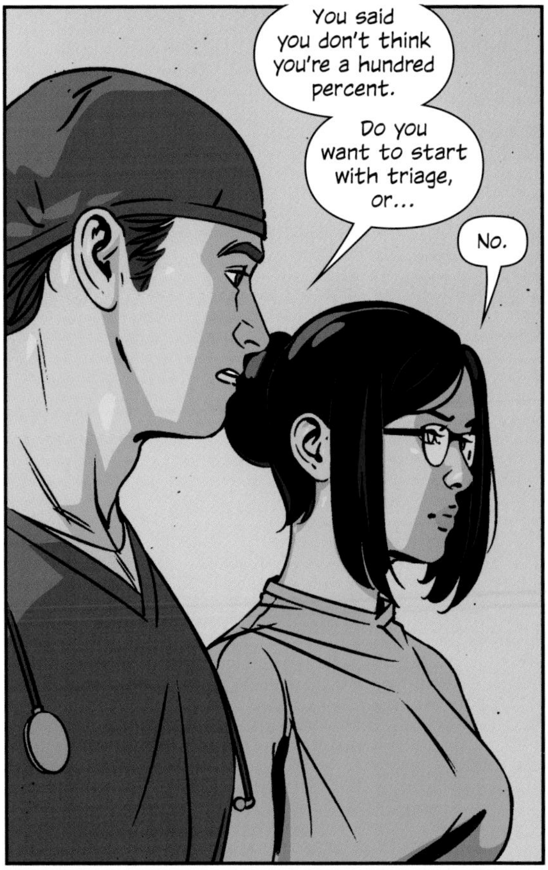
You said you don't think you're a hundred percent.
Do you want to start with triage, or...
No.

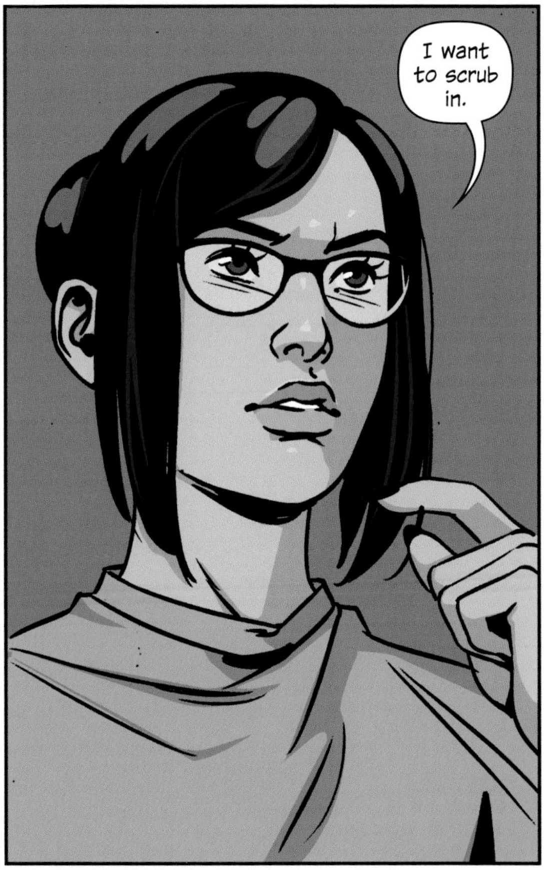
I want to scrub in.

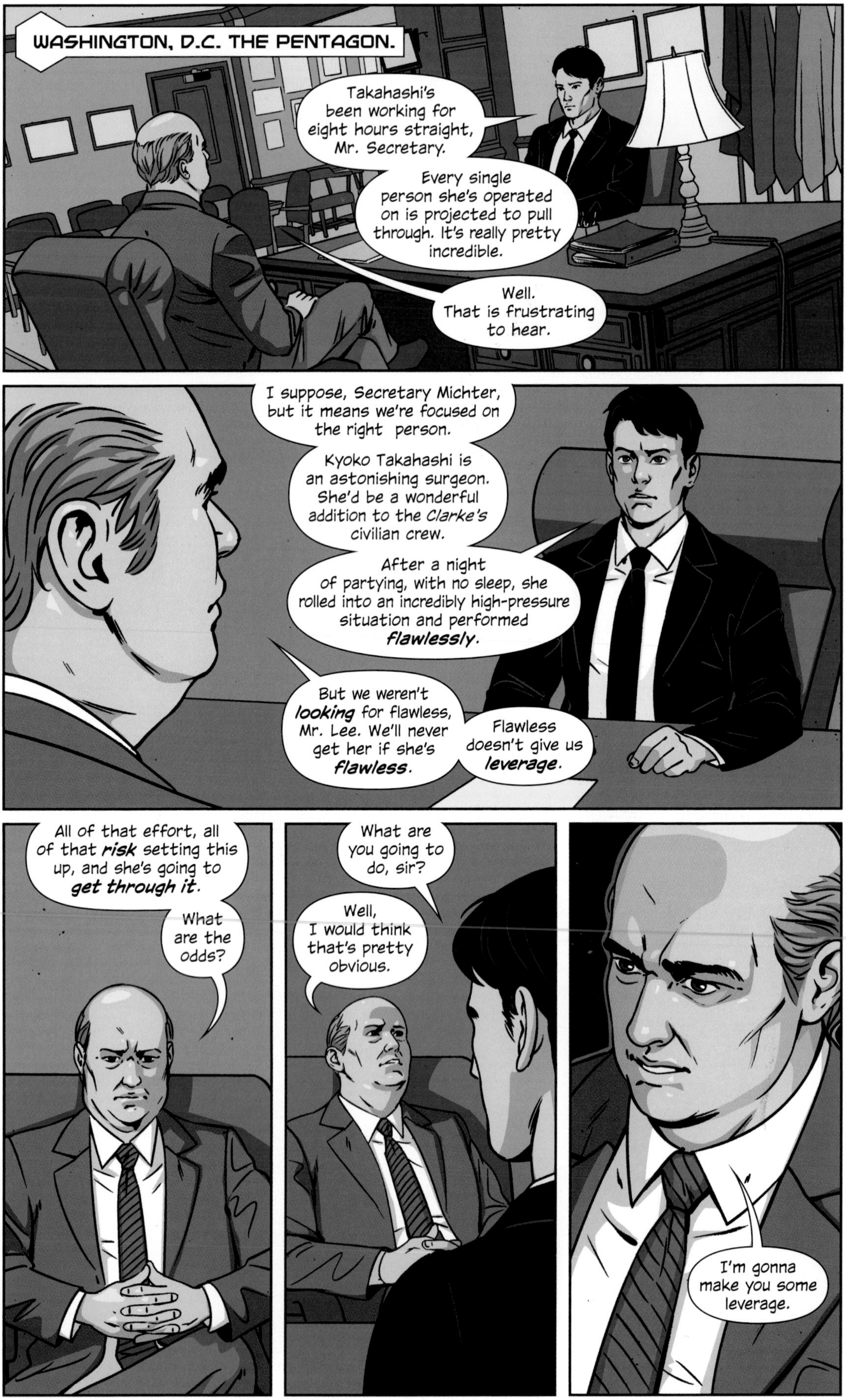
WASHINGTON, D.C. THE PENTAGON.
Takahashi's been working for eight hours straight, Mr. Secretary.
Every single person she's operated on is projected to pull through. It's really pretty incredible.
Well. That is frustrating to hear.
I suppose, Secretary Michter, but it means we're focused on the right person.
Kyoko Takahashi is an astonishing surgeon. She'd be a wonderful addition to the *Clarke's* civilian crew.
After a night of partying, with no sleep, she rolled into an incredibly high-pressure situation and performed ***flawlessly***.
But we weren't ***looking*** for flawless, Mr. Lee. We'll never get her if she's ***flawless***.
Flawless doesn't give us ***leverage***.
All of that effort, all of that ***risk*** setting this up, and she's going to ***get through it***.
What are the odds?
What are you going to do, sir?
Well, I would think that's pretty obvious.
I'm gonna make you some leverage.

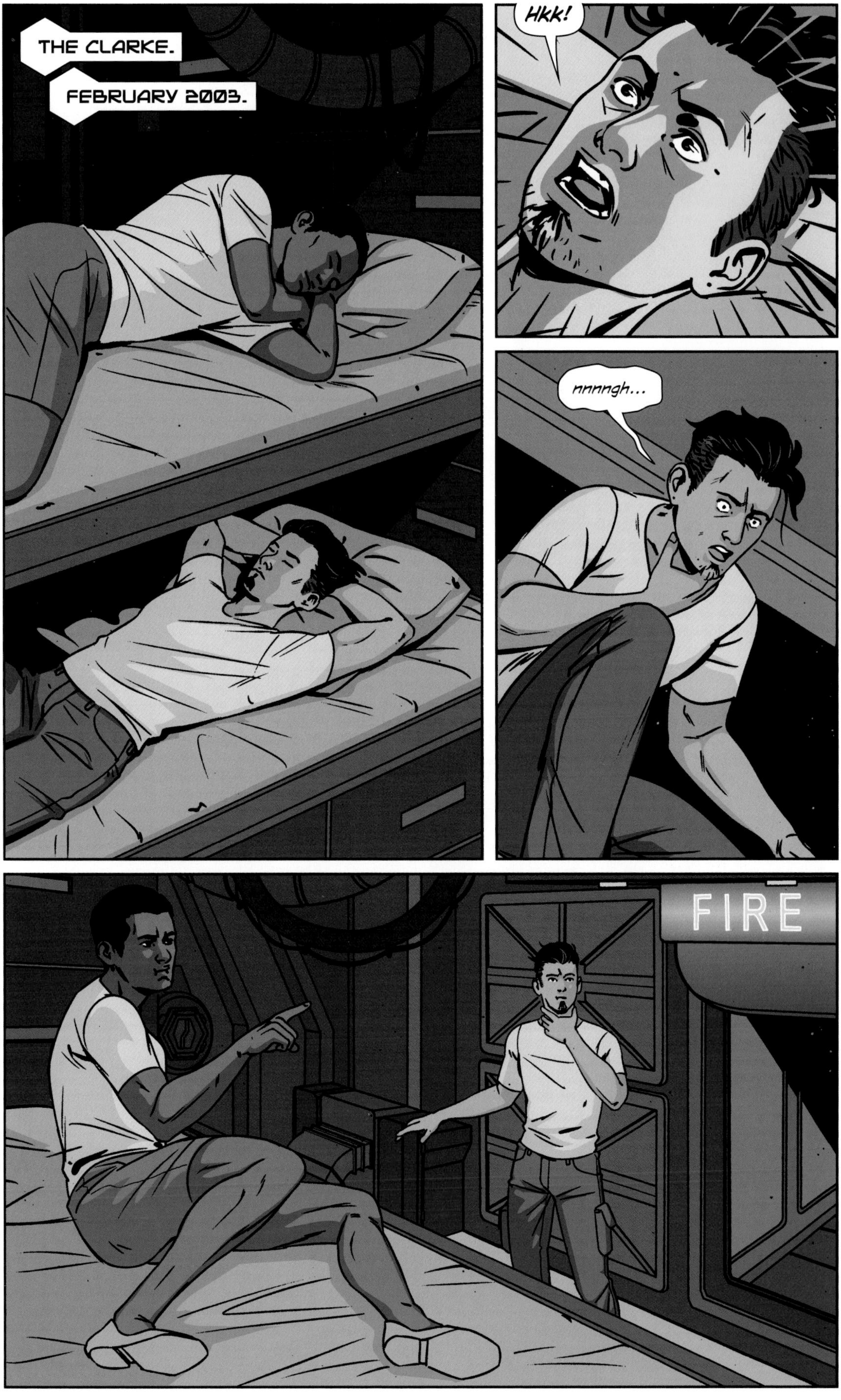
THE CLARKE.
FEBRUARY 2003.
HKK!
nnnngh...
FIRE

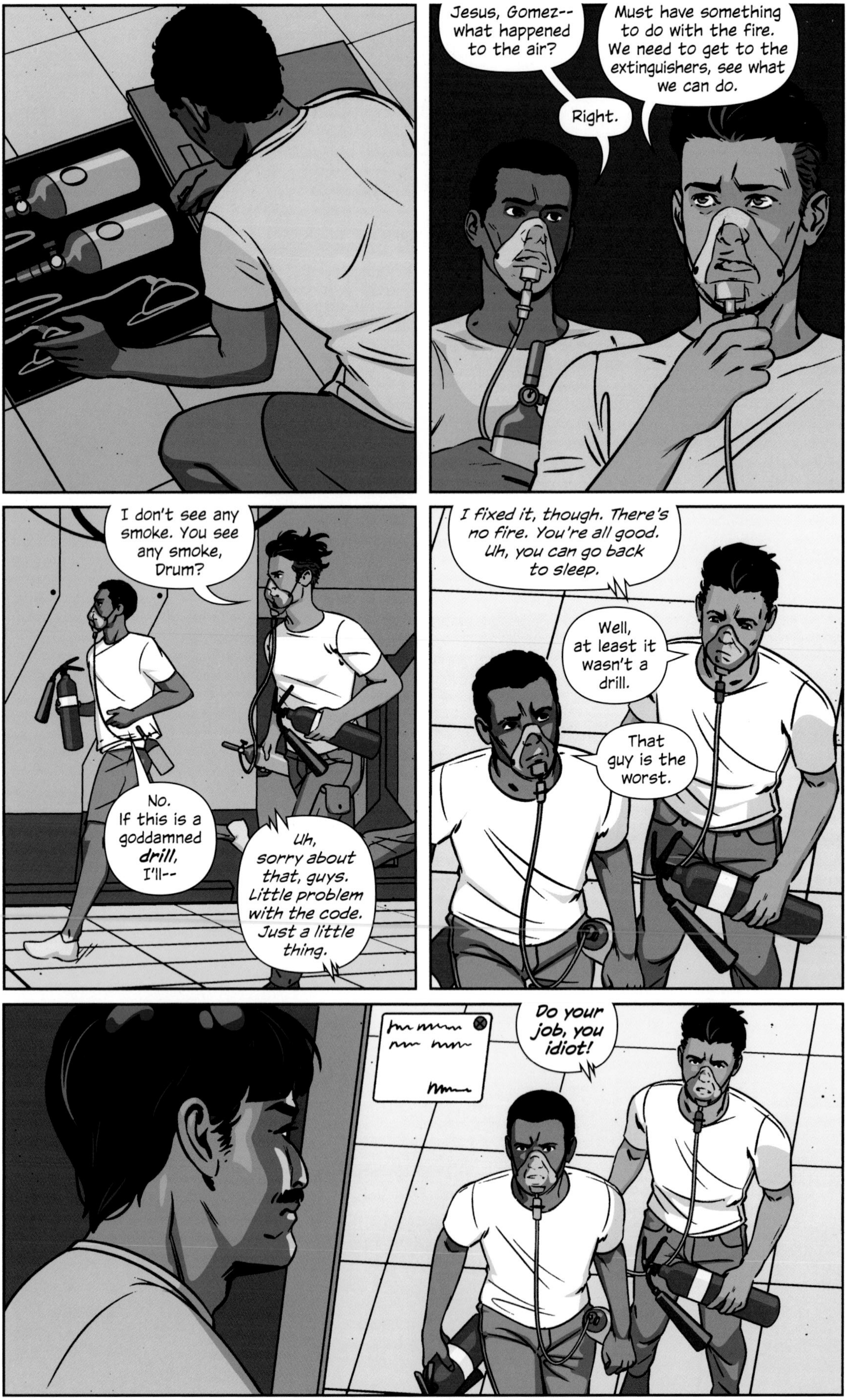
Jesus, Gomez--
what happened
to the air?
Must have something
to do with the fire.
We need to get to the
extinguishers, see what
we can do.
Right.
I don't see any
smoke. You see
any smoke,
Drum?
No.
If this is a
goddamned
drill,
I'll--
Uh,
sorry about
that, guys.
Little problem
with the code.
Just a little
thing.
I fixed it, though. There's
no fire. You're all good.
Uh, you can go back
to sleep.
Well,
at least it
wasn't a
drill.
That
guy is the
worst.
Do your
job, you
idiot!

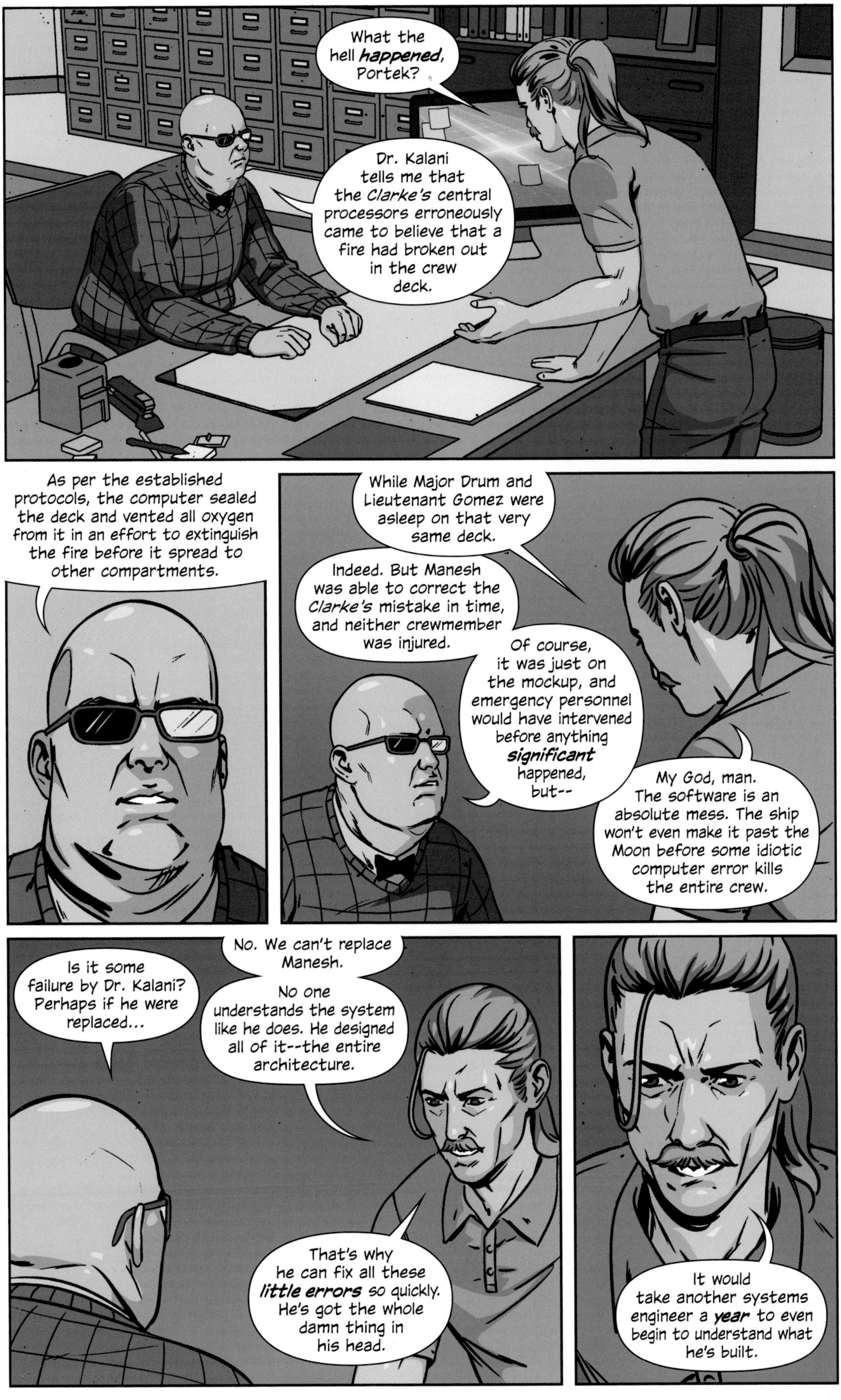
What the hell *happened*, Portek?
Dr. Kalani tells me that the *Clarke's* central processors erroneously came to believe that a fire had broken out in the crew deck.
As per the established protocols, the computer sealed the deck and vented all oxygen from it in an effort to extinguish the fire before it spread to other compartments.
While Major Drum and Lieutenant Gomez were asleep on that very same deck.
Indeed. But Manesh was able to correct the *Clarke's* mistake in time, and neither crewmember was injured.
Of course, it was just on the mockup, and emergency personnel would have intervened before anything ***significant*** happened, but--
My God, man. The software is an absolute mess. The ship won't even make it past the Moon before some idiotic computer error kills the entire crew.
Is it some failure by Dr. Kalani? Perhaps if he were replaced...
No. We can't replace Manesh.
No one understands the system like he does. He designed all of it--the entire architecture.
That's why he can fix all these ***little errors*** so quickly. He's got the whole damn thing in his head.
It would take another systems engineer a ***year*** to even begin to understand what he's built.

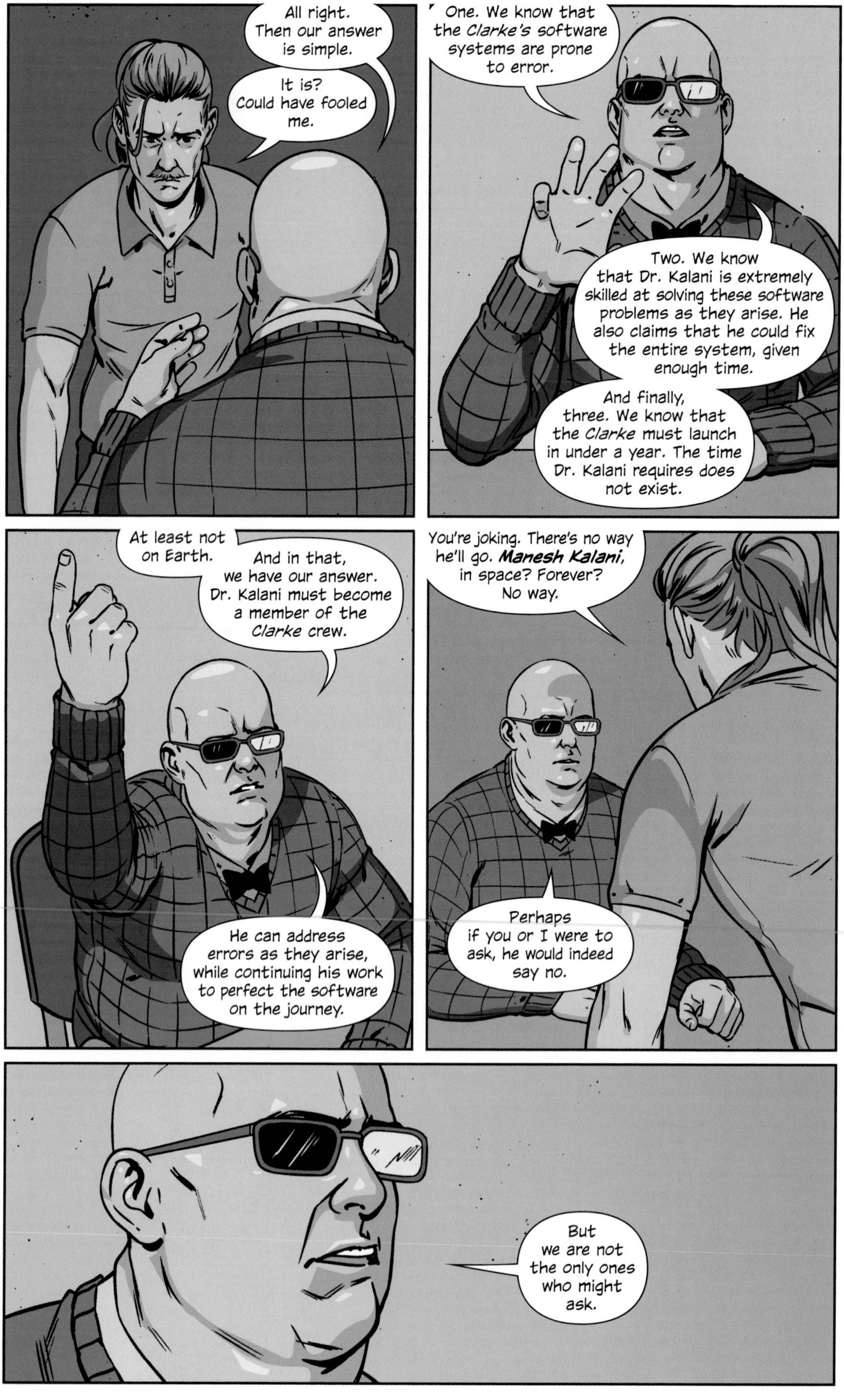
All right. Then our answer is simple.
It is? Could have fooled me.
One. We know that the *Clarke's* software systems are prone to error.
Two. We know that Dr. Kalani is extremely skilled at solving these software problems as they arise. He also claims that he could fix the entire system, given enough time.
And finally, three. We know that the *Clarke* must launch in under a year. The time Dr. Kalani requires does not exist.
At least not on Earth.
And in that, we have our answer. Dr. Kalani must become a member of the *Clarke* crew.
He can address errors as they arise, while continuing his work to perfect the software on the journey.
You're joking. There's no way he'll go. ***Manesh Kalani***, in space? Forever? No way.
Perhaps if you or I were to ask, he would indeed say no.
But we are not the only ones who might ask.

No, this is impossible. This woman was fine. I fixed her.

How the hell is she dead?

I'm so sorry, Kyoko.

That's four patients deceased so far, all from the night the tanker truck rolled.

Don't you think I *know* that? I was *here*. I remember them all.

Were you... all right, when you came in?

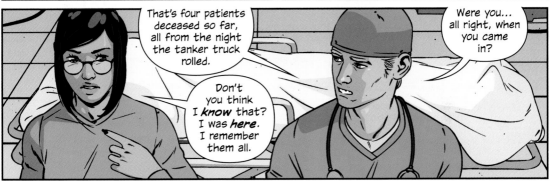

What does *that* mean?

We spoke to the dispatcher, and--

We? Who the hell is *we*?

The administrative board. The dispatcher said you were exhausted. Didn't want to come in.

She *begged* me to pull a shift. I wasn't on call, and I came in anyway. To *help*.

What are you saying, John?

It looks like the Heparin dosage was ten times what it should have been. In all four of them.

And you signed off on it, Kyoko. Your name's right here on the chart.

Fuck. I... fuck.

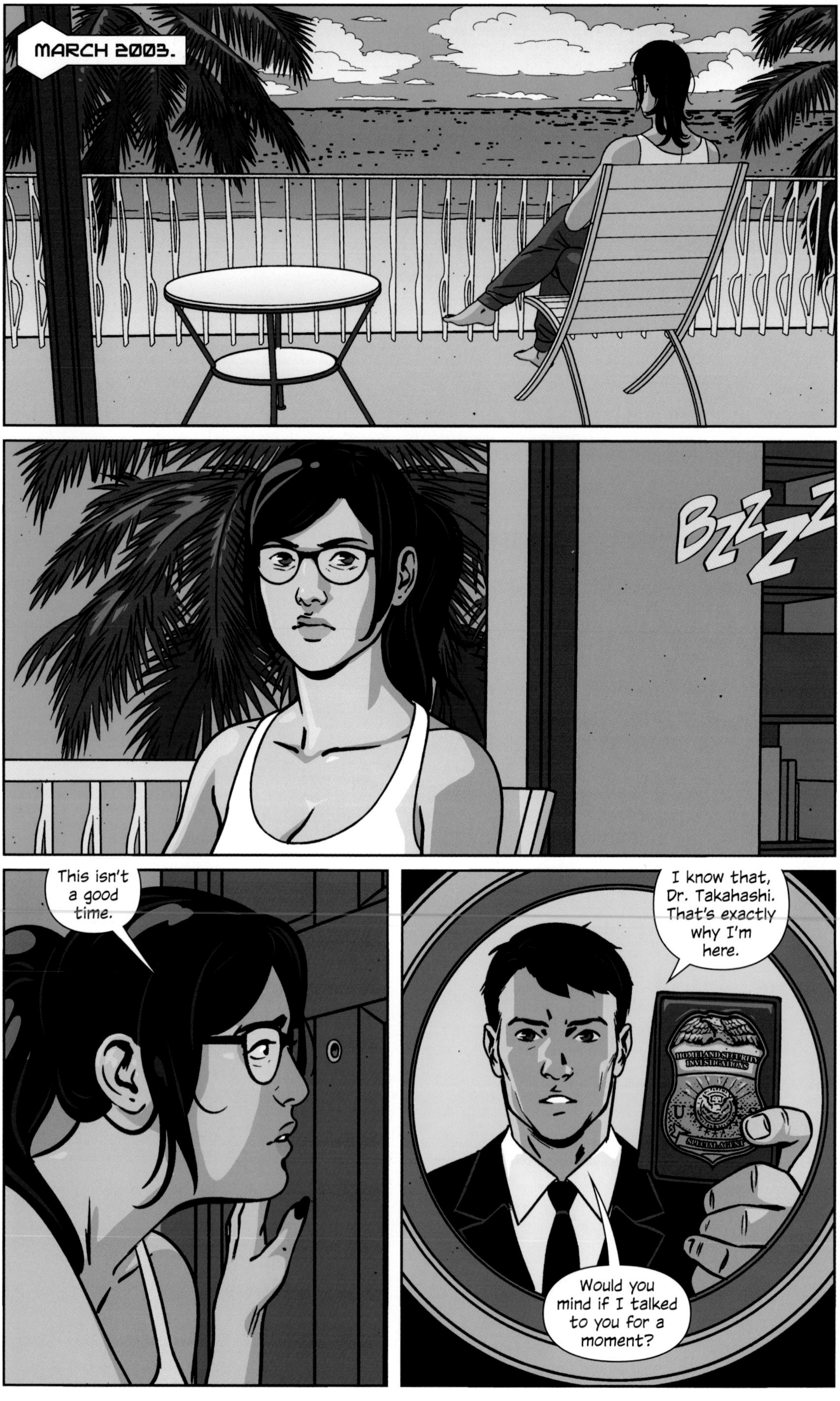
MARCH 2003.
BZZZZ
This isn't a good time.
I know that, Dr. Takahashi. That's exactly why I'm here.
HOMELAND SECURITY INVESTIGATIONS
SPECIAL AGENT
Would you mind if I talked to you for a moment?

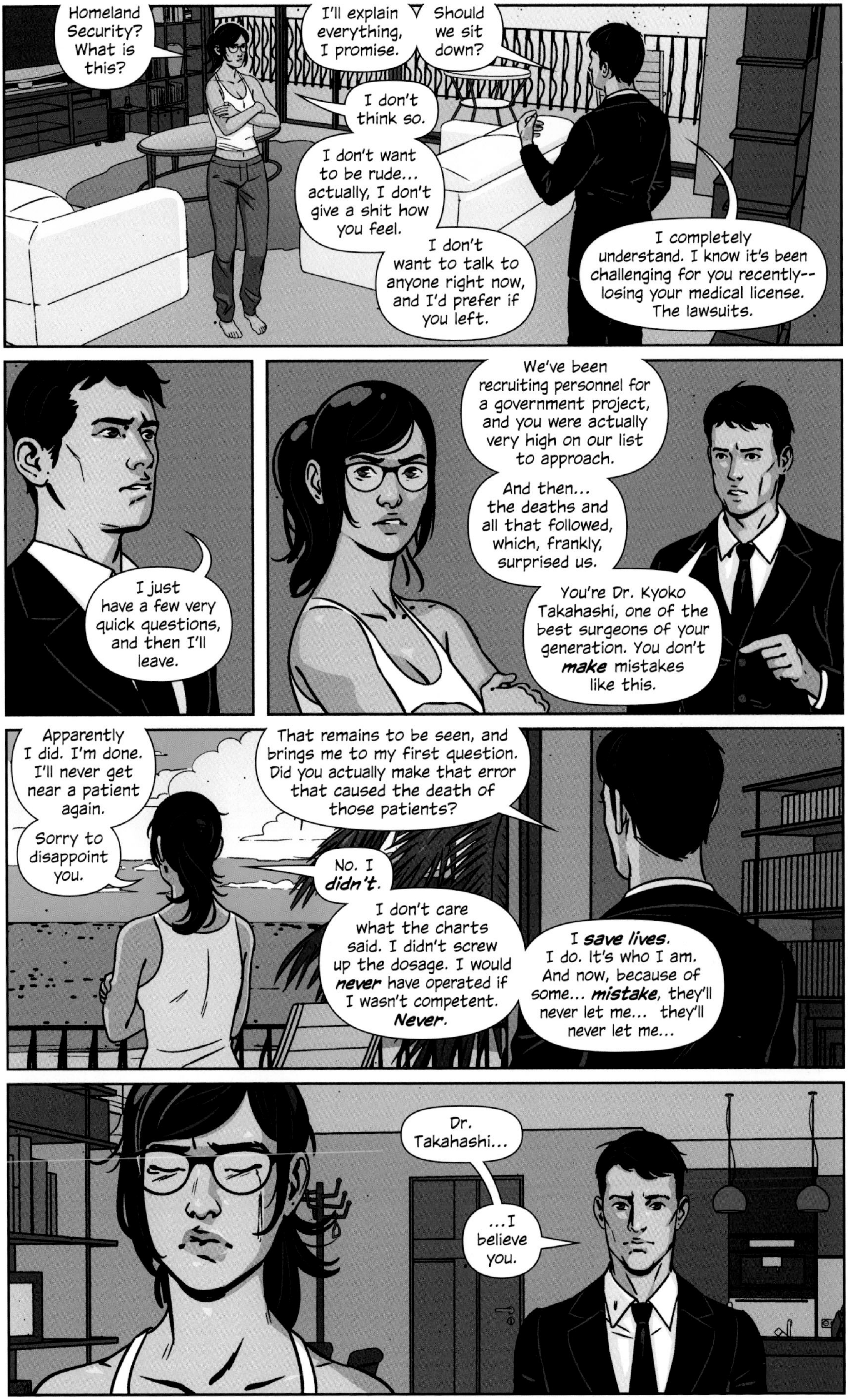
Homeland Security? What is this?
I'll explain everything, I promise.
Should we sit down?
I don't think so.
I don't want to be rude... actually, I don't give a shit how you feel.
I don't want to talk to anyone right now, and I'd prefer if you left.
I completely understand. I know it's been challenging for you recently--losing your medical license. The lawsuits.
I just have a few very quick questions, and then I'll leave.
We've been recruiting personnel for a government project, and you were actually very high on our list to approach.
And then... the deaths and all that followed, which, frankly, surprised us.
You're Dr. Kyoko Takahashi, one of the best surgeons of your generation. You don't *make* mistakes like this.
Apparently I did. I'm done. I'll never get near a patient again.
Sorry to disappoint you.
That remains to be seen, and brings me to my first question. Did you actually make that error that caused the death of those patients?
No. I *didn't*.
I don't care what the charts said. I didn't screw up the dosage. I would *never* have operated if I wasn't competent. *Never*.
I *save lives*. I do. It's who I am. And now, because of some... *mistake*, they'll never let me... they'll never let me...
Dr. Takahashi...
...I believe you.

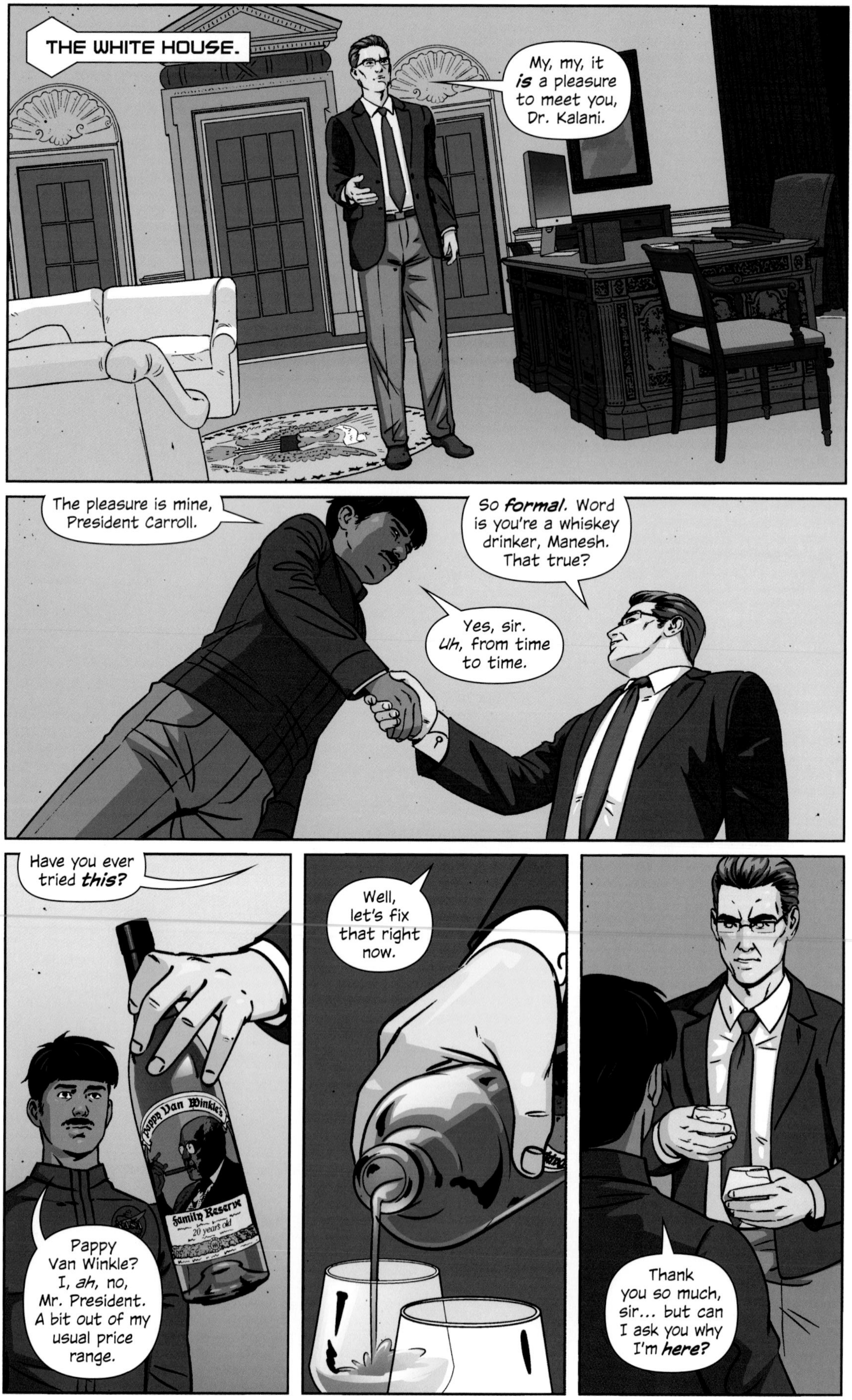
THE WHITE HOUSE.
My, my, it *is* a pleasure to meet you, Dr. Kalani.
The pleasure is mine, President Carroll.
So *formal.* Word is you're a whiskey drinker, Manesh. That true?
Yes, sir. *Uh,* from time to time.
Have you ever tried *this?*
Pappy Van Winkle's
Family Reserve
20 years old
Pappy Van Winkle? I, *ah,* no, Mr. President. A bit out of my usual price range.
Well, let's fix that right now.
Thank you so much, sir... but can I ask you why I'm *here?*

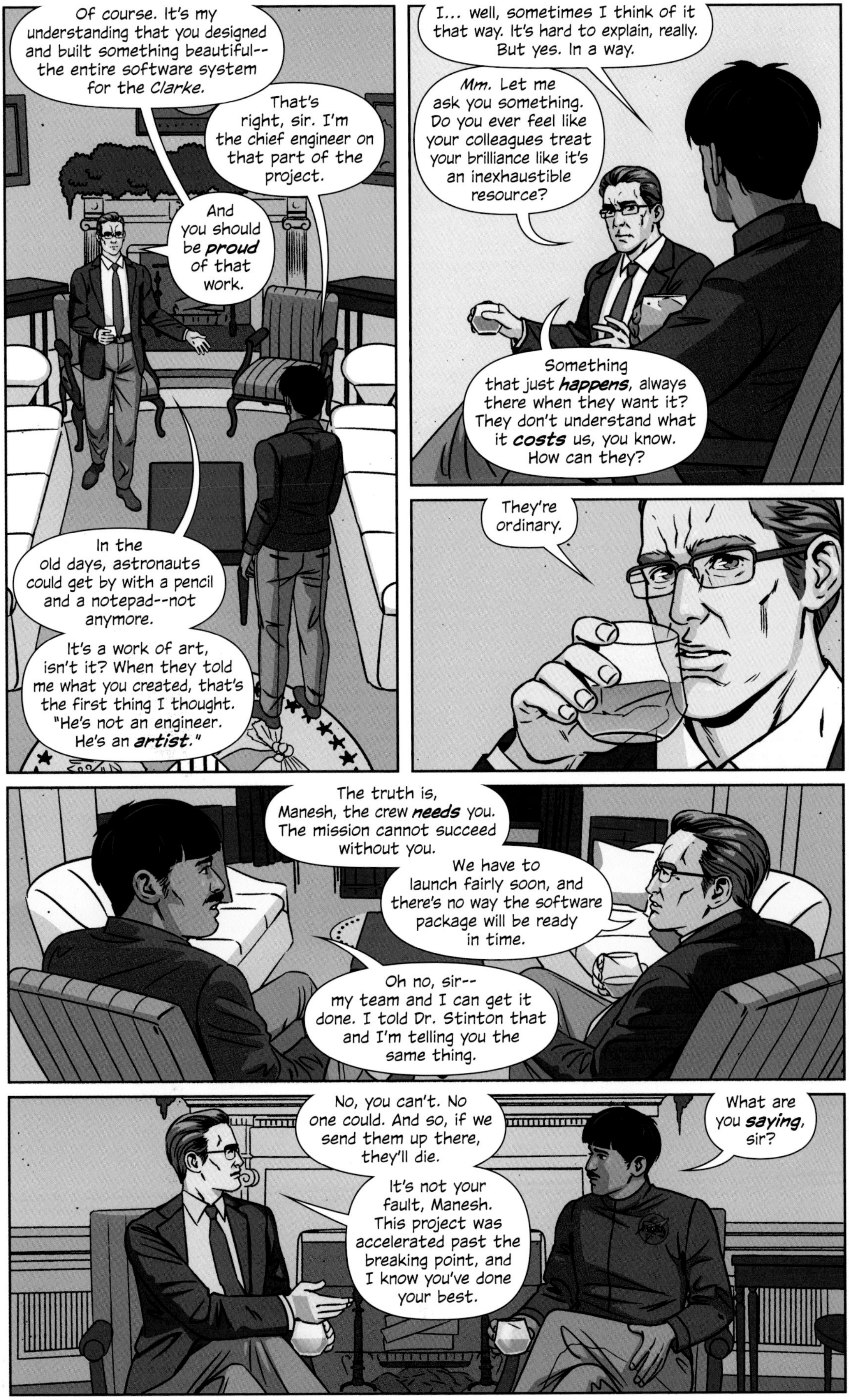
Of course. It's my understanding that you designed and built something beautiful-- the entire software system for the *Clarke*.
That's right, sir. I'm the chief engineer on that part of the project.
And you should be **proud** of that work.
In the old days, astronauts could get by with a pencil and a notepad--not anymore.
It's a work of art, isn't it? When they told me what you created, that's the first thing I thought. "He's not an engineer. He's an **artist**."
I... well, sometimes I think of it that way. It's hard to explain, really. But yes. In a way.
Mm. Let me ask you something. Do you ever feel like your colleagues treat your brilliance like it's an inexhaustible resource?
Something that just **happens**, always there when they want it? They don't understand what it **costs** us, you know. How can they?
They're ordinary.
The truth is, Manesh, the crew **needs** you. The mission cannot succeed without you.
We have to launch fairly soon, and there's no way the software package will be ready in time.
Oh no, sir-- my team and I can get it done. I told Dr. Stinton that and I'm telling you the same thing.
No, you can't. No one could. And so, if we send them up there, they'll die.
It's not your fault, Manesh. This project was accelerated past the breaking point, and I know you've done your best.
What are you **saying**, sir?

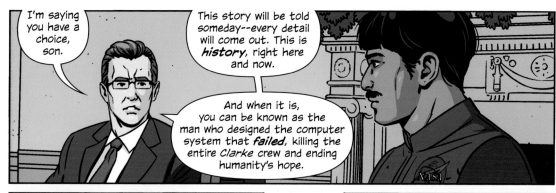

I'm saying you have a choice, son.

This story will be told someday--every detail will come out. This is *history*, right here and now.

And when it is, you can be known as the man who designed the computer system that *failed*, killing the entire *Clarke* crew and ending humanity's hope.

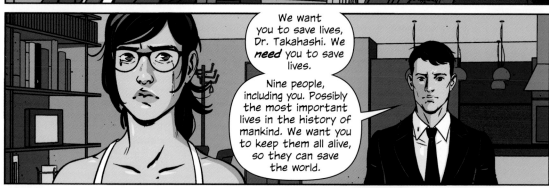

We want you to save lives, Dr. Takahashi. We *need* you to save lives.

Nine people, including you. Possibly the most important lives in the history of mankind. We want you to keep them all alive, so they can save the world.

Or... you can be the man who created the perfect, beautiful systems that made the whole thing possible.

But they have to be finished to make them perfect, and I want you to ask yourself if *anyone* else in the world can actually do that. Who else can *see* it like you do?

As far as we're concerned, nothing has changed. We want you as much as we ever did.

So, now, before I say anything else... my second question. Do you still want me to leave?

Who else has the *art?*

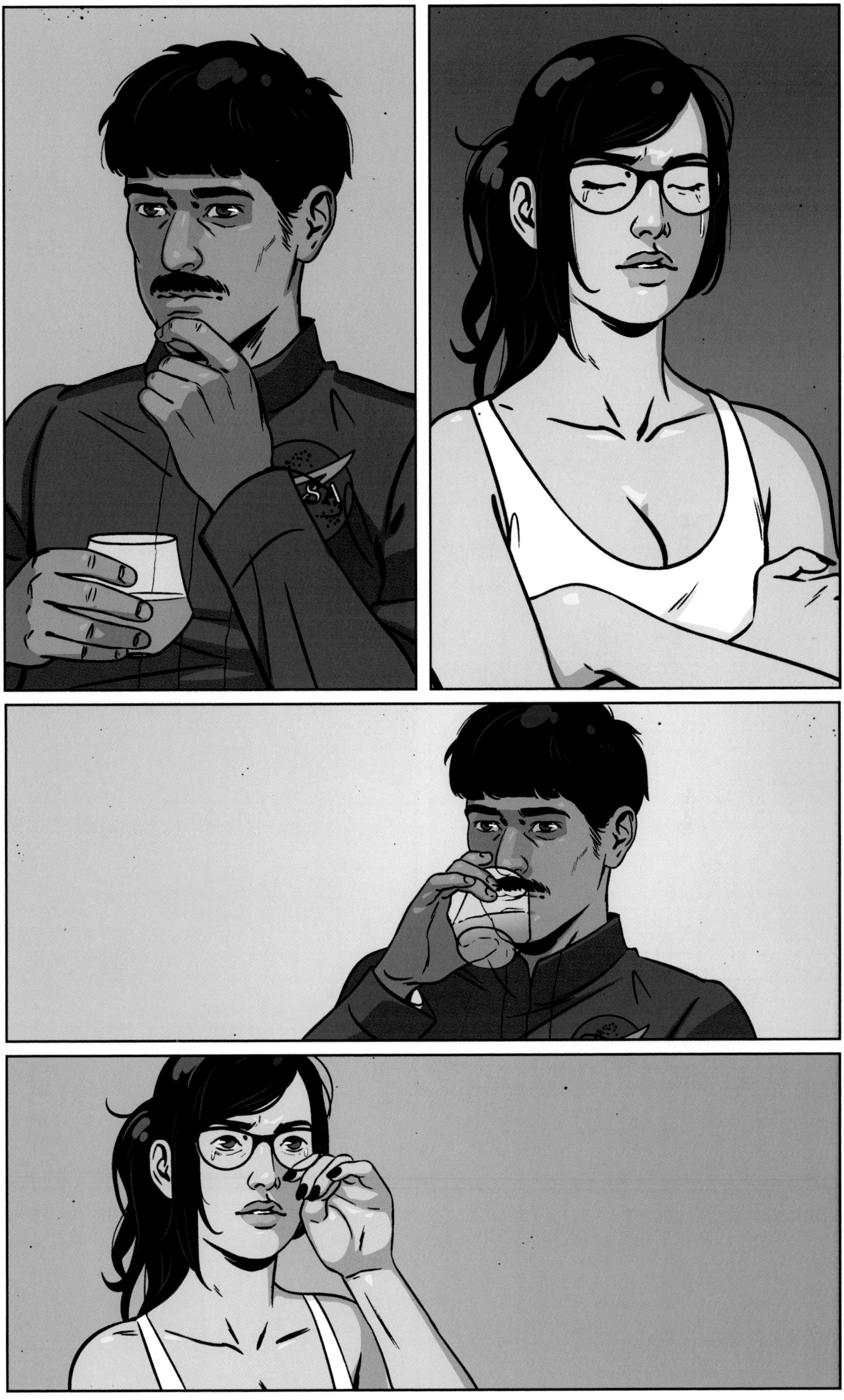

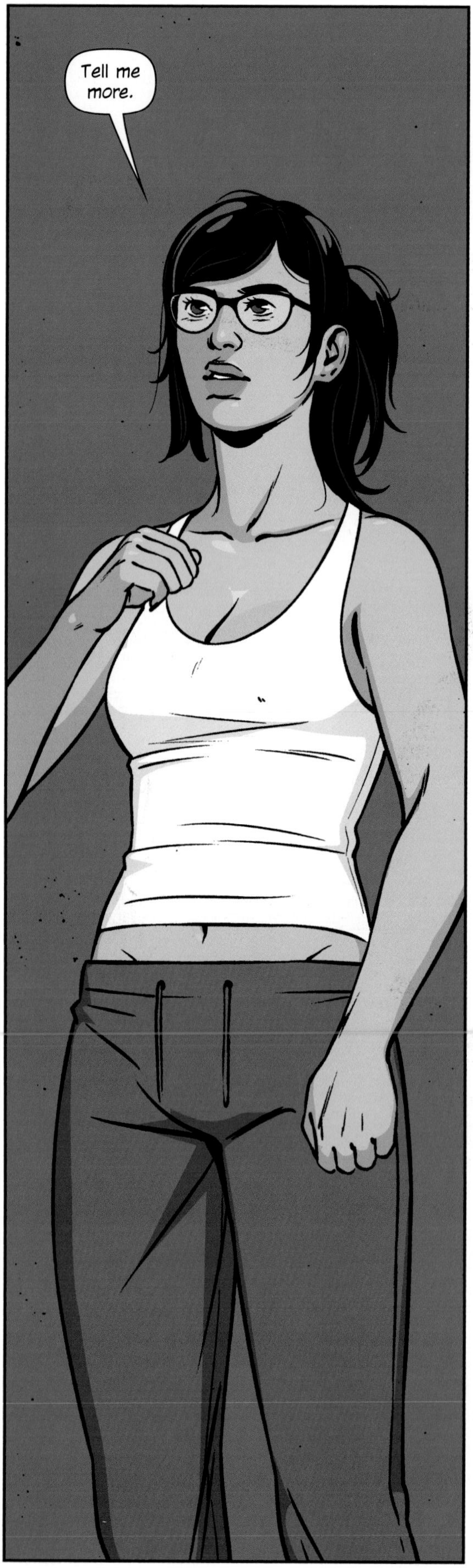
Tell me more.

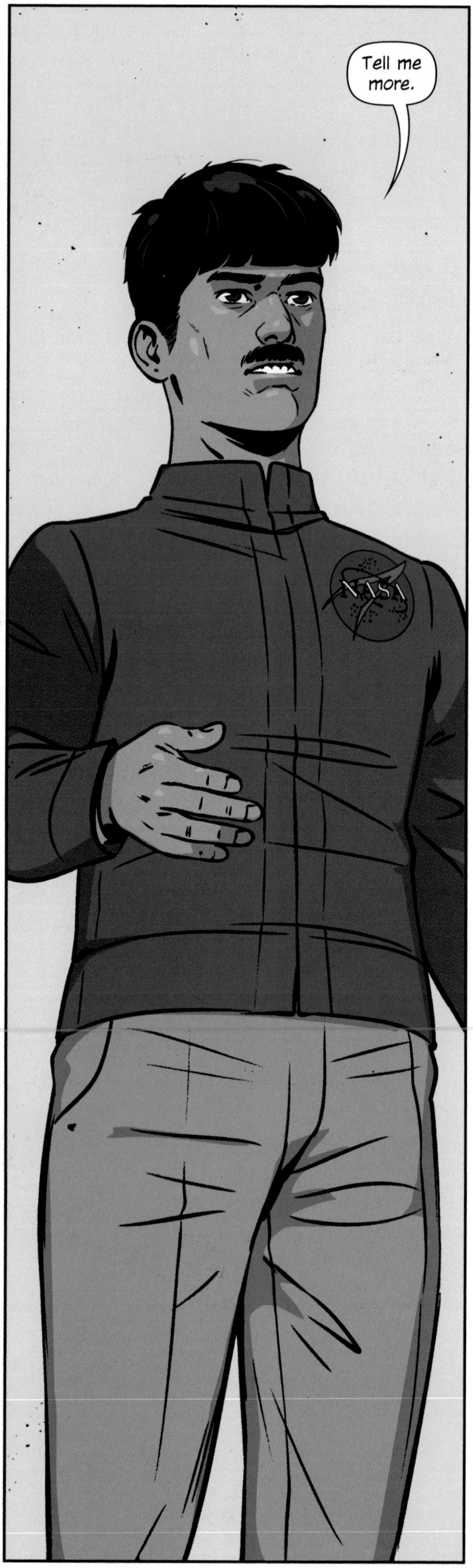
Tell me more.

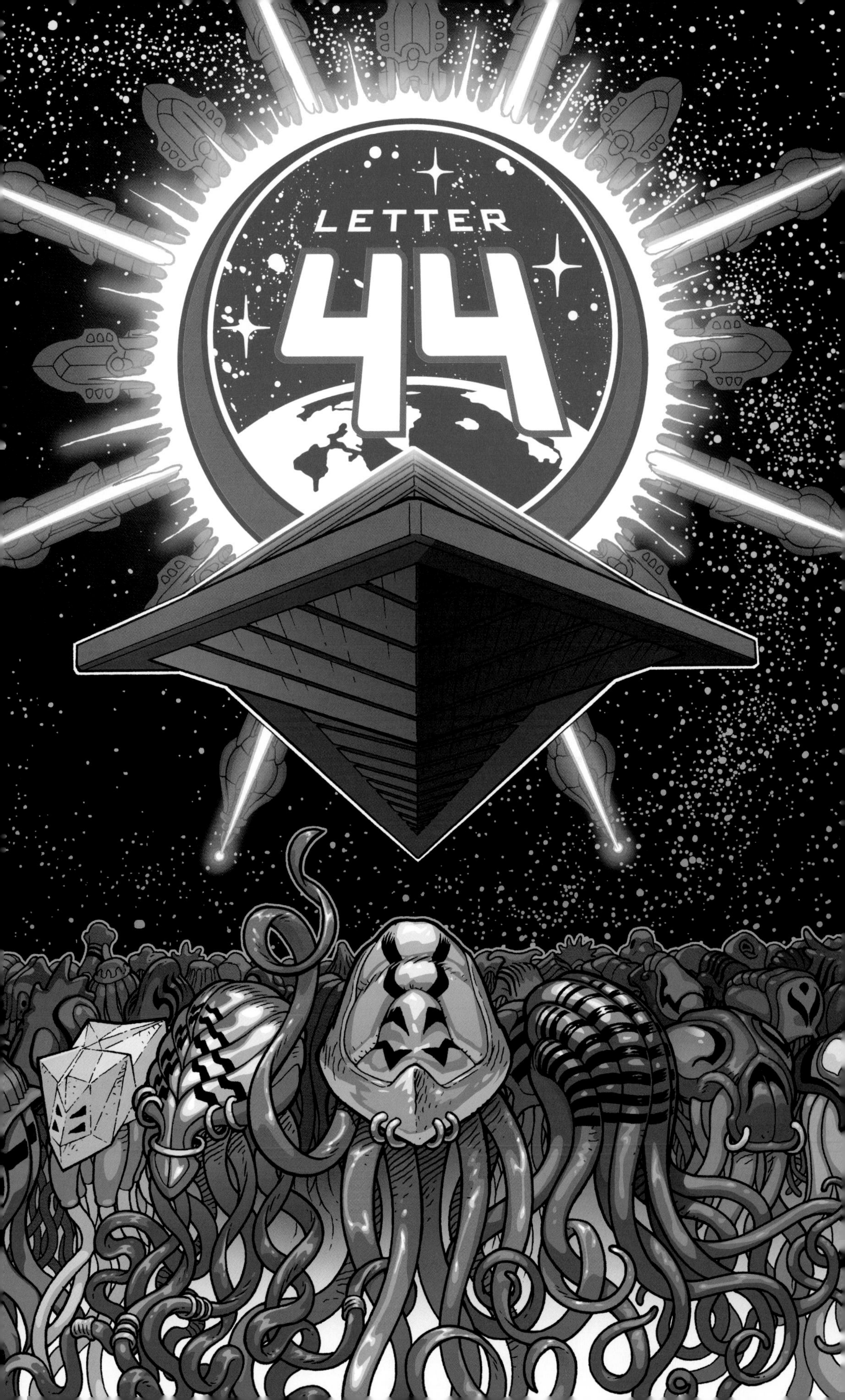
LETTER
44

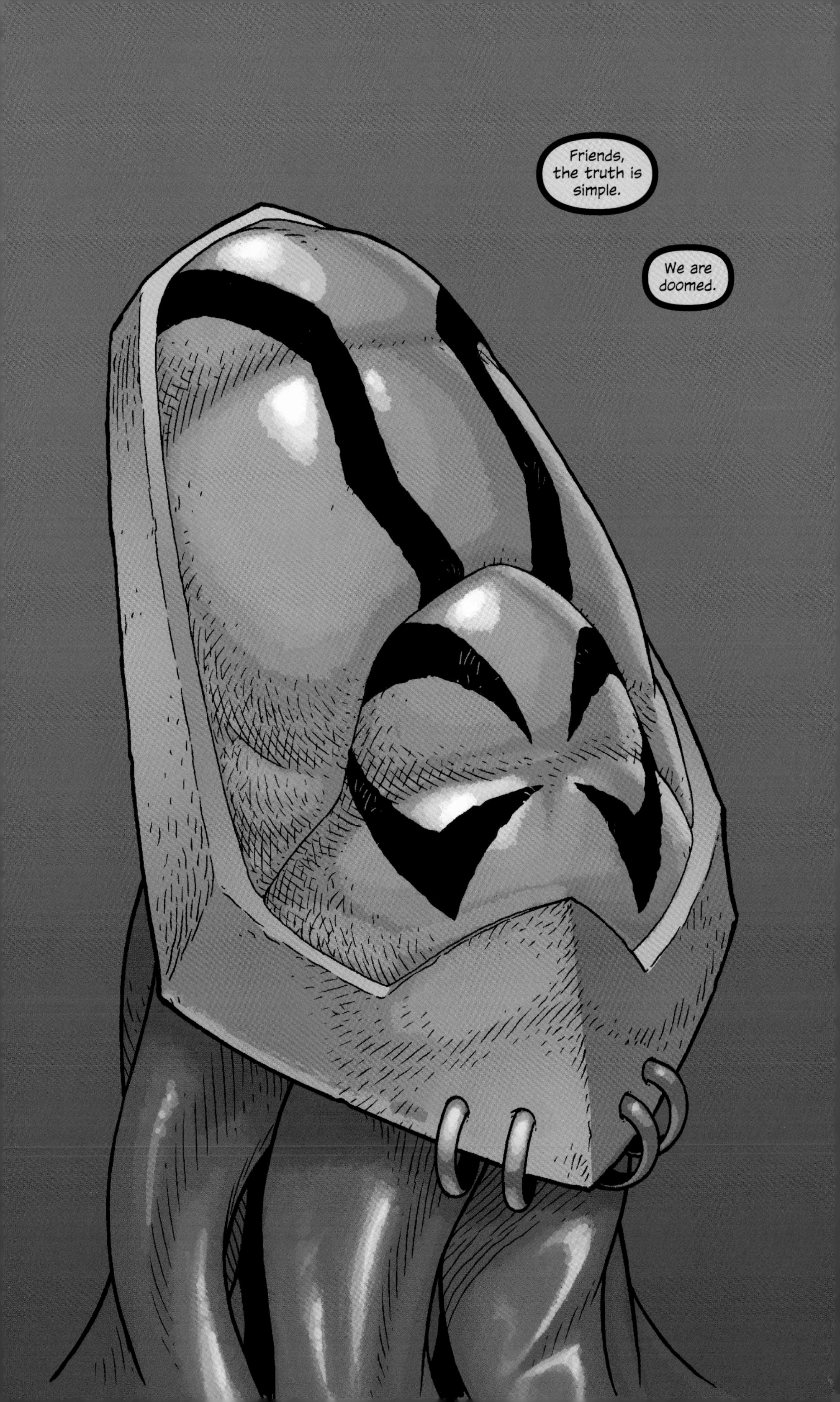
Friends, the truth is simple.
We are doomed.

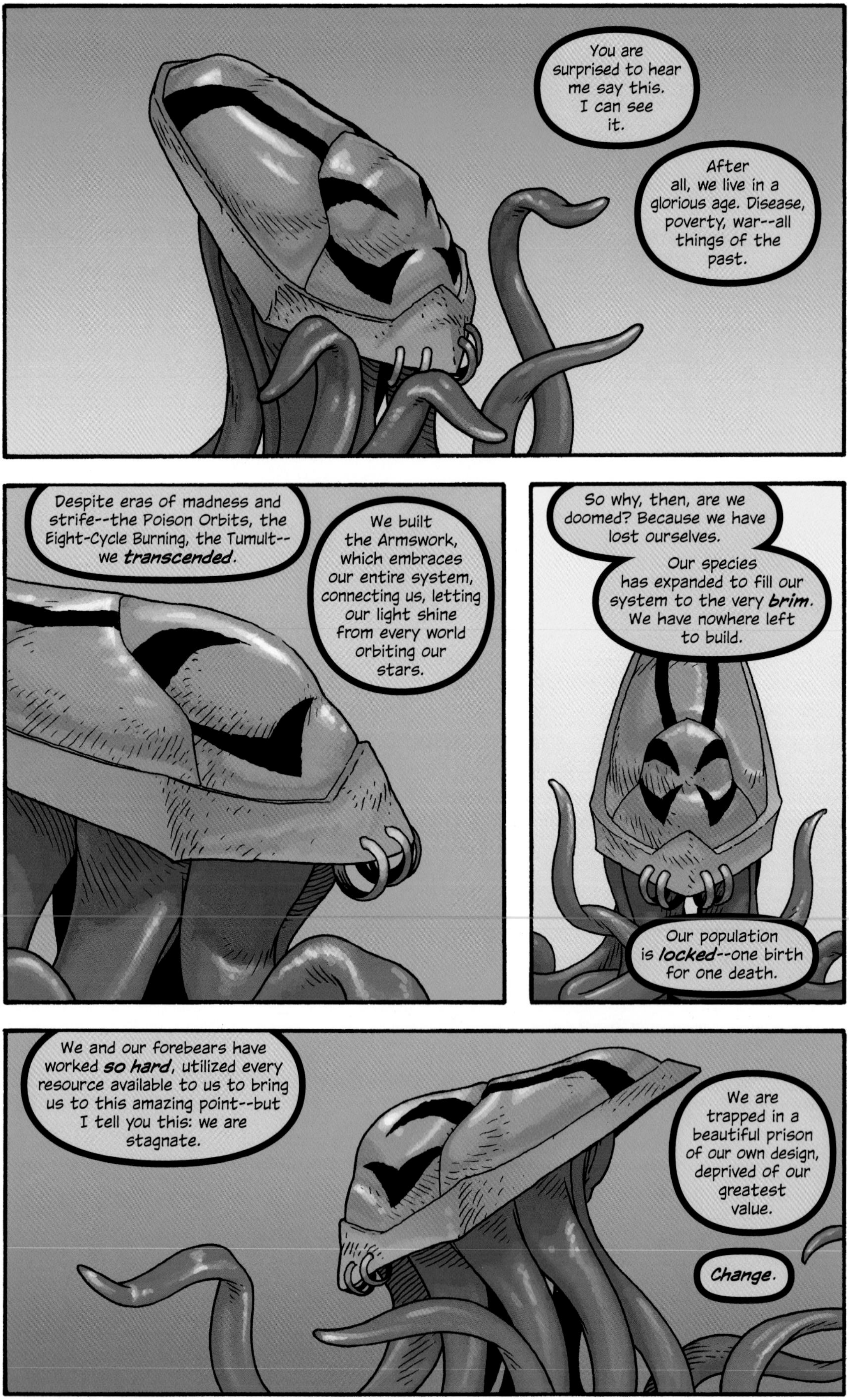
You are surprised to hear me say this. I can see it.
After all, we live in a glorious age. Disease, poverty, war--all things of the past.
Despite eras of madness and strife--the Poison Orbits, the Eight-Cycle Burning, the Tumult--we **transcended**.
We built the Armswork, which embraces our entire system, connecting us, letting our light shine from every world orbiting our stars.
So why, then, are we doomed? Because we have lost ourselves.
Our species has expanded to fill our system to the very **brim**. We have nowhere left to build.
Our population is **locked**--one birth for one death.
We and our forebears have worked **so hard**, utilized every resource available to us to bring us to this amazing point--but I tell you this: we are stagnate.
We are trapped in a beautiful prison of our own design, deprived of our greatest value.
Change.

You elected me to our species' highest office so I could address whatever problems may arise in our present.

The truth is, there are none, or so few as to be meaningless.

And so, I spend most of my time considering our *future*.

What will *we* leave behind? What will we give our buds, as they bloom from our sacred arms?

Will we give them only what we have? Or will we reach for more?

Will we stretch beyond the bounds of this system, so our descendants might bring our light to the great darkness beyond?

I say we *must*.

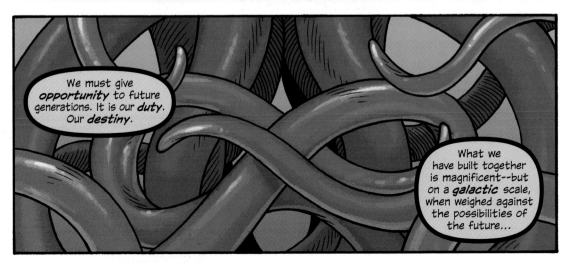

We must give *opportunity* to future generations. It is our *duty*. Our *destiny*.

What we have built together is magnificent--but on a *galactic* scale, when weighed against the possibilities of the future...

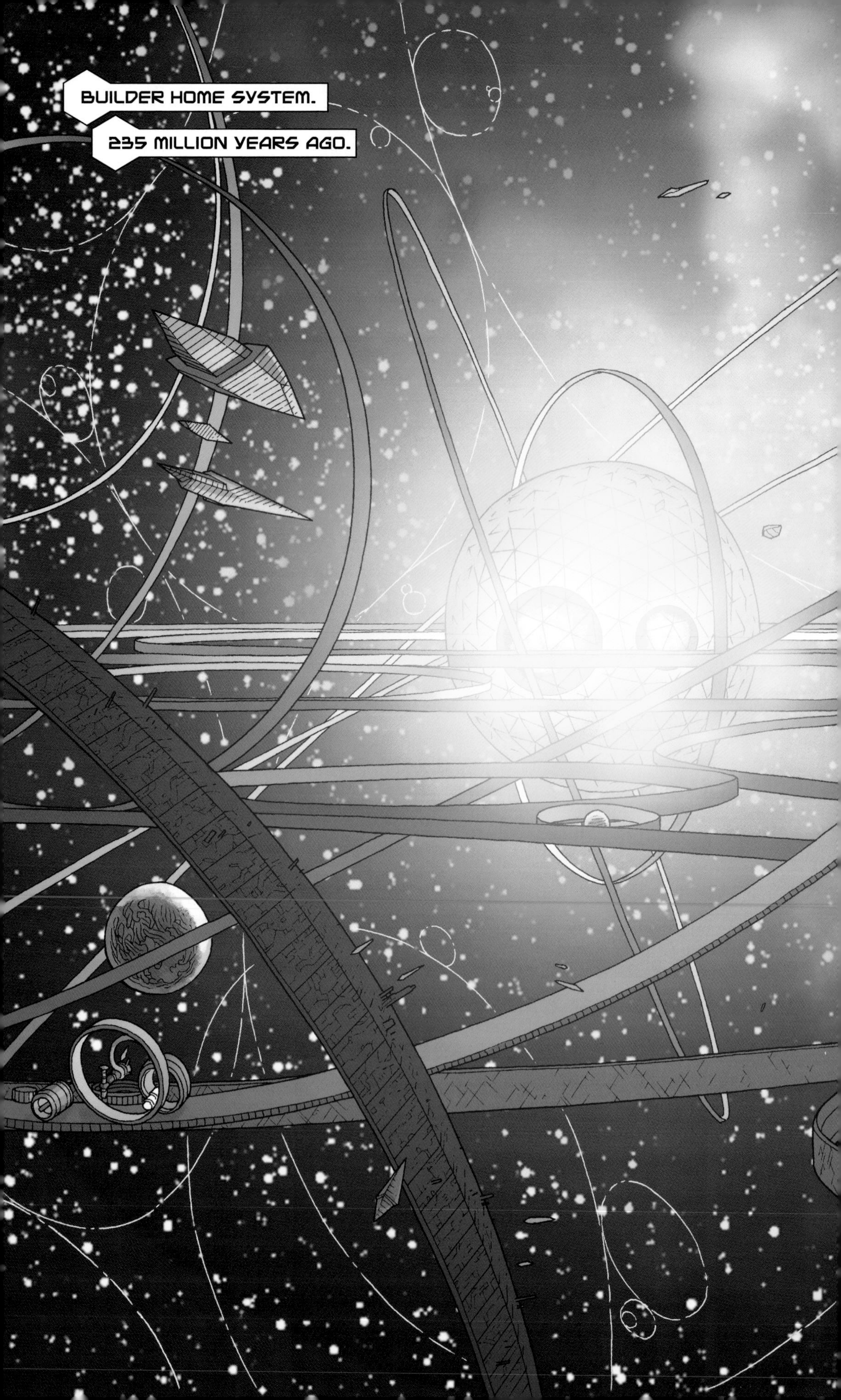
BUILDER HOME SYSTEM.
235 MILLION YEARS AGO.

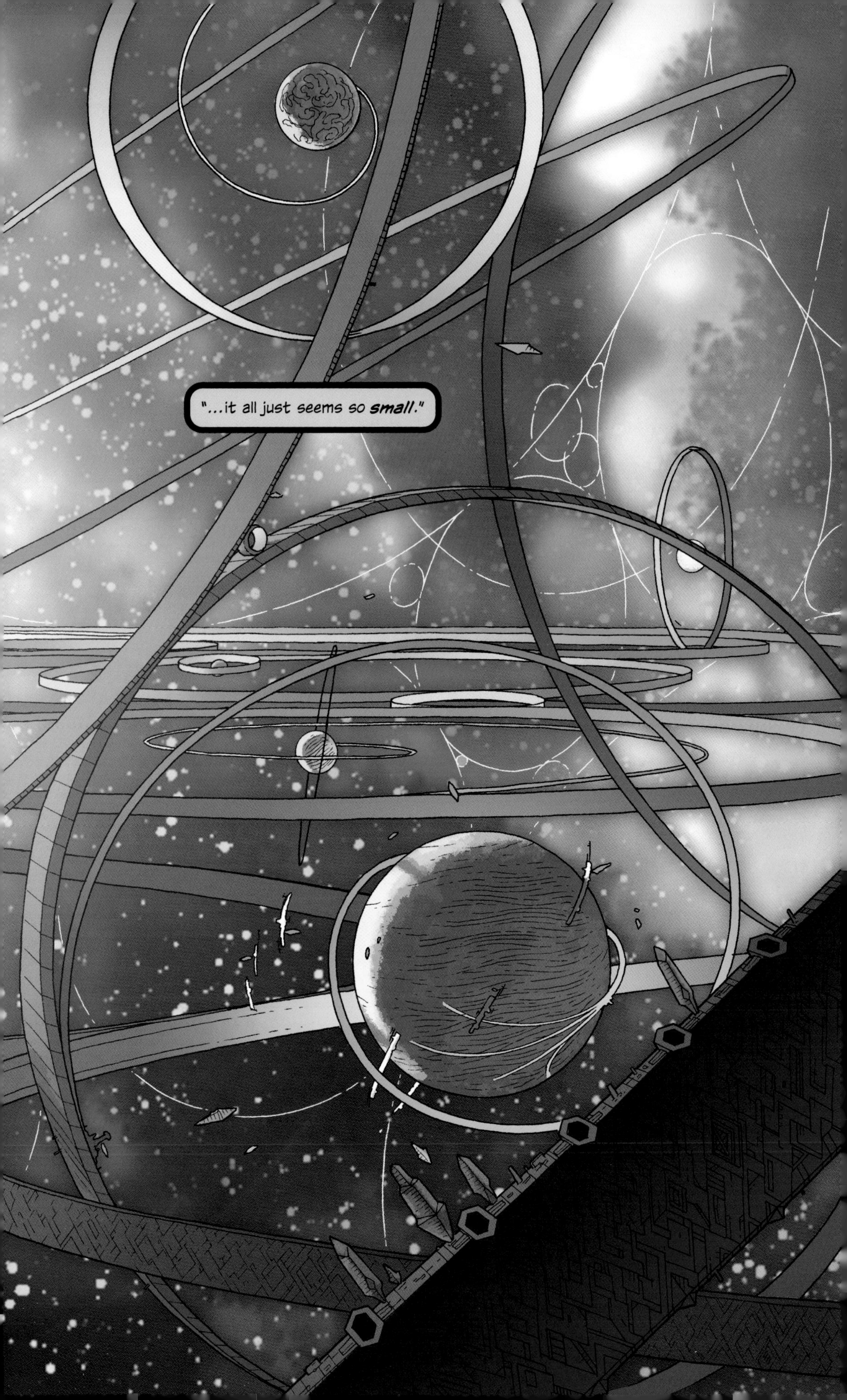
"...it all just seems so *small*."

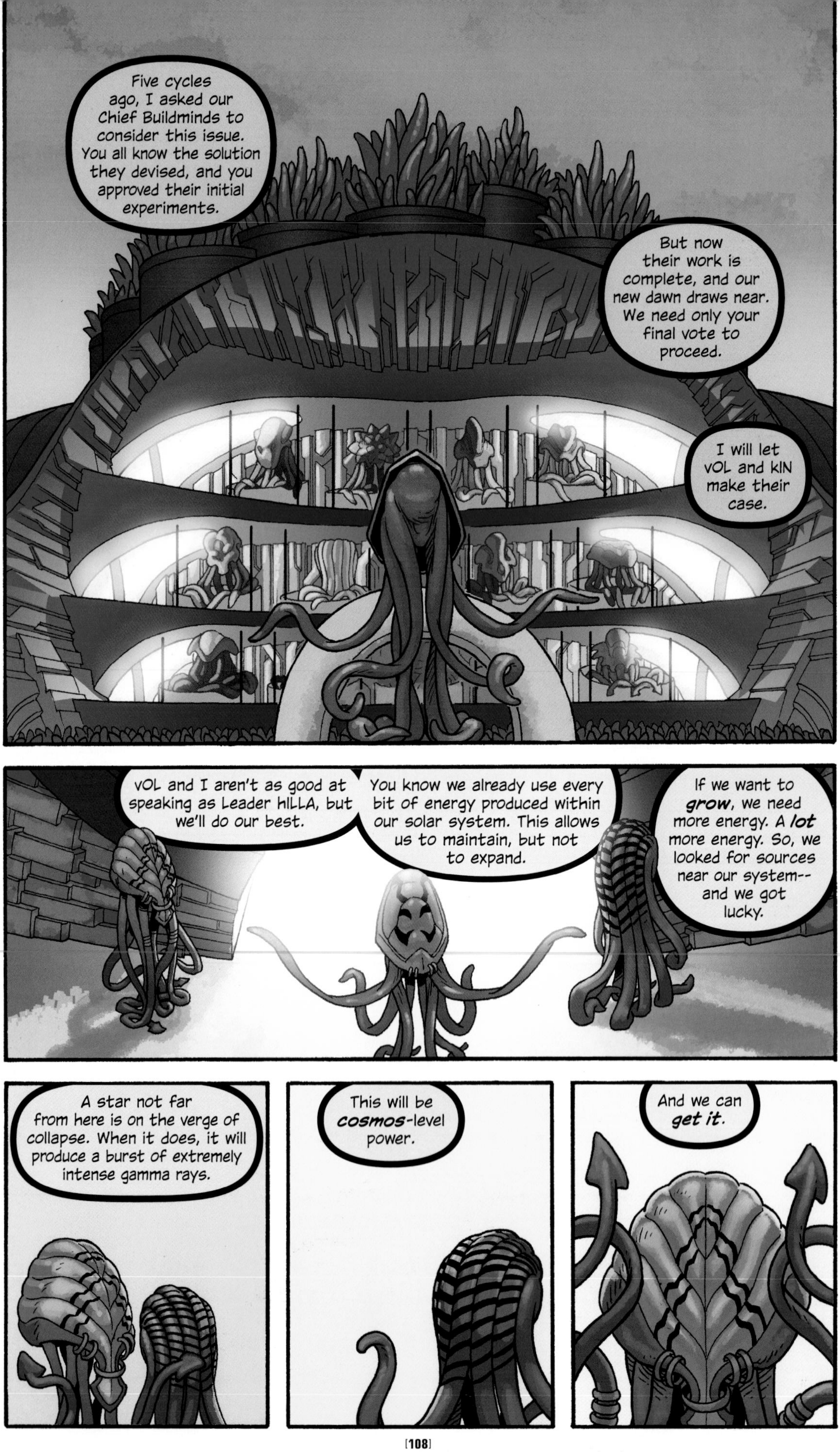
Five cycles ago, I asked our Chief Buildminds to consider this issue. You all know the solution they devised, and you approved their initial experiments.
But now their work is complete, and our new dawn draws near. We need only your final vote to proceed.
I will let vOL and kIN make their case.
vOL and I aren't as good at speaking as Leader hILLA, but we'll do our best.
You know we already use every bit of energy produced within our solar system. This allows us to maintain, but not to expand.
If we want to *grow*, we need more energy. A *lot* more energy. So, we looked for sources near our system--and we got lucky.
A star not far from here is on the verge of collapse. When it does, it will produce a burst of extremely intense gamma rays.
This will be *cosmos*-level power.
And we can *get it*.

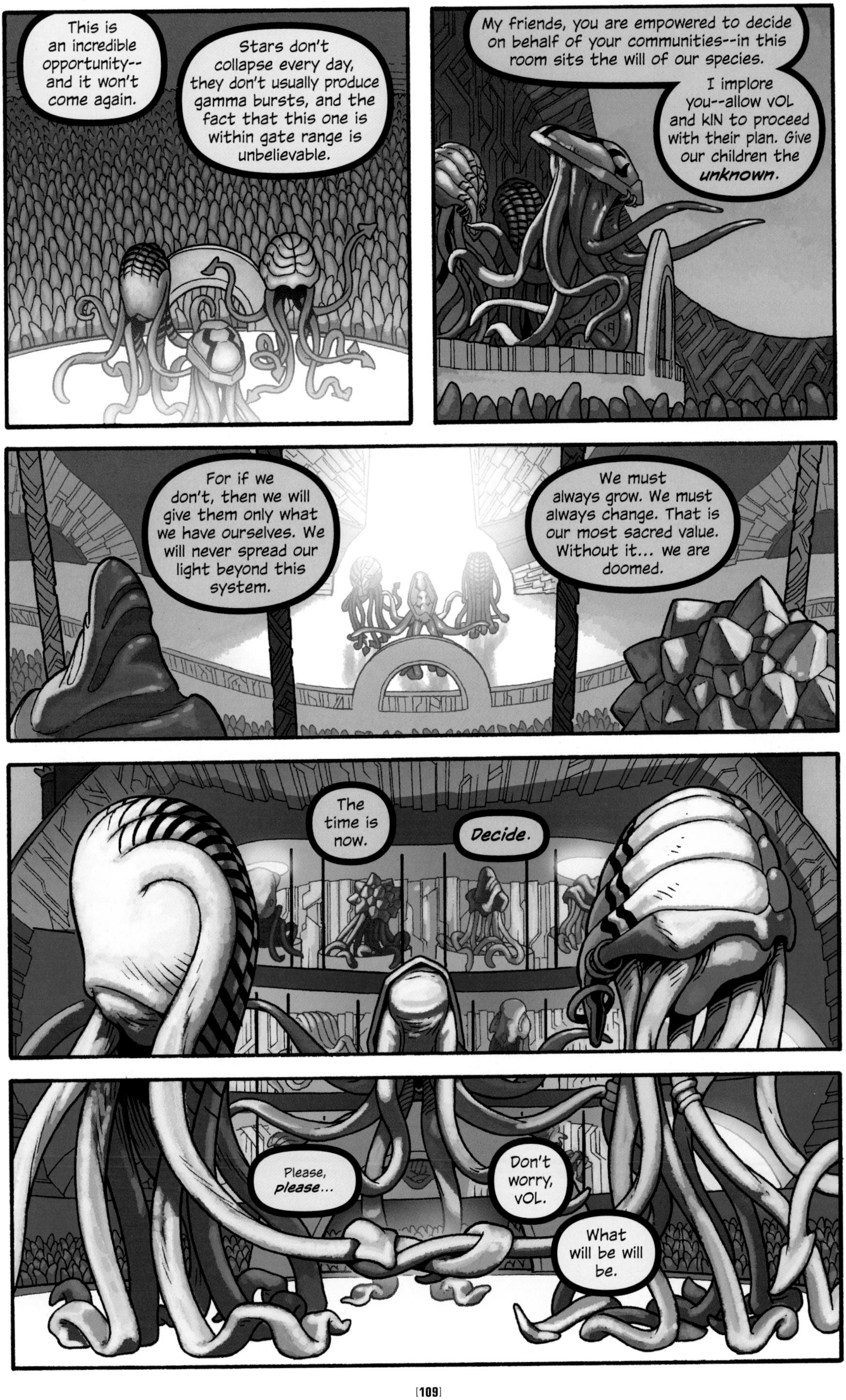
This is an incredible opportunity--and it won't come again.
Stars don't collapse every day, they don't usually produce gamma bursts, and the fact that this one is within gate range is unbelievable.
My friends, you are empowered to decide on behalf of your communities--in this room sits the will of our species.
I implore you--allow vOL and kIN to proceed with their plan. Give our children the *unknown*.
For if we don't, then we will give them only what we have ourselves. We will never spread our light beyond this system.
We must always grow. We must always change. That is our most sacred value. Without it... we are doomed.
The time is now.
Decide.
Please, *please*...
Don't worry, vOL.
What will be will be.

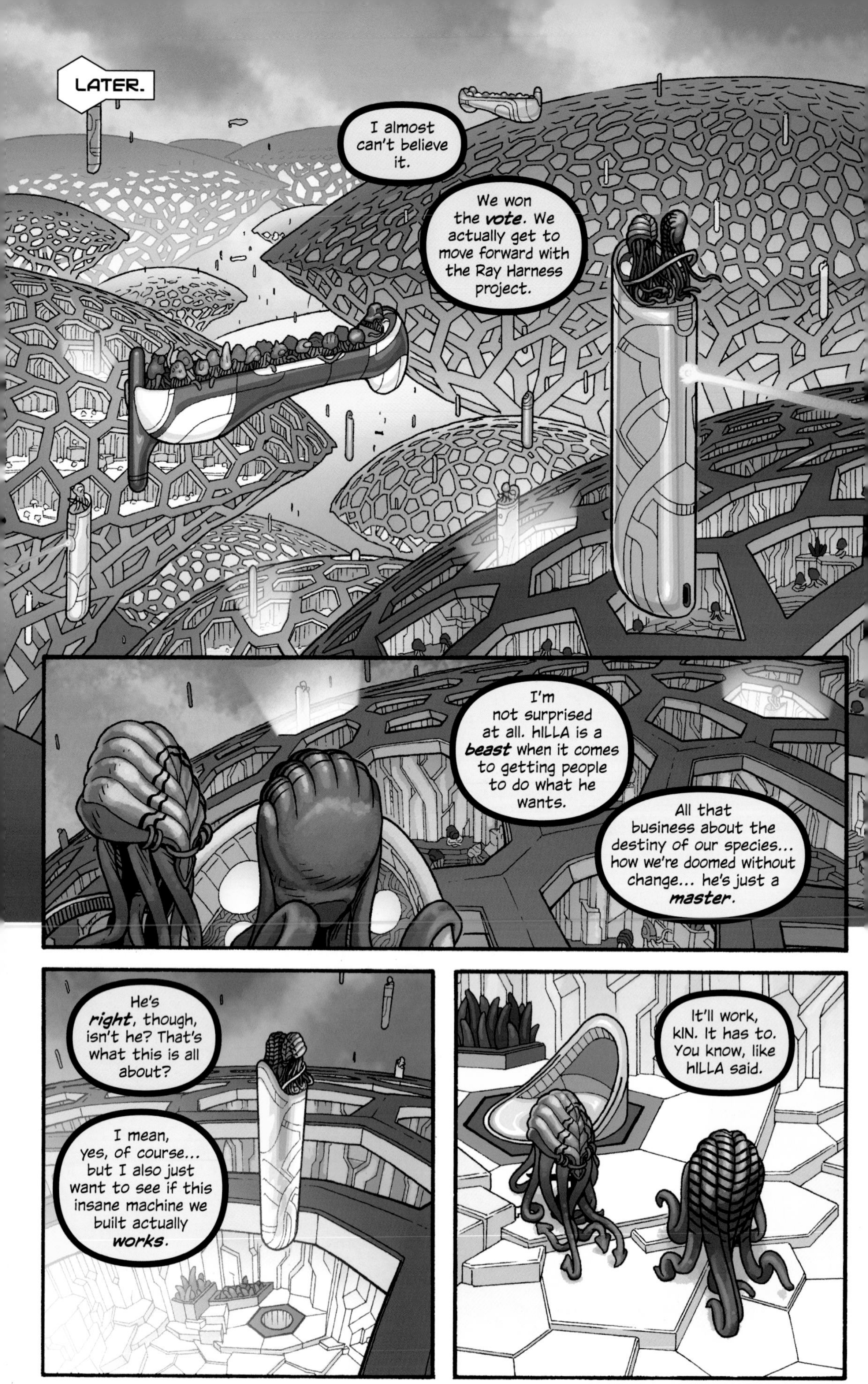
LATER.
I almost can't believe it.
We won the *vote*. We actually get to move forward with the Ray Harness project.
I'm not surprised at all. hILLA is a *beast* when it comes to getting people to do what he wants.
All that business about the destiny of our species... how we're doomed without change... he's just a *master*.
He's *right*, though, isn't he? That's what this is all about?
I mean, yes, of course... but I also just want to see if this insane machine we built actually *works*.
It'll work, kIN. It has to. You know, like hILLA said.

For the *children*.

Did the Council... did they agree?

Yes. A unanimous vote. They're going to let us activate the Ray Harness.

We won't have to *cull*, bUR. All of them can live--not just three. We'll need the population for the expansion out of the system.

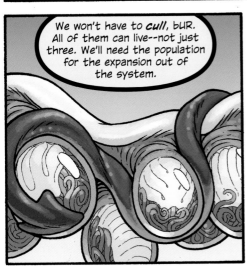

None, I suppose.

All right, loves.

Let's go make some joy.

I... can't believe it. You've saved us. You've *saved us all*.

I'd say we should celebrate, if I weren't *already* gravid.

What difference does *that* make?

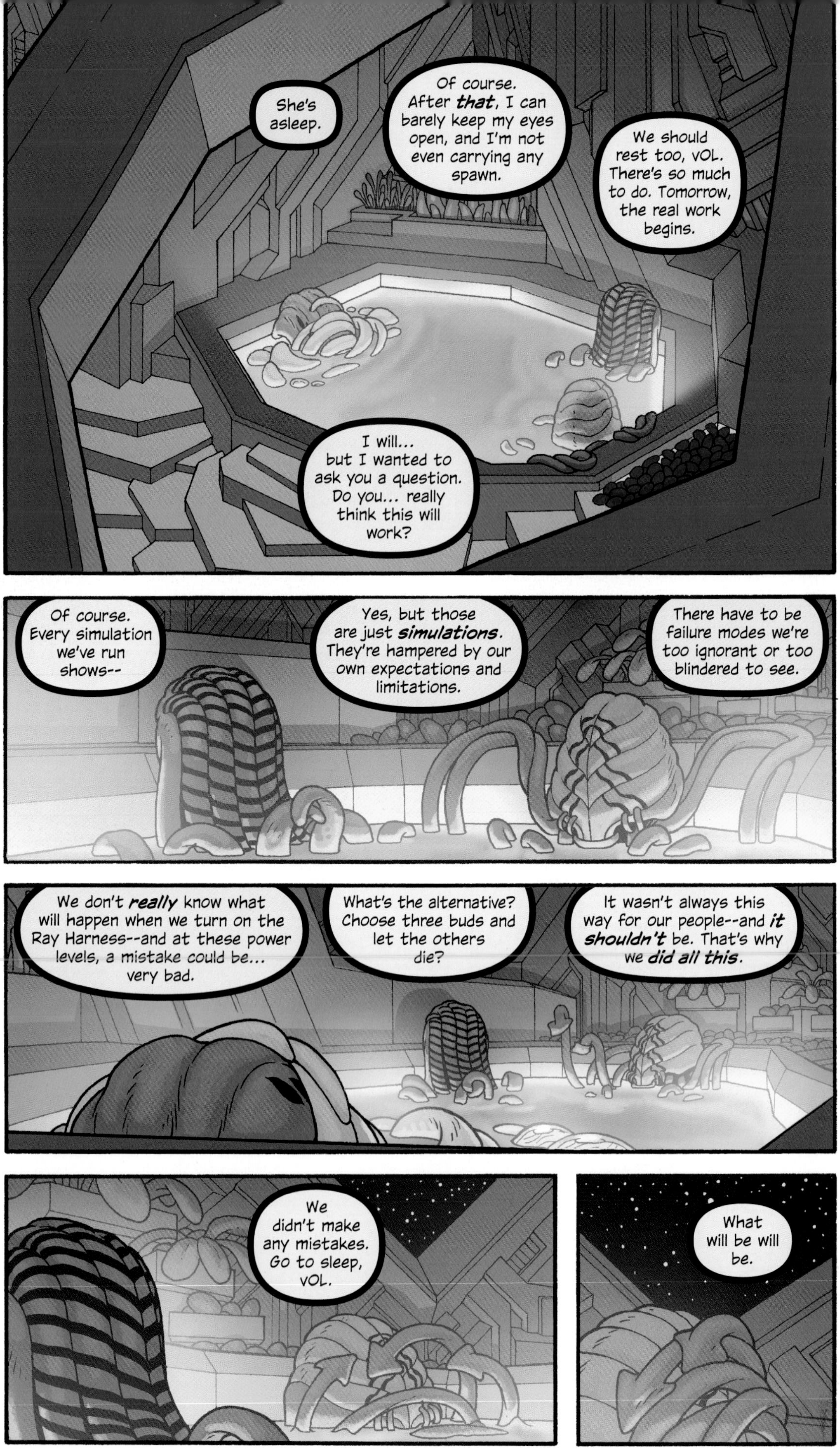
She's asleep.
Of course. After *that*, I can barely keep my eyes open, and I'm not even carrying any spawn.
We should rest too, vOL. There's so much to do. Tomorrow, the real work begins.
I will... but I wanted to ask you a question. Do you... really think this will work?
Of course. Every simulation we've run shows--
Yes, but those are just *simulations*. They're hampered by our own expectations and limitations.
There have to be failure modes we're too ignorant or too blindered to see.
We don't *really* know what will happen when we turn on the Ray Harness--and at these power levels, a mistake could be... very bad.
What's the alternative? Choose three buds and let the others die?
It wasn't always this way for our people--and *it shouldn't* be. That's why we *did all this*.
We didn't make any mistakes. Go to sleep, vOL.
What will be will be.

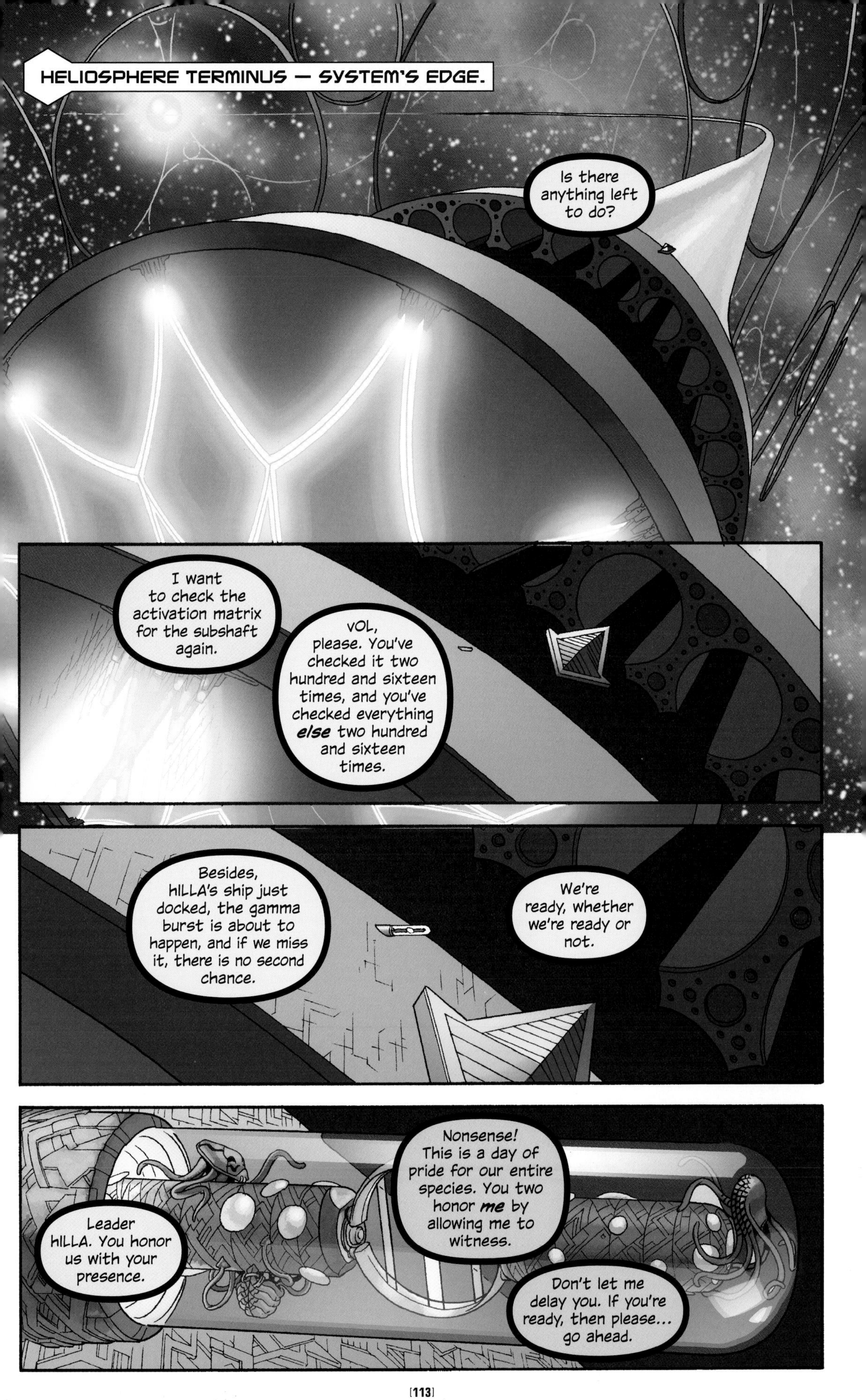
HELIOSPHERE TERMINUS — SYSTEM'S EDGE.
Is there anything left to do?
I want to check the activation matrix for the subshaft again.
VOL, please. You've checked it two hundred and sixteen times, and you've checked everything *else* two hundred and sixteen times.
Besides, hILLA's ship just docked, the gamma burst is about to happen, and if we miss it, there is no second chance.
We're ready, whether we're ready or not.
Leader hILLA. You honor us with your presence.
Nonsense! This is a day of pride for our entire species. You two honor *me* by allowing me to witness.
Don't let me delay you. If you're ready, then please... go ahead.

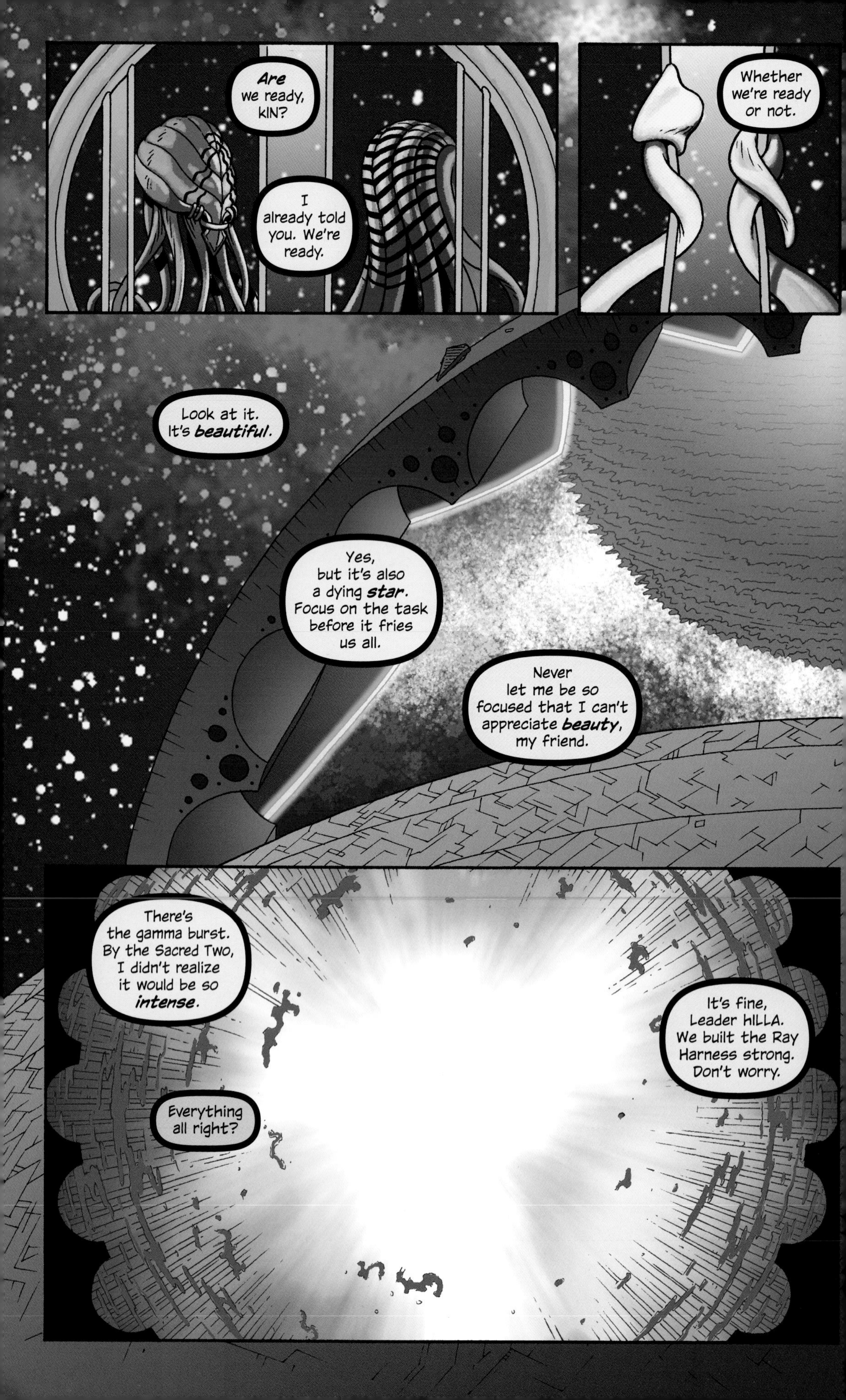

Are we ready, kIN?
I already told you. We're ready.
Whether we're ready or not.
Look at it. It's beautiful.
Yes, but it's also a dying star. Focus on the task before it fries us all.
Never let me be so focused that I can't appreciate beauty, my friend.
There's the gamma burst. By the Sacred Two, I didn't realize it would be so intense.
Everything all right?
It's fine, Leader hILLA. We built the Ray Harness strong. Don't worry.

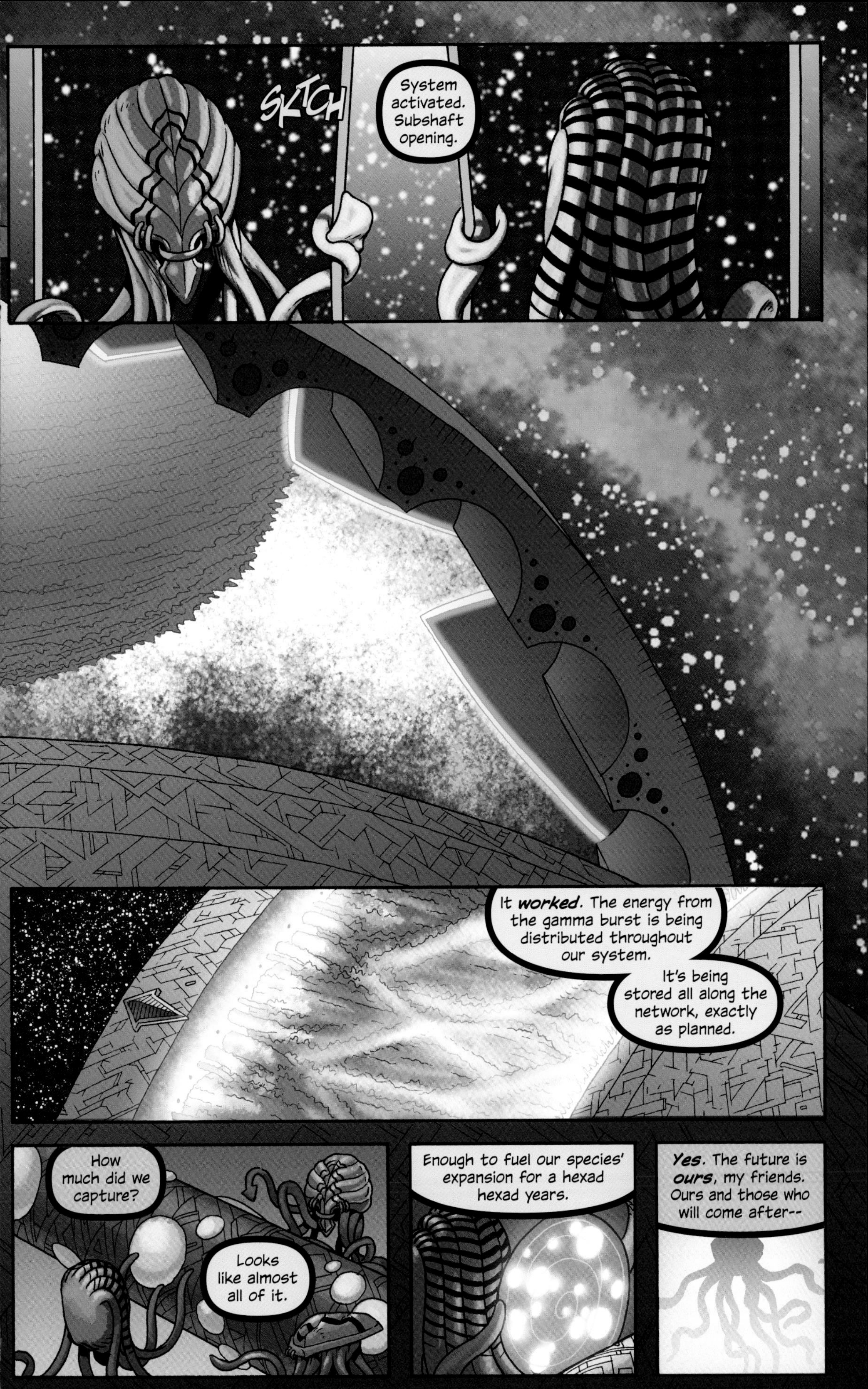
SKTCH
System activated. Subshaft opening.
It worked. The energy from the gamma burst is being distributed throughout our system.
It's being stored all along the network, exactly as planned.
How much did we capture?
Looks like almost all of it.
Enough to fuel our species' expansion for a hexad hexad years.
Yes. The future is ours, my friends. Ours and those who will come after--

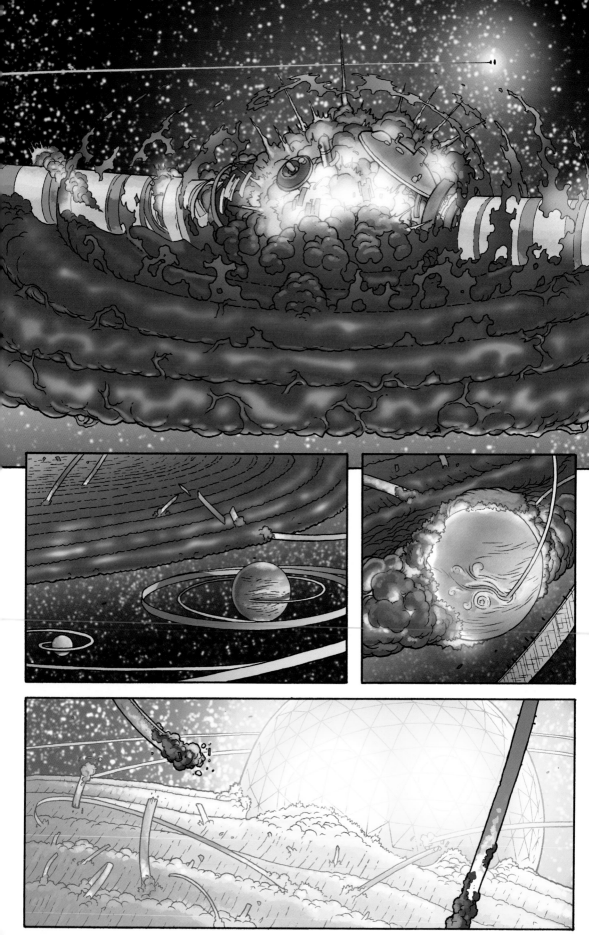

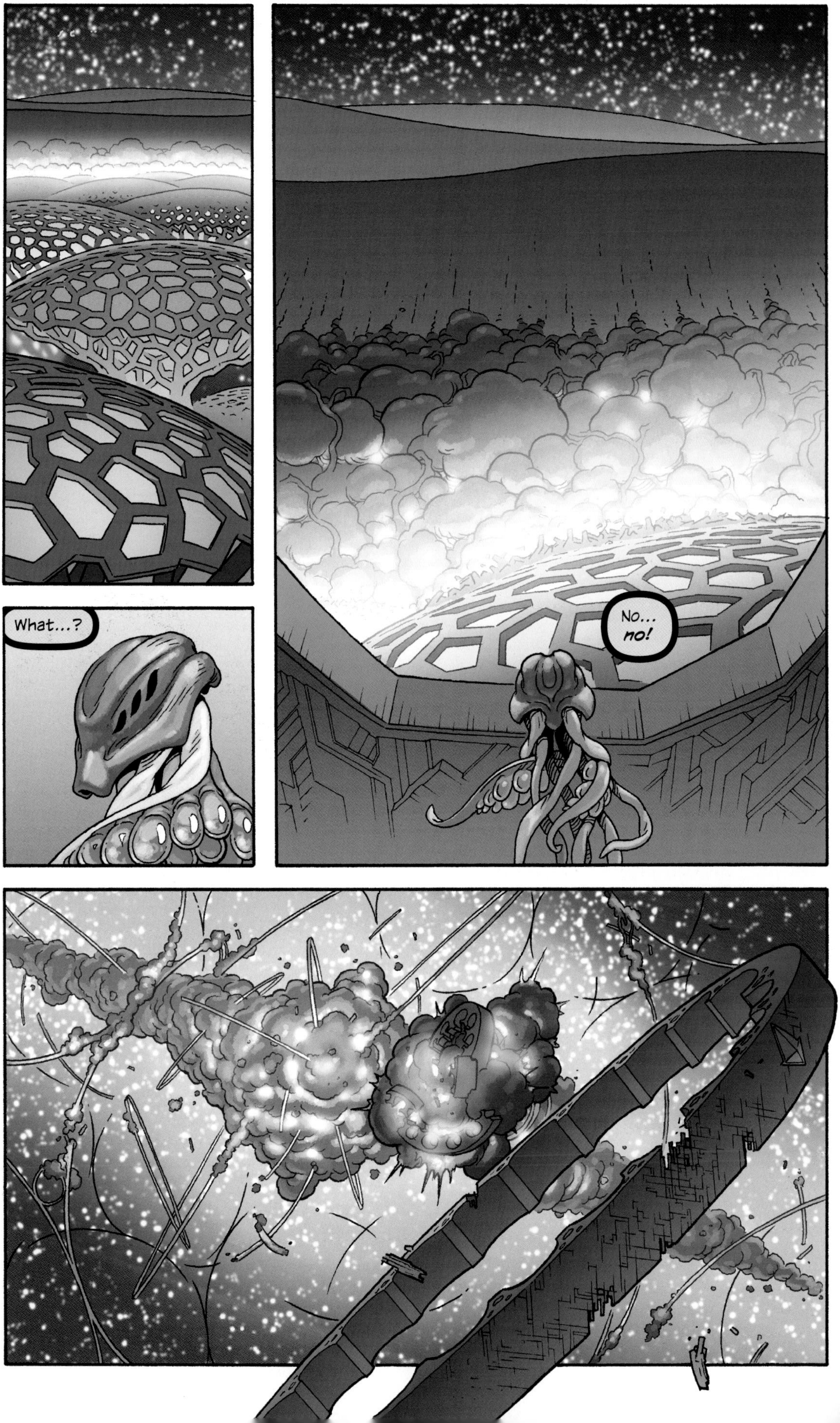
What...?
No...
no!

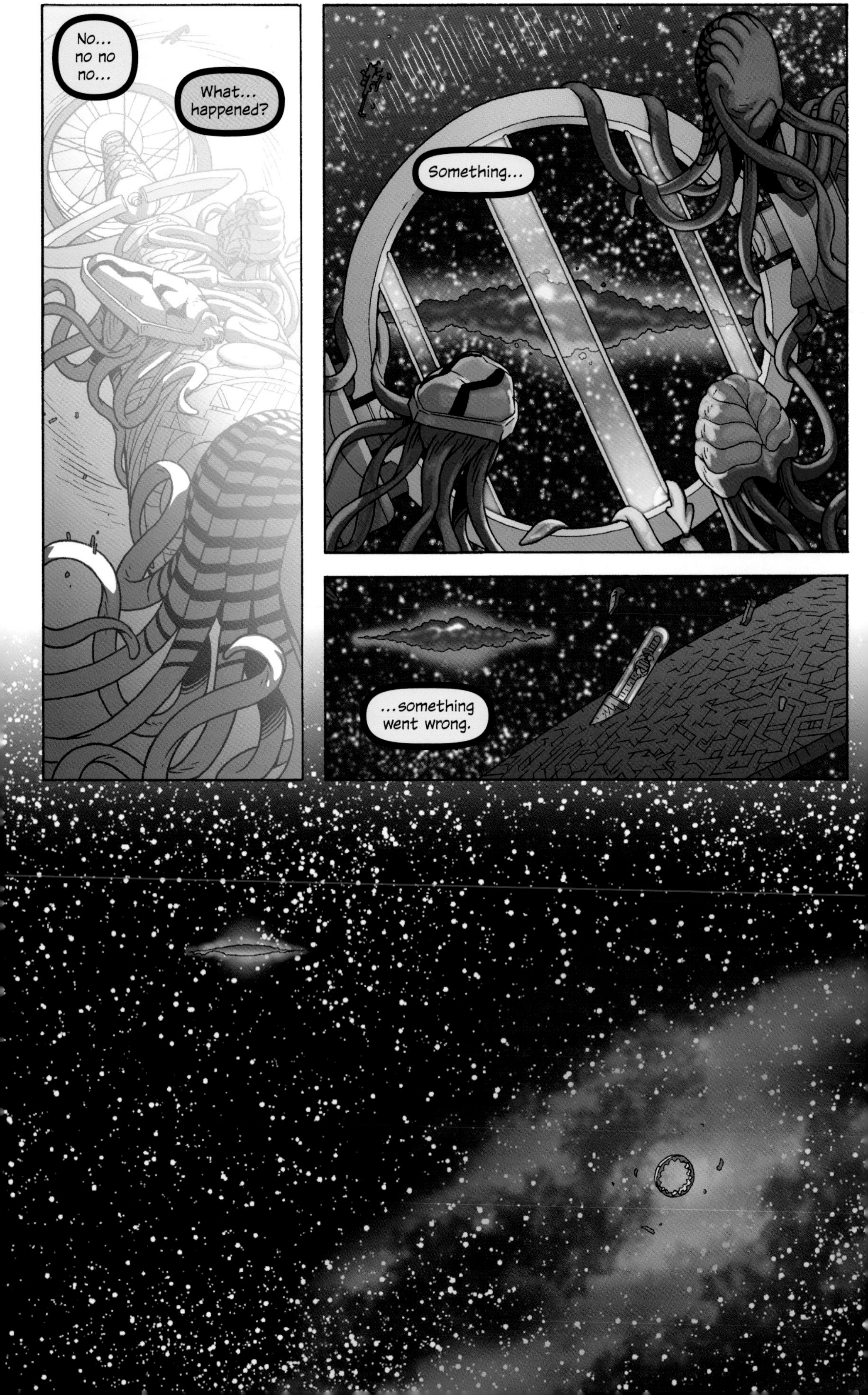
No... no no no...
What... happened?
Something...
...something went wrong.

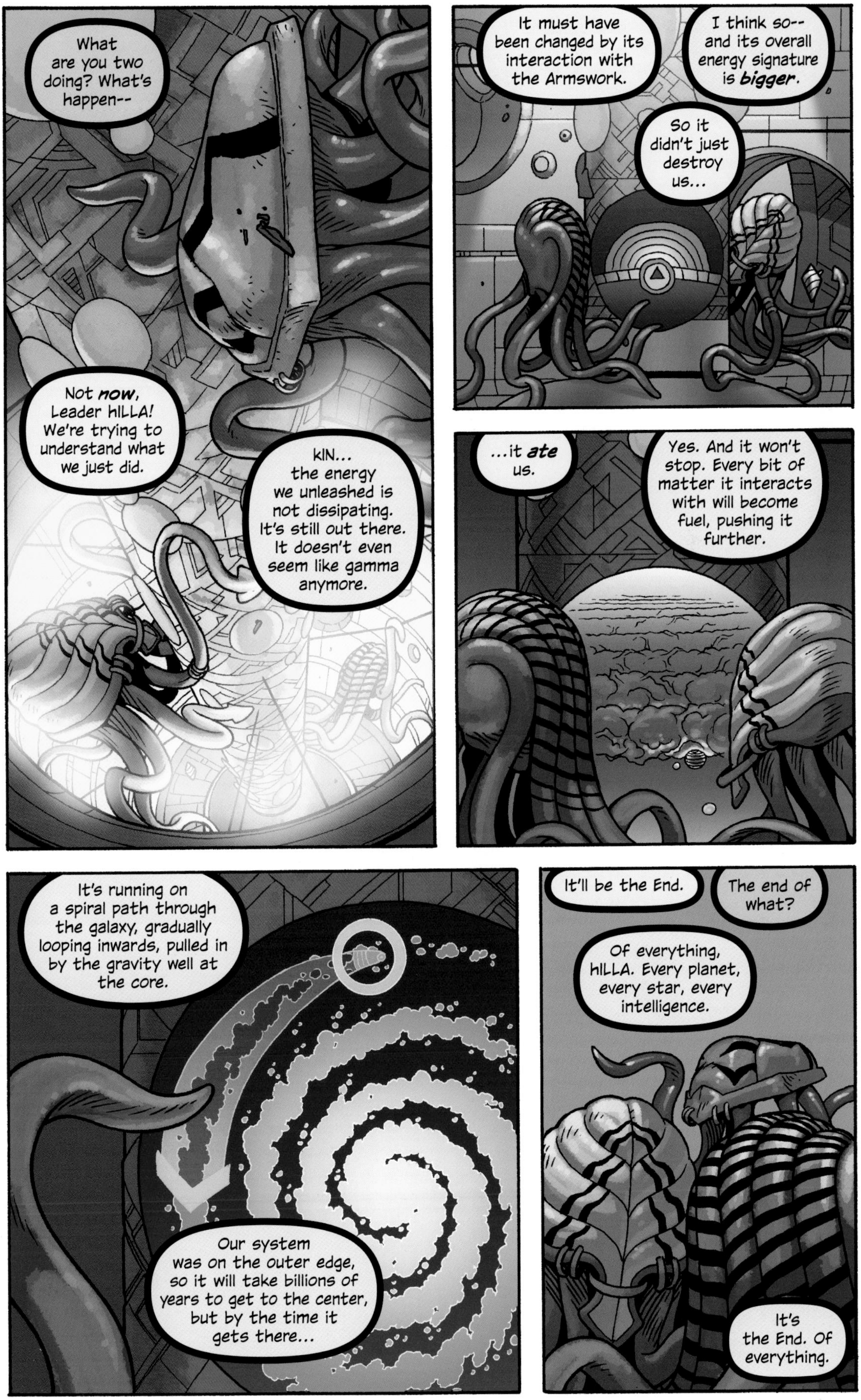
What are you two doing? What's happen--
Not **now**, Leader hILLA! We're trying to understand what we just did.
kIN... the energy we unleashed is not dissipating. It's still out there. It doesn't even seem like gamma anymore.
It must have been changed by its interaction with the Armswork.
I think so-- and its overall energy signature is ***bigger***.
So it didn't just destroy us...
...it ***ate*** us.
Yes. And it won't stop. Every bit of matter it interacts with will become fuel, pushing it further.
It's running on a spiral path through the galaxy, gradually looping inwards, pulled in by the gravity well at the core.
Our system was on the outer edge, so it will take billions of years to get to the center, but by the time it gets there...
It'll be the End.
The end of what?
Of everything, hILLA. Every planet, every star, every intelligence.
It's the End. Of everything.

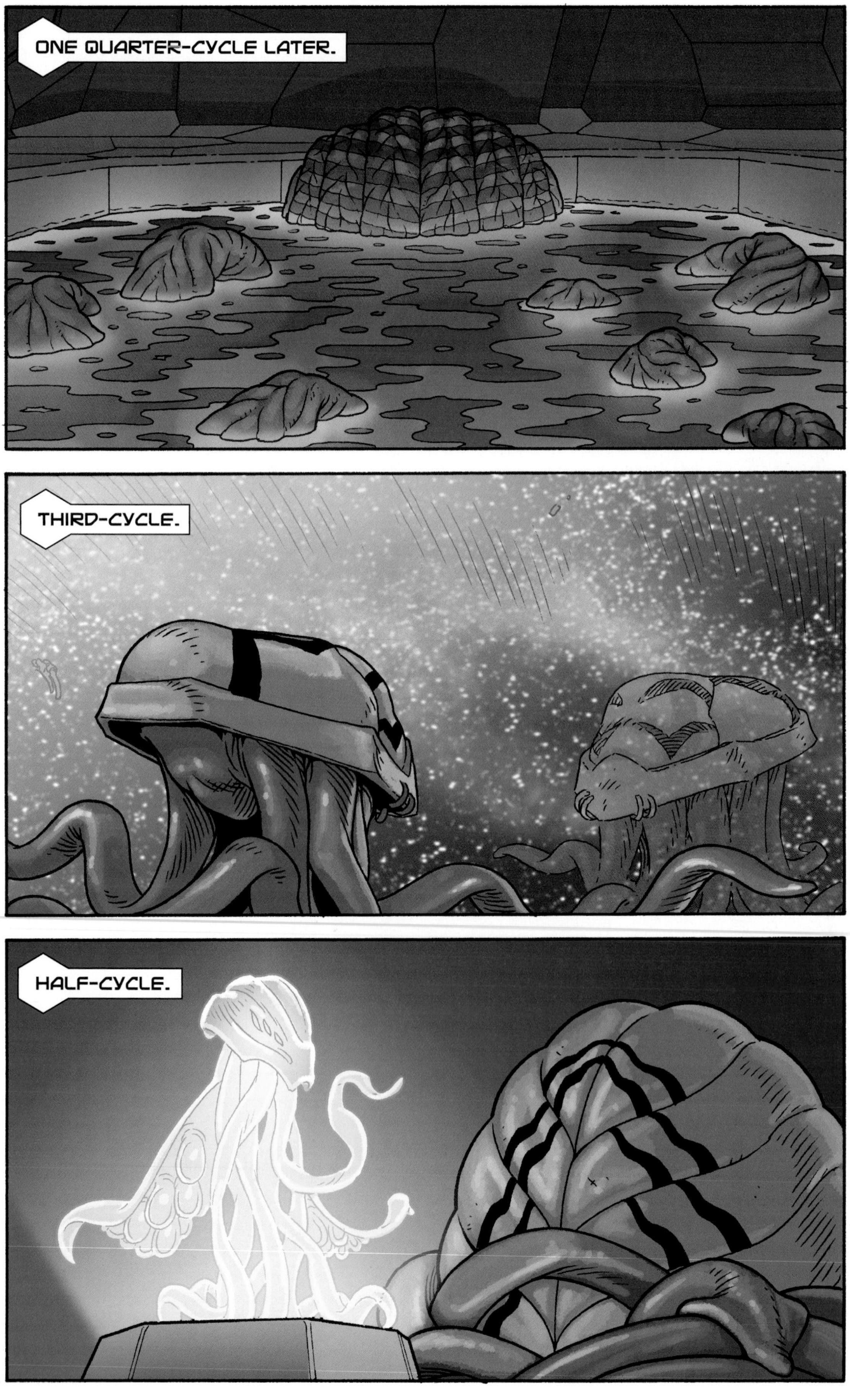
ONE QUARTER-CYCLE LATER.
THIRD-CYCLE.
HALF-CYCLE.

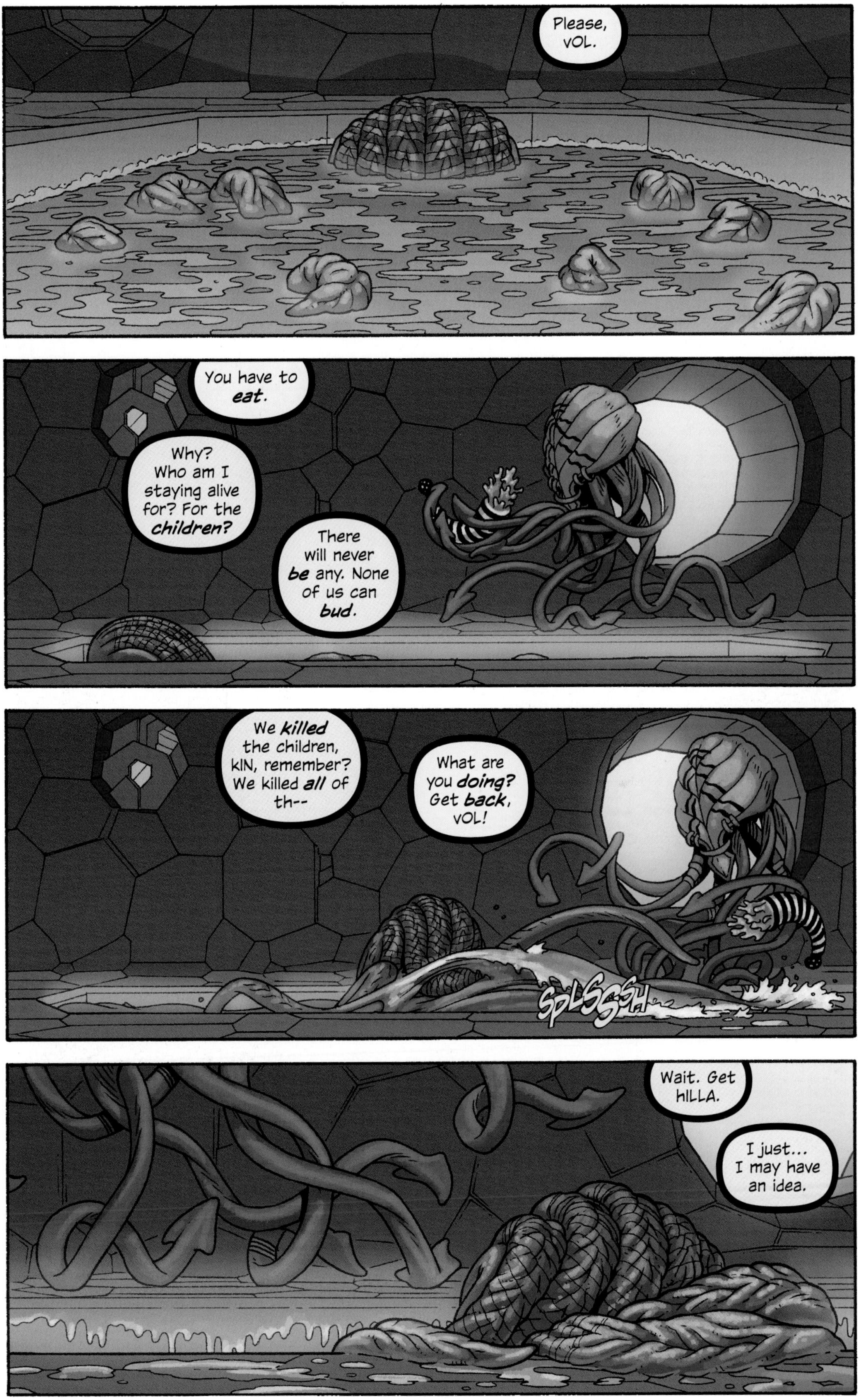
Please, VOL.
You have to eat.
Why? Who am I staying alive for? For the children?
There will never be any. None of us can bud.
We killed the children, KIN, remember? We killed all of th--
What are you doing? Get back, VOL!
SPLSSSH
Wait. Get HILLA.
I just... I may have an idea.

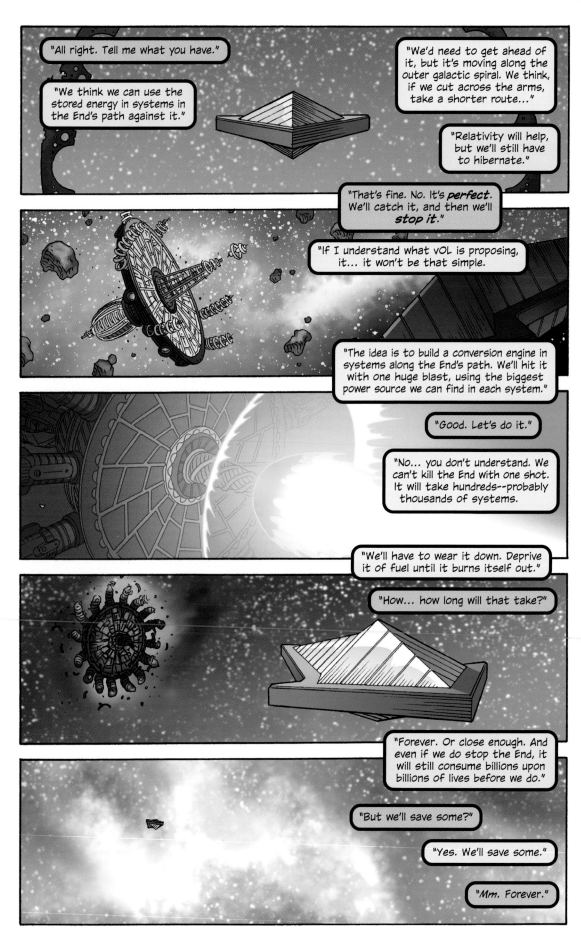

"All right. Tell me what you have."

"We think we can use the stored energy in systems in the End's path against it."

"We'd need to get ahead of it, but it's moving along the outer galactic spiral. We think, if we cut across the arms, take a shorter route..."

"Relativity will help, but we'll still have to hibernate."

"That's fine. No. It's *perfect*. We'll catch it, and then we'll *stop it*."

"If I understand what vOL is proposing, it... it won't be that simple.

"The idea is to build a conversion engine in systems along the End's path. We'll hit it with one huge blast, using the biggest power source we can find in each system."

"Good. Let's do it."

"No... you don't understand. We can't kill the End with one shot. It will take hundreds--probably thousands of systems.

"We'll have to wear it down. Deprive it of fuel until it burns itself out."

"How... how long will that take?"

"Forever. Or close enough. And even if we do stop the End, it will still consume billions upon billions of lives before we do."

"But we'll save some?"

"Yes. We'll save some."

"Mm. Forever."

AFTER AEONS.

"Then we should probably hurry."

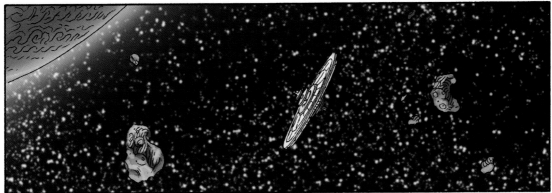

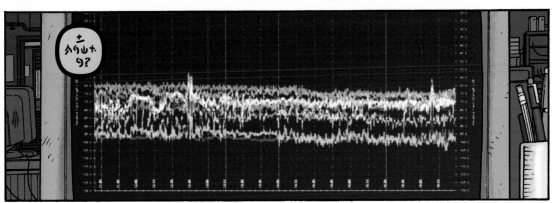

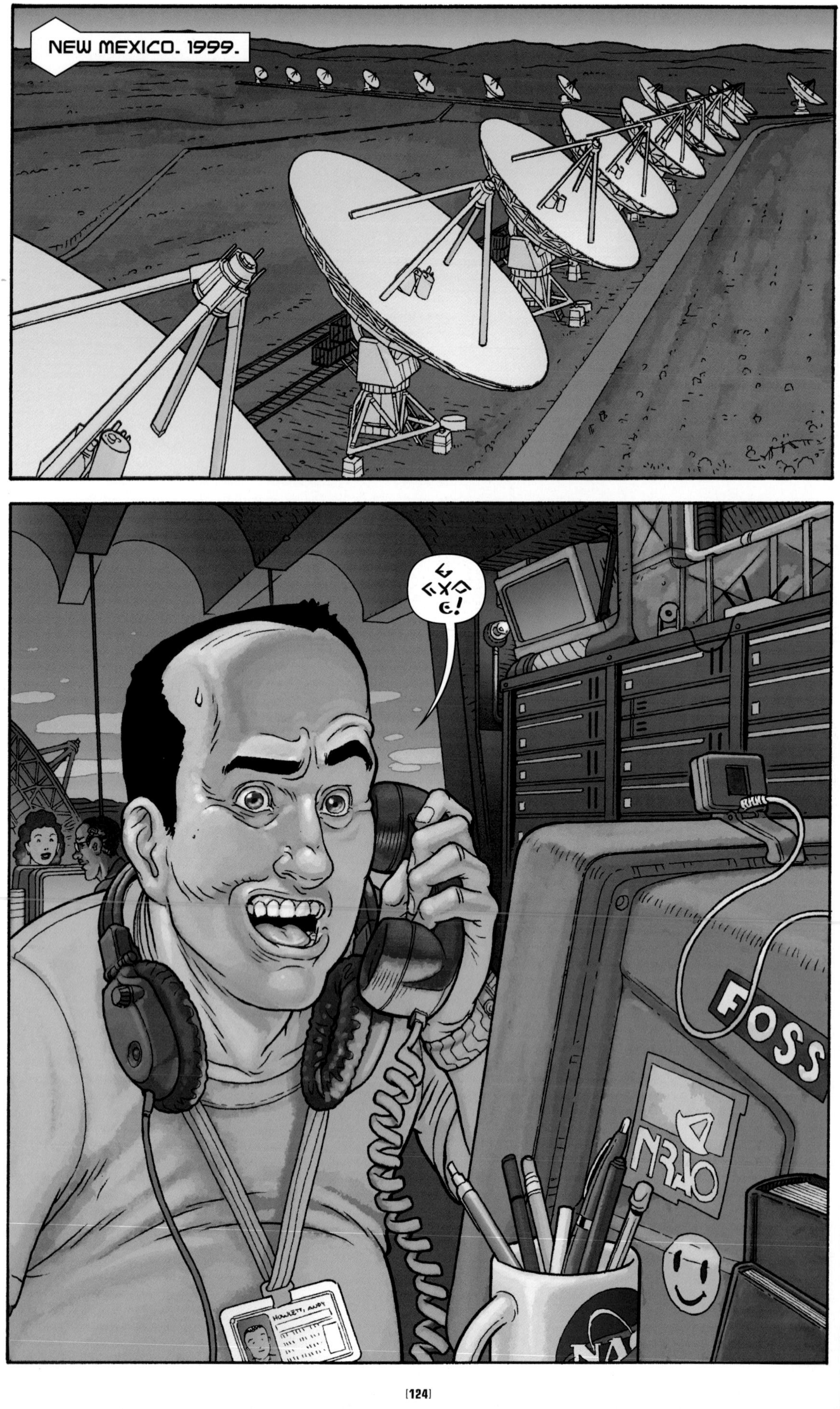
NEW MEXICO. 1999.
FOSS

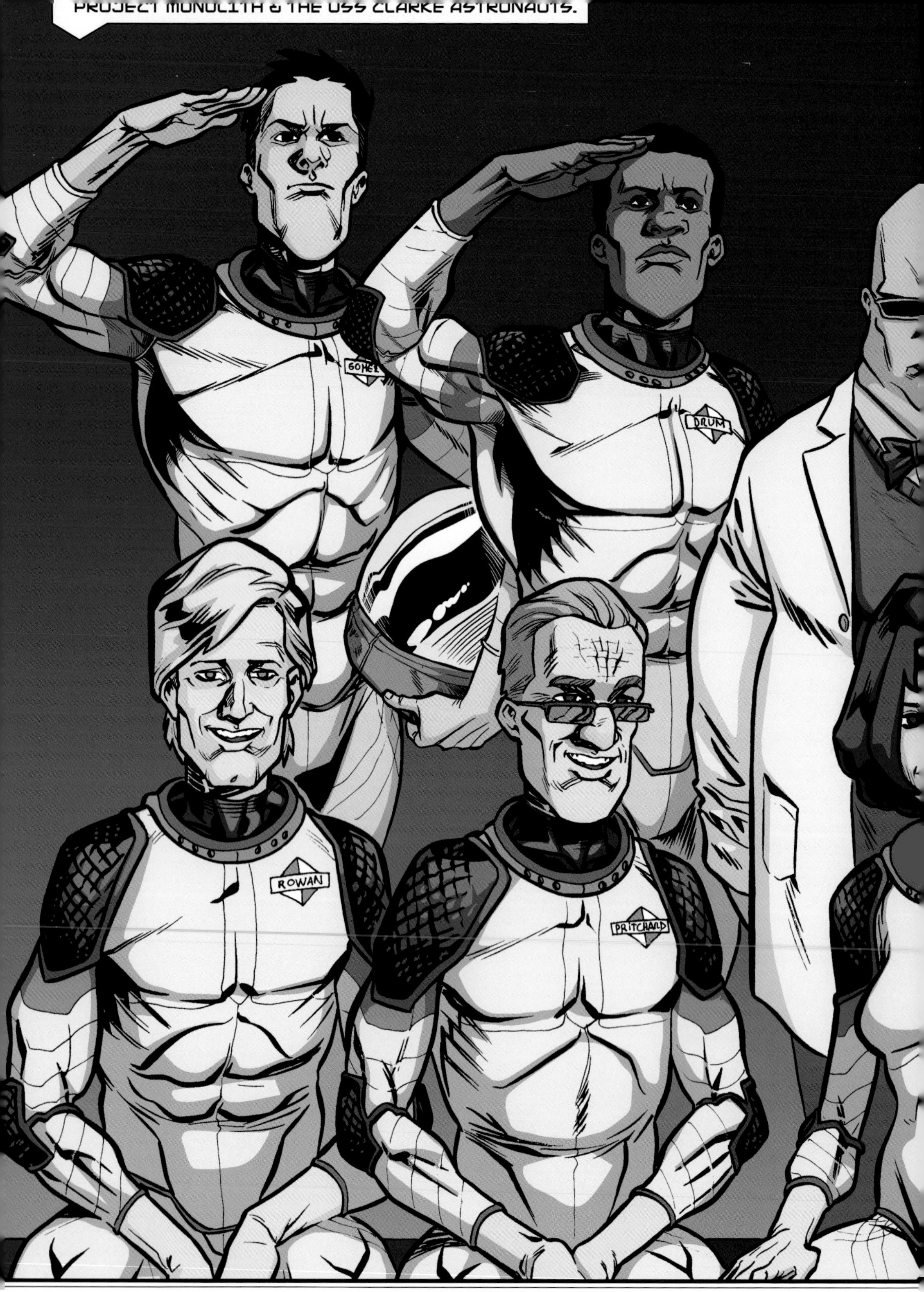
PROJECT MONOLITH & THE USS CLARKE ASTRONAUTS.
GOMEZ
DRUM
ROWAN
PRITCHARD

TOP ROW [FROM LEFT TO RIGHT]:

LIEUTENANT ALBERTO GOMEZ, MAJOR GABRIEL DRUM,
DR. PORTEK [HEAD OF PROJECT MONOLITH], **COLONEL JACK OVERHOLT,**
SERGEANT JOHN WILLET

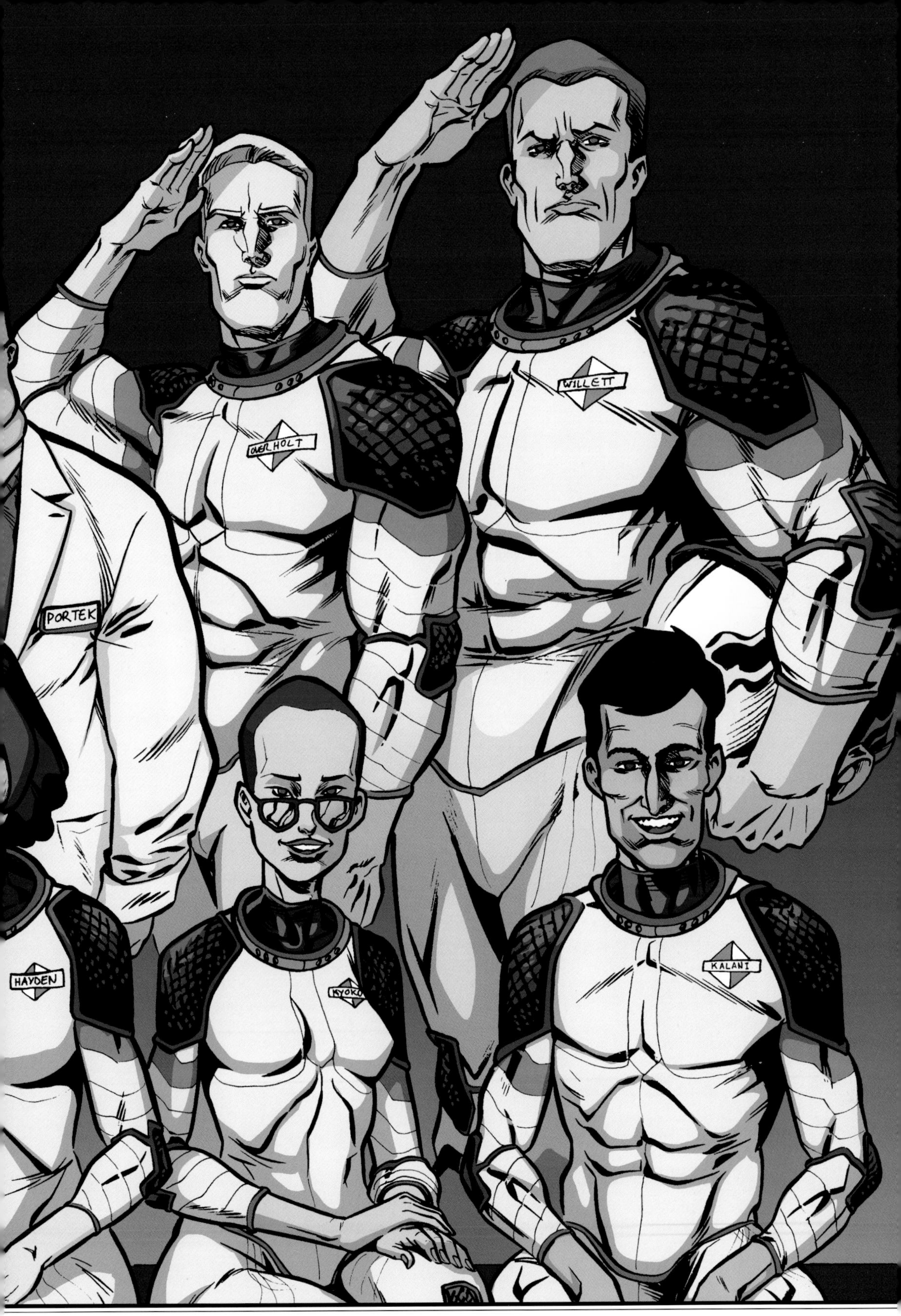

WILLETT
OVERHOLT
PORTEK
HAYDEN
KYOKO
KALANI

BOTTOM ROW [FROM LEFT TO RIGHT]:

CARY ROWAN [GEOLOGIST], **DONALD PRITCHARD** [CHIEF ASTRONOMER], **CHARLOTTE HAYDEN** [SENIOR MISSION COMMANDER], **KYOKO TAKAHASHI** [DOCTOR], **MANESH KALANI** [LINGUIST AND COMPUTER SPECIALIST]

1999 — Non-terrestrial construction project discovered in the asteroid belt by astronomer Andy Howlett.

Edward Stanton

2000 — US President Francis T. Carroll authorizes Project Monolith, with stated mission goal to investigate alien anomaly, under Director Edward Stanton.

The United States invades Iraq.

The United States invades Afghanistan.

2001 — The first members of the *Clarke* crew—Charlotte Hayden and Cary Rowan, both members of the vessel's scientific team —are recruited into Project Monolith.

Colonel Jack Overholt enters into discussions to lead the *Clarke*'s military team.

NOVEMBER— President Carroll wins re-election to a second term.

2002 — Sergeant John Willett recruited to join *Clarke* crew, conditional on agreement of Overholt to lead military team.

Clarke orbital assembly launches commence.

CLASSIFIED.

2003 — Edward Stanton replaced as head of Project Monolith by Dr. Radislav Portek. Portek urges Carroll to take a more militaristic approach to the alien anomaly.

DECEMBER 17— The *Clarke* departs Earth orbit.

2004 — Senator Stephen H. Blades announces that he will attempt to secure the nomination as the Democratic candidate for President in the 2006 election.

Cindy Reed (NSA), Brian Michter (Secretary of Defense), Francis Carroll (P.O.T.U.S.), Bridget Carroll (First Lady), George Cohen (Chief of Staff), Chairman of the Joint Chiefs

2005

OCTOBER—
President Carroll recruits Elijah Green into Project Monolith.

NOVEMBER—
Stephen Blades is elected President with 54% of the popular vote.

2006

JANUARY 6—
Blades receives a letter from his predecessor informing him of the existence of an alien presence in our solar system and the measures that have been taken to deal with it: Project Monolith.

SUMMER—
Ex-President Carroll enters into a secret alliance with Germany, providing them with information about the alien presence in our solar system.

OCTOBER—
US Forward Operating Base Hurricane (Afghanistan) is destroyed in a nuclear attack perpetrated by German operative – the initial military action of World War Three.

2007

NOVEMBER—
In retaliation for the destruction of FOB Hurricane, President Blades uses orbital defense platform LEOPRD to destroy the headquarters of the First Panzer Division outside Hanover, Germany, while simultaneously revealing the existence of the aliens in the asteroid belt to the world.

NOVEMBER-DECEMBER—
World War III. US forces, along with primary allies France and the People's Republic of China, battle Die Allianz der Freien Erde (the Free Earth Alliance, which includes Germany, Russia and Great Britain, among other nations, and is secretly led by ex-President Carroll).

JANUARY-MARCH—
War.

APRIL—
Manila destroyed.

MAY-SEPTEMBER—
War. Escalating losses on both sides.

2008

OCTOBER—
President Blades authorizes Operation Endtime, a ground invasion of the North German coast using all remaining US military assets, intended to capture A.F.E. leadership and end the war.

NOVEMBER 28—
A deal is struck with Russian leadership to betray the A.F.E. and force them to accept the cease fire.

NOVEMBER 29—
★ Ex-President Carroll secretly takes control of the LEOPRD, cau sing it to fire on Moscow, erasing it from the map. The weapon subsequently explodes in orbit.

★ Hours later, the world-ending asteroid slows, changes direction and lands on the National Mall in Washington, D.C.

★ *Clarke* astronaut Gabriel Drum emerges and requests a meeting with President Blades.

NOVEMBER—
Operation Endtime fails. With no remaining options, President Blades prepares to surrender.

NOVEMBER 27—
Thanksgiving Day—
Blades learns that a large asteroid will impact the planet within a matter of days, and forms a plan to use the LEOPRD to destroy it in exchange for a no-fault cease fire.

LETTER
44
ONE. GIANT. LEAP.

Charles Soule
Writer-In-Chief

Alberto J. Alburquerque
Executive Artist

Dan Jackson
Executive Colorist

Crank!
Chief of Letters

THE
WHITE HOUSE
1600 PENNSYLVANIA AVE NW, WASHINGTON, DC 20500

FROM THE DESK OF THE 44TH PRESIDENT, STEPHEN HENRY BLADES

NAME:

Charles Soule

LOCATION:

Brooklyn, NY, United States of America

BIO:

Charles Soule was born in the Midwest but often wishes he had been born in space. He lives in Brooklyn, and has written a wide variety of titles for a variety of publishers, including others' characters (*Swamp Thing*, *Superman/Wonder Woman*, *Red Lanterns* (DC); *Thunderbolts*, *She-Hulk*, *Inhuman* (Marvel); and his own: *27*, *Curse Words* (Image); *Strongman* (SLG) and *Strange Attractors* (Archaia). When not writing—which is rare—he runs a law practice and works, writes and performs as a musician.

One of his biggest regrets is never personally witnessing a Space Shuttle launch.

Charles Soule
Writer-In-Chief

Alberto J. Alburquerque
Executive Artist

Dan Jackson
Executive Colorist

Crank!
Chief of Letters

THE
WHITE HOUSE
1600 PENNSYLVANIA AVE NW, WASHINGTON, DC 20500

FROM THE DESK OF THE 44TH PRESIDENT, STEPHEN HENRY BLADES

NAME:

Joëlle Jones

LOCATION:

Los Angeles, California, United States of America

BIO:

Joëlle Jones is an Eisner-nominated artist currently living and working in Los Angeles, CA. Since attending PNCA in Portland, OR, she has contributed to a wide range of projects and has most recently begun writing and drawing her own series, *Lady Killer*, published by Dark Horse. Jones has also provided the art for *Superman: American Alien* (DC), *Helheim, Brides of Helheim* (Oni Press) and *Mockingbird* (Marvel). She's also done work for Boom! Studios, *The New York Times*, Vertigo and more! Joëlle will be taking on projects for DC and Marvel this year as well as continuing her series *Lady Killer*.

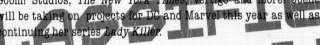

N. L-44Z-ØN1.10.A

Charles Soule
Writer-In-Chief

Alberto J. Alburquerque
Executive Artist

Dan Jackson
Executive Colorist

Crank!
Chief of Letters

THE
WHITE HOUSE

1600 PENNSYLVANIA AVE NW, WASHINGTON, DC 20500

FROM THE DESK OF THE 44TH PRESIDENT, STEPHEN HENRY BLADES

NAME:

Drew Moss

LOCATION:

Hampton, Virginia, United States of America

BIO:

Drew Moss is an illustrator based out of southeastern Virginia.

Drew has done work for IDW (*The Colonized*, *The Crow*) Dark Horse (*Creepy*), Oni Press (*Terrible Lizard*, *Blood Feud*) Image Comics (*Copperhead*) and various other publishers. Drew enjoys fine cigars and whiskeys and spends too much time writing bios. To see more of Drew's work and upcoming projects you can follow him on Twitter @drew_moss or on Instagram @drewerdmoss.

Charles Soule
Writer-In-Chief

Alberto J. Alburquerque
Executive Artist

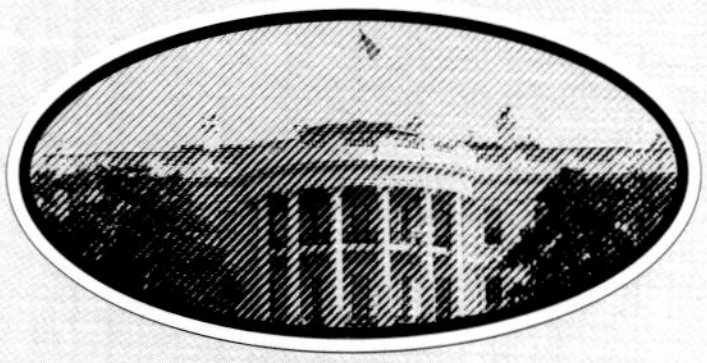

Dan Jackson
Executive Colorist

Crank!
Chief of Letters

THE WHITE HOUSE

1600 PENNSYLVANIA AVE NW, WASHINGTON, DC 20500

FROM THE DESK OF THE 44TH PRESIDENT, STEPHEN HENRY BLADES

NAME:

Ryan Kelly

LOCATION:

St. Paul, Minnesota, United States of America

BIO:

Ryan Kelly has been drawing comics for almost 20 years. After drawing *LOCAL* for Oni Press, he has gone on to co-create a wealth of original books and series; such as *The New York Four*, *Saucer Country*, *THREE*, *Cry Havoc*, and *Survivors Club*. He happily lives and works in St. Paul, Minnesota and is expected to draw even more comics in the future.

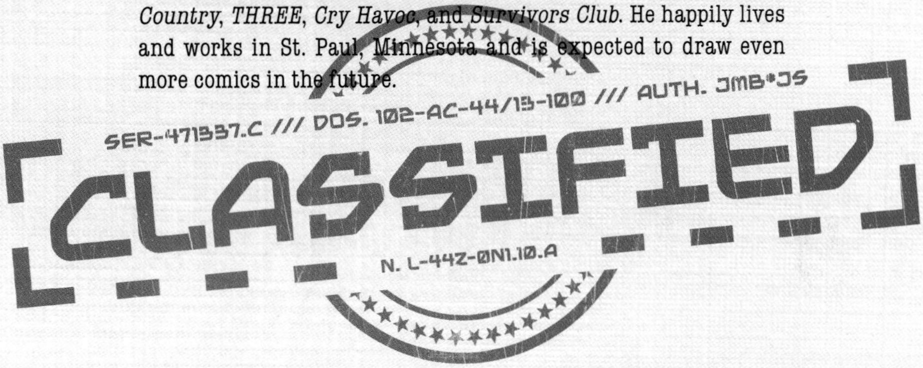
SER-471337.C /// DOS. 102-AC-44/13-100 /// AUTH. JMB*JS
CLASSIFIED
N. L-442-0N1.10.A

Charles Soule
Writer-In-Chief

Alberto J. Alburquerque
Executive Artist

Dan Jackson
Executive Colorist

Crank!
Chief of Letters

THE WHITE HOUSE

1600 PENNSYLVANIA AVE NW, WASHINGTON, DC 20500

FROM THE DESK OF THE 44TH PRESIDENT, STEPHEN HENRY BLADES

NAME:

Alise Gluškova

LOCATION:

Riga, Latvia

BIO:

Alise Gluškova is an artist from Latvia, Riga. Her background work is layout design for print production and motion comics. Her art has been featured in *Aw Yeah Comics*, Dark Horse's *Abe Sapien* and "Bait: Off-Color Stories for You to Color" by Chuck Palahniuk.

SER-471337.C /// DOS. 102-AC-44/15-100 /// AUTH. JMB*JS

CLASSIFIED

N. L-442-0N1.10.A

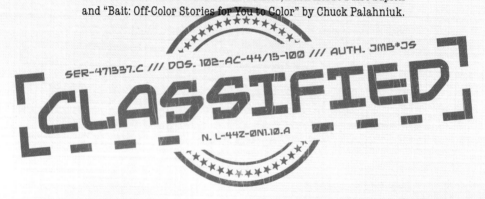

Charles Soule
Writer-In-Chief

Alberto J. Alburquerque
Executive Artist

Dan Jackson
Executive Colorist

Crank!
Chief of Letters

THE WHITE HOUSE

1600 PENNSYLVANIA AVE NW, WASHINGTON, DC 20500

FROM THE DESK OF THE 44TH PRESIDENT, STEPHEN HENRY BLADES

NAME:

Langdon Foss

LOCATION:

Colorado Springs, Colorado,
United States of America

BIO:

Langdon makes art and draws comics in Colorado. He's well-known for drawing Anthony Bourdain's graphic novel paean to food and samurai movies, *GET JIRO!*, *The Surface* with Image comics, and most recently his work for Marvel including *Bucky Barnes: Winter Soldier*, the mini-series *VOTE LOKI*, and others. He's currently drawing indie books and developing other projects, and you can keep track of his adventures @LangdonFoss and at www.LangdonFoss.com. He'd love to hear from you.

NAME:

Dan Jackson

LOCATION:

Portland, Oregon, United States of America

BIO:

What is the most unfair thing you can think of? Got it in your head? Okay, forget that because there's a worse one: There's this guy who gets paid money for coloring comic books. Right. Dan Jackson has been gainfully employed to one degree or another with the coloring of comic books for the better part of 17 years. He's done other Great Big Projects with the fine folks at Oni Press, and he's done a bunch of covers and short projects with them as well. He's a pretty versatile guy. Even writes his own bios.

Mr. Jackson lives in the beautiful Pacific Northwest with his scorching hot wife (see? UN-FAIR!), and two hilarious kids.

MORE BOOKS FROM ONI PRESS

LETTER 44: VOLUME 1 ESCAPE VELOCITY

CHARLES SOULE, ALBERTO JIMÉNEZ ALBURQUERQUE, GUY MAJOR, AND DAN JACKSON

160 PAGES /// SOFTCOVER /// COLOR INTERIORS

ISBN 978-1-62010-388-3

LETTER 44: VOLUME 2 REDSHIFT

CHARLES SOULE, ALBERTO JIMÉNEZ ALBURQUERQUE, AND DAN JACKSON

160 PAGES /// SOFTCOVER /// COLOR INTERIORS

ISBN 978-1-62010-206-0

LETTER 44: VOLUME 3 DARK MATTER

CHARLES SOULE, ALBERTO JIMÉNEZ ALBURQUERQUE, AND DAN JACKSON

160 PAGES /// SOFTCOVER /// COLOR INTERIORS

ISBN 978-1-62010-272-5

LETTER 44: VOLUME 4 SAVIORS

CHARLES SOULE, ALBERTO JIMÉNEZ ALBURQUERQUE, DAN JACKSON, AND SARAH STERN

160 PAGES /// SOFTCOVER /// COLOR INTERIORS

ISBN 978-1-62010-355-5

THE BUNKER

THE BUNKER: VOLUME 1

BY JOSHUA HALE FIALKOV AND JOE INFURNARI

136 PAGES /// SOFTCOVER /// COLOR INTERIORS

ISBN 978-1-62010-442-2

THE SIXTH GUN
BUNN
HURTT

THE SIXTH GUN: VOLUME 1 COLD DEAD FINGERS

BY CULLEN BUNN, BRIAN HURTT, AND BILL CRABTREE

176 PAGES /// SOFTCOVER /// COLOR INTERIORS

ISBN 978-1-62010-420-0

ONI PRESS
www.onipress.com

FOR MORE INFORMATION ON THESE AND OTHER FINE ONI PRESS COMIC BOOKS AND GRAPHIC NOVELS, VISIT WWW.ONIPRESS.COM. TO FIND A COMIC SPECIALTY STORE IN YOUR AREA, CALL 1-888-COMICBOOK OR VISIT WWW.COMICSHOPS.US.